Love Yourself Into Life

select teachings and wisdom of

RAMTHA

Love Yourself Into Life

select teachings and wisdom of

RAMTHA

Master Edition

Sovereignty Publishing Company

This Master Edition is a limited first edition printing of *Love Yourself Into Life*. It is being released prior to the formal publication of this book to permit interested readers more timely access to a presentation of the teachings of Ramtha in written form.

Sovereignty Publishing Company

PO Box 483, Eastsound, Washington 98245

BEHOLD, there come unto a reckoning a wondrous Master from a far land who be mystical and elusive and calls himself a "Ram."

AND BEHOLD, the entity takes unto his Kingdom a small gathering of disbelievers who seek for hope. And much to their surprise, the Master picks them up and lifts them and says, "Behold, God is given, the perfect of His Image, now and forever." And Life is jubilant within them.

AND BEHOLD, an image of a God Spectacular is born in the Consciousness of Christ.

AND BEHOLD, life abounds in a succulent Joy, a Happiness and Peace and Life that will be Forever.

AND BEHOLD the Master who loves them all, who has given them Hope. But greater than He is the Word that Lives, that gives them Life in the spectacular movement of the Father, the Life Force.

That is how it is, even this hour.

—Ramtha

DEDICATION

This work is dedicated to you and the words of Ramtha. May these words live forever in your thoughts and give to you Life in the spectacular movement of the God you are.

PREFACE

Love Yourself Into Life is the first of a series of volumes which collectively will present the scope of the teachings of an entity identified as "Ramtha The Enlightened One." It is composed entirely of verbatim transcriptions of tape-recorded public and private audiences conducted by Ramtha between 1979 and 1983. Ramtha does not appear in bodily form at these audiences, but instead "speaks through" the body of a woman named J. Z. Knight who functions as a "channel" through which Ramtha can communicate his "understandings" or teachings.

The primary purpose of this and future volumes is to facilitate an understanding of these spoken teachings while at the same time provide accurate, verifiable transcriptions of them. Thus, this book is designed to function both as "teaching book" and as a reliable "sourcebook" for the teachings of Ramtha.

The teachings presented in public audiences, and reflected in this book, are of two types. The first is a general teaching presented to the audience as a whole in the form of an address or as a teaching on a select topic. The second, and more common, is a spontaneous and directed teaching to a patricular member of the audience in response to his or her question or on a "need to know" basis. The reader is thus urged to view the teachings from the context in which they were presented.

To facilitate comprehension of the spoken teachings, the verbatim transcriptions have been edited. However, extreme care has been taken to insure that no editorial procedure would alter the meaning or intent of the teaching. Nevertheless, it is important to understand that editing the material, removing it from context and organizing it into a coherent presentation may alter to some degree the meaning and intent of the original presentation.

Additions to or clarifications of the transcribed material are noted by the use of brackets. When a pronoun was used in the original presentation but the noun to which it referred was unclear, the noun has been substituted for the pronoun. This has been noted by the use of brackets only when there was not absolute certainty as to the referent for the pronoun. Words, phrases, sentences and paragraphs were occasionally re-ordered within the text of the teaching to facilitate comprehension and readability. Material deleted from the original text has not been noted. To enable the reader to better identify with the teachings, the pronouns "you" and "yourself" and the adjective "your" has been substituted, as appropriate, for indefinite, general or impersonal pronouns and adjectives (e.g., he, they, them, one, our, their).

Punctuation and emphasis added to words and phrases have been used in an effort to parallel the timing and emphasis of the spoken word from the original presentation. Ramtha's vernacular language has been preserved as much as possible and has been presented without comment or clarification if the meaning of unique or slang words and phrases is understandable as presented or from the context of the text.

Portions of the material presented, including the entire Preface and Introduction, are composed of teachings presented in several audiences woven together to provide a summary of information or to integrate related teachings to facilitate comprehension.

To permit the reader to understand the material through their own frame of reference, no interpretation or editorial comment has been made other than indirectly through the editing and organization of the materials.

No written presentation of Ramtha's teachings can fully capture the eloquence, beauty and power of his spoken word, nor can it present the full informational value of such teachings conveyed through inflection, timing and other aspects of speech patterns. The reader is urged to supplement **Love Yourself Into Life** by listening to tape recorded audiences. Information regarding the availability of tapes of especially informative audiences can be obtained by writing to: Ramtha Dialogues, Post Office Box 1210, Yelm, Washington 98597.

FORWARD

Beloved entity, I am Ramtha The Enlightened One. I have brought with me the Winds of Change upon this plane. I have lived upon your plane and ascended in life. I did not die. And after me, many have ascended.

I am [now] that which is termed Light Synthesis. I come to you in that which is termed the "illusion." I am a mystic, the Unseen Voice, the Unseen Power. I am, in the totality of my being, that part of God that has found a foreverness, that is complete in and of itself.

I am a reality as you are a reality. I have returned from whence I came, not to tell you what lies "beyond," but to teach you how to see [it] for yourself, for the glory I already possess; yours is for you to have.

I have come unto you in script to give unto you truths [so] that you, my beloved, may understand yourself and the conditions of existence that you are in on this Plane of Demonstration. These [truths] are not what you would term new teachings. They are as ancient as time immemorial, as it were. Indeed, they are basic truths, basic laws that are in harmony with all things. They be, indeed, God, the Principle Cause, the Spirit Divine, unveiled, as it were.

I am here because I love you. And I am no messiah. I am not! I am not your Savior. I am not your Deliverer [or] your Lord. I cannot deliver you from your own personal bondage, for only you can do that. Indeed, I cannot save you from the irony of your life expression; only you can do this. I cannot be your Lord, for only you can be Lord of yourself.

I am not to be worshipped or to be idolized or to be sought after. I am to be loved. I wish none to sit at my feet but to look me in the eye. I wish to exalt all men as I have been exalted. I wish no followers, only leaders. And I will free you, but it will be by your own conviction that you are, and that be better indeed.

I am not a sage, I am not a fortune-teller, I am not a priest. I am but a teacher, servant, brother unto you. And through the power of my being and for the love of your being, I will teach you how to become [unto your sovereignty] as I have taught myself to become. And I will laugh with you, entity. And when you weep, I will send a wind to dry off your tears.

I am speaking to a nation of peoples--and soon the world. All that I teach you, the world is going to learn. And little by little, the army will grow. Upon the road you will see vagabonds, wretched men, kings, famous and infamous and all peoples coming. And you will see them advancing. And the abreastness of the road will widen, and all will join a line that advances into an eternity that is not linear. And you will see them come. And behold, as the March goes on, there will be a clamouring of experience, a rushing of gladdened hearts.

I have chosen to do this because I was once, like you, [in] an embodiment and I went through the slings of a torrid experience--from great hate into great love into understanding God and His wondrous mysteries. That has brought me a tie unto Mankind that has never been broken, for the love of who be you, for the love of who be I.

I have chosen to do this, entity, for there is no one else capable to do this! They all get lost in dogma and clamour into laws, regulations, judgements and all the like. I have chosen to do this for God is an Unlimited Thing: It is a Vast Emotion, and none on this plane know how to express that or explain that; they are all busy influencing everyone else around them.

What you will learn here, all will learn--simply! For what you learn here is about you and God and the deepest intimacy between the two of you. [And] you will learn to love yourself by recognizing who you are.

And who are you? You, my illustrious and beloved brothren, you are more than mortal. You are more than mere human. You are more than an entity lost in the mass of consciousness. You are a great God-Force, a great Fire that ignites the thoughts that are within you that gives you immortality.

You are more than the transcendent creature called Man. You are God! You are not the "bastards of the Universe," nor are you helpless creatures, nor are you forgotten. You are divine entities. You are a "collective thought" that never ceases. You are a great creator.

You, my beloved brothren, are God. You have always been. The mystery of yourself and how you think and how you feel is a collection of lies you have lived thousands of years. Who are you? You are God-Man called "Christus." Christus means "God-Man," God [living] in the embodiment of Man on this plane.

In your society, my beloved brothren, you have found it difficult to believe upon your own being, for always the heros of some mystical sort gave credence to a power greater than you. Thus it gave unto you lesser responsibility to become all-perfect, all-wise, all-beautiful. You [have] sought to find yourself in temples, in marbled figures, in sunsets and birds and all creatures. You looked everywhere but "in."

In this [teaching], we look "in." In **you** shall we find the hero, shall we find the God, shall we find the perfect Ideal that you are needing to become. The "unknown" God, entity, is at the altar of your [own] goodness.

Many leaders or teachers that have been upon this plane have been hard-pressed, as it were, to teach a solemn truth that they had perceived in their wondrous consciousness to a world that despised them, hated them, and even went to great lengths to destroy them, for they reminded [mankind] unceasingly of its studpidity [and] ignorance. These teachers have made a great indent upon your learning. But unfortunately, because it has been handed down from truth to truth, it has taken many avenues and planes to come back [to the original teaching], to what you now are learning.

This teacher has plotted and planned, if you will so forgive the terms, to bring to you what I am [teaching] in an undying manner. And what you will come to know **is,** and you shall be uplifted and glorified, for what I tell you **will** become, and this truth [that I teach] shall be substantiated on all levels, [from] Man's weakness to his greatest strength.

There is a war, entity, upon this plane even this hour [between] what is called "intelligence" and what is called "spirit." Already the forces have assimilated themselves and stand erect to gather their beloved brothers into a realized opportunity to think for themselves. That is what I am doing with you.

Your age is advancing very quickly to a change in consciousness level. Those that are the lovers of Mankind will be brought to the surface very quickly in the hours to come. They will be like beacons, and they will be magnetized, and they will act like living channels of thought for a great mass of humanity that will be divided against one another, not in war, but in "belief acceptance."

This "new" consciousness is not really a new consciousness. It is **the** consciousness: it is consciousness without restriction, without limitation and without doubt! All those who have aligned to such a consciousness--and I assure you there are many of them--shall come to this place, for I shall be the place of parlay. And you shall be able to witness them. Everyone will!

We are going to unite the Consciousness of God to all peoples--not only of this plane, but [of] other planes. Think you that you are the only thing that exists in this universe? How arrogant of you! Think you, indeed, that your embodiment is the most sublime and beautiful creation there is? There are many more [peoples] who are very different, but all--who are your beloved brothers--have the essence of God the Father, and we are going to bring them together.

The coming age comes forth as a deliberate change in time and the values of time. Time will become rapid up [until] the turn of the century, and as that is done so, [those] who are caught up in the past will never see the future; those who are caught up in the Now will find hope in the future; those who obtain according to themselves, according to the God that lives within them, indeed **are** the future.

That which comes forth [is] what is termed The Age of God. War, pestilence, disease, inharmonic creeds, imbalance, hate and despise--they are no longer a part of the Age of God for the natures of Man [will have] been accelerated.

The understanding of God sublime upon this plane shall be seen, not only in the great light in the heavens, entity, but [in] the Great Light that gives the light in the heavens purpose in being and meaning--the Light within each individual entity.

No longer shall there be an extermination of life but life continuous. No longer shall there be the suffering of the pitiful and aimless, for all accelerate to the turn of time. And time itself will cease at the Age of God and permit Life to become the Essence of God ever-flowing in Man--Man being as God, God being as Man. That is the New Age.

All who be despisers of his brother, of freedom, and despise all things will not see [the coming age] and will not be permitted upon this plane until they have aligned themselves with the Holy and Divine Force of God. Then they are permitted to participate in a Kingdom that is forever.

There are no "avatars" of this Kingdom. There are no leaders of this age. All are leaders!

You are all beauteous. You are all cherished. I and that which stands with me have begun a great protection upon this, your wondrous plane. [We] shall begin to deflect the terrible prophecies that are lying latent and waiting to be fulfilled [so] that life can go on [and] the Glory of God which is "within" [can] become "without."

All of you are important in that, [for] through the sovereignness of your being you are going to reverse [the prophecies]. All of you will live to see a magnificent Kingdom emerge and civilizations come forth that you had not even the slightest vision existed. And a new wind will blow. And God, the Eternal Isness, can get on with His sublime design called Life.

My beloved brothren, you are greatly loved in all that you are and in all that you do. Unto those that call this [teaching] "madness," if this indeed be madness, then woe unto that which is termed "sanity," for it narrows the horizon of human fulfillment and permits the decay of hope.

[This teaching], it is indeed grand madness, as it were, for it creates fertile fields, heavy with manifested hope and truth that will sustain a Perfect Kingdom on your plane at its harvest time. You, my beloved, are the seeds! So be it!

CONTENTS

INTRODUCTION

"I am Ramtha The Enlightened One that speaks the truth of my being [to] give unto you a more perfect ideal, a more perfect understanding, a loftier understanding [from] which you may reason and understand your heritage, indeed your kingdom, indeed your destiny."

There is an hour before dawn that the night hath a host of stars in its heavens and there is great activity there in the silence. And if you would peer into the sky, into the silence, and find the loveliest star of all and watch it shine forth in its brilliant display of color and its fury of life unspoken, and if you have found this to be your favorite star, then you have found God.

And when the morning comes upon the horizon and you look clearly, you will see in the east a faint hue of color, and the color holds a splendor of a rose-hued sky that blazes with such life, yet is always quiet. And if you look towards the east at dawn and see this to be lovely and find it to be beautiful, then you have loved God.

And as Ra approaches upon the horizon, and the blaze becomes more intense, if there is a quickening spirit that hath alighted itself in a nearby tree and begins to sing its first song, for it is greeting God in the onslaught of His day, and if that be your favorite sound, then that be the Loveliest Voice of God.

And as you are standing there and you perceive a brilliant light casting forth itself into magnificence upon the horizon, and what you see sets forth your soul into a blaze, and Ra hath become your favorite light, then you have seen God in His Splendor.

To see these things, to find them lovely and beautiful, is to be God, for that which is looking at God is merely a reflection of God Himself. And when they are seen and felt in a most spectacular surrender, then you will learn to love yourself, for you are part and a creator of all this loveliness. Then you will learn the depth and the beauty and the foreverness of who you be, for you are grander than all these things I have spoken—All!

YOU ARE THE HOPE, THE REALITY, THE FOREVER

AN INTRODUCTION

I am Ramtha The Enlightened One, indeed. And who be I that stand before you in the enigma of your illusions? I be that which is a servant unto God Almighty. And who be He, as it were?

He be the Principle Cause, the life force element that be the principle basis of all that is. He is called the Source. He is called the Principle Life Force. He is called the All-Wise Knowing Intelligence. He is called the Platform of Life. He is the Giver of Thought: Unmanifested Emotion.

"You Have Been Summoned"

This day in your time, as we are gathered in what is termed a proper audience, you have come forth [from] all over your lands for you have been summoned. You, my most beloved brothren, are here for I have desired for you to be here!

I am unto you but a simple teacher. Indeed, I am unto you a brothren. I am unto you, indeed, a God that understands and loves the totality of his being as you shall readily in your time, as it is so seen and ascertained, indeed love that which you be also.

You be unto me that which is termed my beloved brothren, for you be all that is in the greatest hope that shall ever be. You be unto me that part of my being that we share unto one another that is called the semblance of life understood within one another. We be unto one another a brotherhood, the composite, the make-up, as it is most properly termed in your language, of the Mind of God. Unto you I am a servant and salute you in the perfectness of your being.

I am Ramtha The Enlightened One that speaks the truth of my being unto you that I give unto you a more perfect Ideal, a more perfect understanding, a loftier understanding, to the abilities of your abilities, [from] which you may reason and understand your heritage, indeed your kingdom, indeed your destiny; that you may understand the importance and worth and

"The God that you have been taught who has harrangued, who has judged, who has persucuted, who has despised, who has made you 'imperfect,' does not exist but in the hearts of Man."

value of your life upon this plane; that [it] give unto you the understanding that Life be forever, that Life, in the moments as they are so seen in their perfect eloquence, can be designed into however illusion or disillusionment that you so desire.

Thus it is so given . . .

Everything Is God

What you term "God Almighty" or that which is termed the "Divine Father," you think of [as] the Creator, the sublime Creator, and [you] imagine Him in the form of a singular entity, the entity possessing all-conclusive power, all-knowingness, all-isness. The Father is indeed all of these things, [but] the Father, or Source, is not a singular entity. Though He is one entity, He is every entity.

God, the Benevolent indeed, is an all-consuming entity that is everything:

He is the wind upon the water,
the changing of the leaves,
the laughter of a child,
the simplicity of a rose
deep within its hue and color;
He is indeed a sunrise,
a twinkling star,
a full moon, waxing and waning
across the midnight sky;
He is a humble bird in flight,
a beauteous insect,
a vile and ugly worm;
He is, indeed, everything!

That which is, **all** which is, be that which is termed the Principle Cause. God, the Sublime Excellence, is the Creator, for He is the Mass [from] which all things are; He is the Embodiment which all things spring [forth] from. Thus all things that are issuing forth from His Beauteous Self are [nothing] other than God.

God Has Never Judged You

The God you have been taught has been a fiery entity that hath created a two-fold plan of existence: that which is termed "heaven," that which is temed "hell," and that which is termed

"The God I teach you of loves you with greater love than you have ever fathomed for He is the life that you are. He is the ground that you walk on, the air that you breathe. He is the color of your skin, the magnificence in your eyes, the gentleness of your touch."

the "proving ground" that lies betwixt the two. This God is judgemental indeed, a warlike God that causes all to worship and to live in exile and fear. This is not the God that I teach, that I am the servant of, [of whom] the complexities of my simplicity is.

The God that you have been taught who has harrangued, who has judged, who has persecuted, who has despised, who has made you "imperfect," does not exist but in the hearts of Man. The Father be not a singular God possessing an "ego" that knoweth that which is termed "right" or "wrong"; in other words, possessing that which is termed "judgement." [That] is not this God that I will teach you of this day.

The God I teach you [of] is egoless. He does not possess an ego that He can determine that which is termed "good" or "bad," "negative" or "positive," "right" or "wrong," for He is the wrong as well as the right; He is the ugliness as well as the beauty; He is the vileness as well as the divinity. He is All Things.

The Father, [the] Life Source [that] I teach you of this day, hath never judged you. Indeed, He never will, for if He judges but one of you for one act, if He judges any of you for one thought, then this beloved, sublime, perfection of that which is termed Isness hath judged Himself, indeed "altered" Himself--which He has never done and never will do!

The Father sees no wrong; He sees only Himself. The Father sees no "failure"; He sees only His Isness ongoing into that which is termed foreverness. Only Man has brought together a "culminating" God that brings forth judgement on some and exalts others. That is the God of Man, thus the creation of Man and of his will.

The God I Teach You Of Is The Life That You Are

The God I teach you of this day loves you with greater love than you have ever fathomed for He is the life that you are. He is the ground that you walk on, the air that you breathe. He is the color of your skin, the magnificence in your eyes, the gentleness of your touch. He is all-encompassing, infinite.

He loves you regardless of what you have done for He **is** what you have done. He knows that there is nothing you can ever do to alter life--indeed you never will--and that you have never failed for failure equates "the ending of," and nothing has ever ended. Thus, you have never failed.

Only You Have Ever Judged Yourself

Only **you**, in your own collective emotional attitude, have caused yourself to feel failure for is not [the] ultimate failure the ceasing of the Life Force that permits you to be? Yet you are living even this moment ongoing. Indeed! You have always been and you will always be. You have never failed.

The thought that you be "imperfect" in this kingdom--that is not how it is! You are quite perfect, you are quite beauteous, and all that you have created has been quite acceptable, for if it were not, you would be no more and the essence of you would be no more. You create the blossoms of life and even the vileness of it, and the Father will become the vileness and the blossoms and yet never judge the two of them as to which is greater and which is less. He simply is!

You will live this day and the tomorrows in your time and all eternity to come. Your form will change because you **desire** it to change, but you, the total essence, shall never die. The Father loves you beyond what you think love is for His Ideal of you holds your very cells together: it is the Spark of Light that surrounds your eminent being.

You Are God Expressing as Man

And who be you that be so worthy of the love of a most Grand Source that rebukes you not, that judges you not, that despises you not, but loves you, exalts you, continues your being forever? Who be you to deserve this?

You be, unto the Father, Himself! You have been referred to, eloquently, as His "Son." That is what you are. But you are also Him:

In the beginning, if you will, when the Father contemplated the expanse of His Being, all was the void called Thought--The Ultimate, Supreme Creator. When the Father contemplated Himself, He took the Thought within Himself, and the Contemplative Thought expanded Itself into Light, the First Body of Thought.

Of the expanded part of the Father who impregnated Himself with Thought and begat Himself, you became: of each particum [of Light] was born an individual. And when the Thought reflected Itself into the prism of Light, all It saw was Itself. And when [each] Particum of Light reflected itself into the Thought, all it saw was God.

Of each Particum of Light, God Is, for He gave life to each Particum of Light by seeing Himself in it--of course, [for] that was what He was. Thus, He will always see you as Himself, for that is what you are; you are an "altered phase" of that which He be, but nonetheless, you are Him.

[Thus] who be you indeed in all that be divine and splendor and lovely? You be, indeed, the Son. You be God expressing as Man. You be Man expressing as God.

God Expresses His Purpose Through Your Unique Will

The Principle Cause, the Source, has delivered unto you all that the Father is in all of His splendid affirmation, in all of His purpose and being. The Father indeed hath given unto you the movement of a singular entity. You be, indeed, God explicit, God unique, into the sublime beauty that you have become.

Though you are all [Sons] unto the Father, the Life Force, the Principle Understanding, you are all unique in your beauty and intellect and individualized Self, thus giving unto you a difference of opinion, a difference of will, and, most certainly, a difference in truth. God, through all that He is, has expressed His truth and purpose through the individualized truth, purpose, illusion and disillusionment of all that you be.

You Are Spirit, Soul And Ego: The Lord God Of Your Being

Who be you? Gods! You have heard about them, indeed. You have read about them. Great Gods, bodiless Gods, Gods of Light--that is what you are. You think you are mere mortals who possess a fatal body? You think that is all your kingdom is? Nay.

Sublime Gods that you be, the composite of your being is this: Your "auric field," which your scientists have determined [to] exist around your embodiment, is called your Spirit [or] the "God" of your being. It [is a] direct connector [to the] flow of that which is termed the River of Thought.

That which is termed the possessor of thought that brings forth Thought into memory [is] the Soul of your being, which is called the "Lord" of your being. The Soul's sole purpose is to record Thought [that has been] felt and exchanged through the kingdom, the body of the God that inhabits it. The Soul records memory, not in vision, but in feelings. Hence, from feeling, [a] word is formulated to describe [the feeling]. Without the Soul, you cannot occupy Thought, you cannot have memory, you cannot create, for you cannot make a thought stand still [to] contemplate it.

"I will tell you who created this universe and all ninety-nine universes that surround even a greater sun cycle. You did! Indeed!

Everything is God, but the designer of it, as it were, is exclusively the Artisans of Artisans which you be—His beloved Son."

[Your] Ego is the "God Totality" of your being. The God Totality of your being has a will of its own to accept certain thoughts and to reject others; to feel certain ways and to store feelings. [Thus it] represents, collectively, a unique entity, different from his brothers.

And finally, [you possess] the body [with] which to express on this [plane], the first and lowest of seven planes--[the Plane of] Mass and Matter.

You are made up of Spirit, Soul, and Ego. That is the Lord God of your Being, The Lord God of your Totality.

You Are The Great Creator

I will tell you who created this universe and all ninety-nine universes that surround even a greater sun cycle. You did! Indeed!

Everything that you see is called mass [or] gross matter. The Father is the mass, but His beloved Son, [having] the will of fluid thought, put together collective ideals through the memory of his Soul [and] created the ideals and [the] mass which he created [the ideals] from. Everything was formulated from a thought, embodied in the electrum of light, and became the solidity which it is. Everything is derivative of Thought.

You designed this universe--simply! It is magnificent! Each moment you designed each thing (each thought contemplated) expanded the experience, which allowed feelings--the truest treasure of Thought--to occur within the Soul. [And through feelings] this plane of seven planes was created, which is the lowest facet of Thought--Mass.

Everything **is** God, but the designer of it, as it were, is exclusively the Artisans of Artisans which you be--His beloved Son.

Your divinity lies in that you are indeed The Spark of Light, and that you, the Creators, have created from the Father, the Sublime Source, through your unique wills, all that is. All! God did not create the Universes--He **is** the Universes! His Sons created [the Universes] from their thinking processes by feeling it in their Souls, [and] they came forth readily.

The Father has given to His Son and **always** will give unto them whatever they desire. [Thus] Planes of that which is termed Advancement were lowered [so] that His Son could experience from Light, into Heavy Light, into Electrical Matter, into Gross Matter, into Manifested Form, all of their Creations.

"What you are in your essence as Son of this Totality, of this God, is not seen. What you really are is not your body, though it is a part of your totality. What you are hides behind your eyes and your hair and your skin, [lies] deep within your body, and is seen by no one. Your body is the illusionary instrument to play the game of Illusions of Life—a vehicle to ride within to experience this totality of Creation [so] that the Soul may learn [of] Emotion."

You Created The Embodiment of Man As A Vehicle To Experience Matter

In order for that which is termed Gods of Light, [the] Great Creators, to possess a feeling of mass, they had to have a "vehicle" of mass [of] the same vibration. [Thus the embodiment of] Man was created [by] the Gods, but [only] as a vehicle [so] that that which you are may ride within [the embodiment] and experience this Kingdom of Matter.

Now, ponder this for a moment. What love you about another? Be it their body? Nay. What love you of another is the "unseen essence" that makes the body work, that makes the eyes flicker, the voice melodious, the hair with sheen, the hands with touch. It is the essence of an entity called their "personality self" that you love, not their embodiment.

What is a body? It is a wonderful, refined "machine," but it is a no thing without that which works it, which is you. If I remove your body and leave your thought directly where it is, you would still be there but no one would see you. What you are, indeed, in your essence as Son of this Totality, of this God, is not seen. What you really are is not your body, though it is a part of your totality. What you are hides behind your eyes and your hair and your skin, [lies] deep within your body, and is seen by **no one.**

Your body is the illusionary instrument to play the game of Illusions of Life--a vehicle to ride within to experience **this** totality of Creation [so] that the Soul may learn [of] Emotion.

You Have Forgotten The Purpose Of This Life Experience

So who be you? You are all Gods, Sons of the Living Cause, indeed. You have created upon this your plane a Paradise of Matter. And you have created to the point that you have forgotten **why** you create!

For ten and one-half million years in your count, you have been upon this place called your Earth [or] Terra. And for ten and one-half million years you have come from divine, splendid entities [to be] "lost" in matter, enigmas of the creation called "religion." [You have] separated into warring factions of creeds, intellectual evolvements [and] social evolvements [and are] immersed in superstition, disease, death and war. **That** is your kingdom!

You Are Embroiled In Limitations And Have Lost Your Identity

You once could create a flower. Now you create your own doom, your own misery, by creating and accepting the feelings within your being as your "lot."

Try to create a flower now. You know how to purchase the seeds and put them into fertile ground and add aqueous substance to them and see them bloom. But what is it you create now? You create for yourself, indeed, a shorter life [in] which you accept certain modes of existence here as "beliefs," [which] become "knowingness" within your being. And you grow into limited statures to where you judge all things, all peoples, and even yourself! You live by a code of fashion called "beauty" and surround your life with the things that will cause you to be accepted by a "collective consciousness" of Man which accepts nothing but its own ideal--not even you!

Thus your interactions of "limited" thinking has caused you to have a limited life. You are babes that are born to grow up, to lose the vitality in your body, to believe yourself into old age until you perish. And what was it all for? What did you do? Will you be remembered? Who were you? Will you have ever mattered? Life upon life, being upon being, existence upon existence, you have embroiled yourself into limitations. Indeed.

Who is the creator of your destiny? You believe a great God outside of your body created your destiny, that all things that happen to you are of His doing? Nay, that is not, indeed, how it is known. You create your own destiny, for each of you are a Sovereign Prince, a Queen, a Mighty King, a Herald of Peace. Thrown together by your own choosing, you have lost your identity.

You Choose Your Life By How You Think

You who have created the magnificence of the stars, universes yet untold, have also created your destiny, your prejudice, that which is termed your worships, your religions, your despise, your likes and dislikes and all of your judgements. And you have created your own life.

You choose your life by how you think. Thoughts accepted through the "light flow" [or aura] of your being create the feelings within the Soul, and [that] draws unto you circumstances that [the feelings] can be enacted in.

Everything you think, every fantasy you have ever had, all the things you have spoken, have all come to pass [or] are waiting to come to pass. For how think you everything was created? It was created by Thought! Every thought you have ever had will manifest into an attitude and from an attitude into a reality.

Thought is the true Giver of Life that never dies, that never can be destroyed. And you have used it to think yourself into life, for it is your link to that which is termed the Godhood Isness.

This Life Is A Grand Illusion

God--He be a grand stage. The illusion is this plane in its material form. You have written your own script and are playing it eloquently, part by part upon the stage. It is all an Illusion.

When your curtains are drawn, [when] the last word is spoken, the last bow taken, you die. And for what reason? What about all the times you worked so arduously? For what? What about all the things you so zealously pursued? For what? And what of your temples you have erected to insure your immortality? Someone else owns them!

This is an illusion. All of it is! But you who are the players have come to believe that it is the **only** reality. And yet the only reality that ever existed and ever will exist is that which is termed Life--a free, extenuating, ongoing essence of "being" that allows you to create your games however you wish to play them.

Ponder this for a moment: It only takes a moment for you to envision happiness, that your whole body begins to feel joyful. It only takes a moment indeed to play the part of a saddened, wretched creature who no one has befriended to cause you to weep and to feel sorrow and pity for yourself. It only takes a moment to do that! It takes you a moment to stop laughing, to become sad. It takes you a moment to stop judging, indeed to judge. Now, who is doing all of this? You! And hath anything around you changed? While you have had this fancy of creating feelings within your being, has anything changed? Nay, but everything [that] is You has!

You are **precisely** what you are thinking. The thought comes in [and] is fulfilled in your body as a feeling. [The feeling is] recorded in your Soul, [which then] sets a precedence for the actions in your life.

The less you think of yourself, the less you shall become. The less you love yourself, the less you have the ability to love others. The less you give credit to yourself for intelligence, the more of an imbecile you shall become. The less beauty you think you are, the more ugly you shall become. The poorer you think you are, the more wretched you will become.

"Who are you? You are born here, you have chosen a body. You, the Unseen Essence, have come through it and played your games. And you will die because you have forgotten your divinity. You have forgotten the purpose of this and you have not even the ideal of what reality is."

You Have Forgotten Your Divinity

Who are you? You are born here, you have chosen a body. You, the Unseen Essence, have come through it and played your games. And you will die because you have forgotten your divinity. You have forgotten the purpose of this and you have not even the ideal of what reality is.

You are so immersed in that which is termed fear—fear born out of collective religion that took the divinity out of Man and put it somewhere in the sky and told everyone that they were imperfect. You have believed that and accepted that as a truth!

Ponder this for a moment: Listen to your thoughts. Are you not alive this moment and having the wisdom of your own thoughts occuring right here and now? Are you not a Sovereign who has this? You are not "a bastard" of this universe; you are the **creator** of it! You are the Lord Gods of your Beings. You are the Great Gods of Antiquity. You are the Great Gods of this Now. And you are the Gods that pave the highway into Eternity.

You have lived thousands of lives. You have been every face, every color, every race. You have warred and been warred upon. You have been king and servant alike. You have been sailor and captain. You have been conqueror and conquered. You have been everything. Everything!

Your life did not begin this day or when you issued forth from that which is termed your mothren's womb. It [began] when the Father contemplated Himself and you were. You have always been and always will be.

You are the Lord Gods of your Totality, Supreme Creators. You have created your body—what you look like. You have created your life—everything around you. [And] you have never been "victimized," [for] everything that has happened to you, you have thought of. [Thus], you are at the hands of your own undoing.

God Is Always Loving You Because He Is You

What hath The Father to do in all of this? The Father does not weep when you are woesome and broken in spirit. He does not do that. And when you are the thief, He does not judge you. And when you are the liar, He cannot condemn you, for there is no such thing as a liar. And when you are being slayed, He does not weep. And when you are the slayer, He does not weep. He is always loving you because He **is** you.

"God is always loving you. And it is a good thing He is that way, for if He truly were the God of Man, all of you indeed would be put into that which is termed the 'pit' and burn forever. And there is not one of you that would have ever seen what is called 'pearled gates.' Not one of you! For there is not one of you indeed that has lived up to the expectations of the God that was made by Man."

In your limited thinking, you will think things are "wrong," "disasterous," that they are "evil." That is **your** selection of truth and He lets you have it. His "truth" is what is called "Isness." He will love you regardless, because when you think things are at an end or they are getting worse, He is allowing you the life for you to see that they only get better. He is ongoing.

And when you pass from this plane and you ponder steadfastly all the things you have done in your life--and you will--and you enter the Unseenness [and] are without your body, He will still be there, for He is the Totality which you can exist in. He knows that you will be forever, for He is Foreverness in that which is termed a "Now," a moment. And it is a good thing He is that way, for if He truly were the "God of Man," all of you indeed would be put into that which is termed the "pit" and burn forever. And there is not one of you that would have ever seen what is called "pearled gates." Not one of you! For there is not one of you indeed that has lived up to the expectations of the God that was made by Man. Thus all of you would die!

All Experiences Provide The Virtue Of Wisdom

Be pleased that this Father I speak of is Life, for each wrong that you do, that **you** determine a wrong, has equated a feeling in your Soul; and when the "storm of emotion," torrid as it may be, subsides, you [will] have gained [wisdom], for there is "purposeful good" in everything.

And what happens to the wisdom that is gained in your Soul? It means you never have to do the "wrong" again for you have experienced it and know what it feels like [and] have the "record" of it in your Soul called "feelings"--the truest treasure of Life. And when you have "wronged" and feel guilty of that wrong, when that [feeling] passes away into wisdom in the Soul [and] there is no more emotion behind it, it means you have gained from that and you are becoming virtuous.

Infinite, virtuous Man is infinite, virtuous God who has not abstained from Life to be "holy and divine" in all things that are boring! [A] virtuous man is one who has lived and done everything in the totality of all the lives that he has lived for the experience of them, that the Soul now has the wisdom of All Life within it, that it is not lacking in anything.

There will come a time in all of your lives--whether in this life or those to come--that you will have reached a point that you will have no desire to do "this" or to do "that" but only "to be." You will have no desire to curse or to judge the harlot or whoremonger or the thief or the murderer or the warring country for all [of] their deeds. It will not be in you to do that any

"All of this [plane] is an illusion. Everyone thinks that it is the reality. It is not! It is the Illusion. This is all created to evoke emotion within the Soul.

The real world is that which lies within. This world would never exist if Man did not have the eyes to perceive it in "moving emotion" in his Soul, for it would be a no thing.

The real world exists only on emotion—[emotion] not governed by logic but [by] moving Love."

longer for you will have been all of those things and will have learned from them.

Then one day you are so complete in your experience of this plane--[recorded] in your Soul [as feeling]--that you never have to come back here again for there is nothing here that draws you any longer. That which is termed higher learning, higher becoming, and greater planes will draw you there. And then life is an adventure there. There is life, indeed, on yet other Planes of Consciouness for you to explore. That is the Joy of God the Father, for He is the Platform through which you work through your illusions, your imagination, your dreams.

You Do Everything In Life To Gain The Wisdom Of Emotion

The reason you are here is not to become famous or to become poor. The reason that you are here is "to become." To become what? Yourself! And to do **what** once you have become that? To create in this life whatever you choose. Your purpose here, your destiny, is to live and in that living "to be."

All of this [plane] is an illusion. Everyone thinks that it is the reality. It is not! It is the Illusion. This is all created to evoke emotion within the Soul. The world that lurks ouside of the doors, that be in that which is termed the murk and the mire of the marketplace, is an illusion, for [there] entities wear "cloaks of ego" to be permissible and acceptable to all others who are participating in this wonderment of folly.

The real world is that which lies within, that [which] is indeed the encounter with emotion--to see the world for what it truly is through the moment you feel it. This world would never exist if Man did not have the eyes to perceive it in "moving emotion" in his Soul for it would be a no thing.

The real world exists only on emotion--[emotion] not governed by logic but [by] moving Love. When one deals with the real world, he is not dealing with the Illusion; he is dealing with Emotion, indeed, with Feelings. It is the emotion that is unseen that transcends death and matter. In life, you do everything for Emotion and Feeling. And the ultimate feeling is Joy.

Love And Joy Are The Emotions That Lead To God

This God, whose basic element is Love-Joy, knows that everything that you do is for the learning of it and the experience of it, and [that] no matter what you do, your life will never end; that each time you do [something] you gain from it respectively. And one day, when you have encompassed all of the

"What has kept you from knowing these things? Fear! Fear has ruled your entire destiny! You do everything as a prompting through fear. Fear is a deep-rooted emotion that goes back to the beginning of time on this plane when everything [was] governed by survival. Fear is great and powerful sword that has been used in your society, in [your] religions, in your government, in your schooling. It is a wonderful tool to enslave."

emotions in all of Life's spectrum, you return unto Him. That is [called] Ascension: [returning] back unto the Father pregnated heavily with "fruit," with feelings, for the worlds, the eternities to come are based on virtuous feelings--on God-Man's Love for all things rather than his despise for them.

Each time Man gains the joy of that which is termed Wisdom and Love within his perpetual Soul does he become more unlimited to encompass more Unlimited God. [Thus], your children's children's children of a million years to come will dance in the sun, will be part of galaxies you have not dreamed of. Dance in the sun or a hundred suns from here? An Unlimited God hath the pleasure of doing that! Thus, God--who is the Reaching of Forever in All Spectrums--have you who return unto Him the advantage to be.

Fear Has Ruled Your Entire Destiny And Kept You From Knowing These Truths

What has kept you from knowing these things? Fear! Fear has ruled your entire destiny! You do everything as a prompting through fear. Sadly enough, you do it because if you don't you will not be accepted, which means you will not be loved, which means you will not be esteemed and honored, which means that you contemplate yourself as a no thing. Fear is a deep-rooted emotion that goes back to the beginning of time on this plane when everything [was] governed by that which is termed survival.

Fear is "not knowing." Understand it--fear is not knowing! Mankind, once great and noble Gods, has become the squalor of herd-like animals. They cling together for security yet they fear their own kind. In this herd-like disposition, they have lost the knowingness to understand. When Man does not know, he lives in fear. Thus, fear is prevalent everywhere. And it is a great and powerful sword that has been used in your society, in [your] religions, in your government, in your schooling. It is a wonderful tool to enslave.

When Fear Is Removed You See The Folly Of This Illusion

We remove fear through the Lord God of your Being. And the way we remove it is by removing the "altered Ego"--not Ego, but alteredness, meaning fear. You are all God but you are ruled by that which is termed an altered Ego. Ego of itself is God, meaning "unaltered." The altered Ego is that which has been termed the "Anti-Christ." The altered Ego sees limitation and alteredness in everything.

"When you learn to accept and be the receiver of all thoughts, you are actually in that which is termed The Mind of God. That is where genius is born, brilliance is seen, love that passes all words and understanding exists in."

When we remove fear, we allow unlimited thought to occur within the brain, the receiving unit [for thought]. We allow the brain to expand through its pituitary and pineal glands, [which] allows unlimited thought to enter the receiver, to go through the central nervous system and to be a different feeling than you have ever felt before--[one] that the Soul has no record of and no word [for]. And the more unlimited you become, the more joyful you become and the more folly you see in this Illusion and this Game.

The more you become [unlimited], the lighter your body will grow and become. And one day, through unlimited feeling, unlimited thought, you can complete your Soul and ascend this life--by raising [the bodily] vibrations and going back into the Source. [That] is called "divine ascension," meaning the body will never have to die.

Death is a blasphemy to an isness. The body was built to last forever. It has within it this moment the potential to never grow old and to live a million years; that is what it was programmed for. That which exists within it insists on dying because it insists on having birthdays of "joyous occassion" [in] which you celebrate a year of "olderness." That is a truth!

When You Remove Judgement The Love Of Self Is Born

What has kept you in limitation? Limited thought! What constitutes "Limited God?" The refusal to accept **all** thoughts. Thought has no judgement against it until it is entered into your being and weighed against your pious attitude.

When you learn to accept and be the receiver of **all** thoughts, you are actually in that which is termed The Mind of God. That is where genius is born, brilliance is seen, love that passes all words and understanding exists in. When you lose judgement, then you gain wisdom; then you have the ability to love. And the first love that will come is of Self.

And when you look at yourself and you look over all of your life, you will look and say, "Alas, when I did [each] thing that I feel so remorseful for, at the time [I did it] I did not know [I would feel] remorseful; I was [only] experiencing it. Why should I feel guilt for that? Because it changed afterwards? It only changed into another understanding."

And you shall begin to look at yourself and say, "Alas, I never failed!" And you will look back on your life and all the things that you did--and didn't do--and you will see the "purposeful good" in it. Then you will begin to love yourself, and you will remove your harsh judgement against yourself. And behold, the Love of Self is born, and you will never be critical of yourself in

"You never knew how beautiful you were for you never looked at yourself. You never looked at who you are and what you are.

You want to see what God looks like? Go and look in a reflector and look at yourself—you are looking Him straight in the face! Know that you are Worth. There is no value to your worth. And there is no image to your beauty. And there is no end to your kingdom!"

your action ever again.

When love is established you can look at all entities, and no matter what they have done, it was all good; and no matter what they look like, they are all beauteous. For the [same] "fire" burns within them—and as long as it burns within them, it is a certainty it is burning in you.

To Love And Worship Self Is To Love And Worship God

You never knew how beautiful you were for you never looked at yourself. You [have] always compared [yourself] to someone else. And when their beauty began to fade, it caused you to fear and to find someone else to compare yourself to. You never looked at who you are and what you are.

You want to see what God looks like? Go and look in a reflector and look at yourself—you are looking Him straight in the face! Know that you are Worth. There is no value to your worth. And there is no image to your beauty. And there is no end to your kingdom!

If you are God, then who do you worship? Self! To love God, whatever you conceive Him to be, is to love yourself completely, through and through; to have compassion, pity, warmth, love, understanding, and, above all, forgiveness of Self. When you learn to be that way, then there is no need to follow any ideal except your own. Then you have found the truth of what God is and what your destiny is. And the greater the love grows within you, the greater your kingdom shall manifest abundantly around you in this your reality. And the more it manifests, the more unlimited you will become.

God's Only Desire For You Is That You Be Happy

Everyone, indeed, wants to know what is "God's Plan" for them, aye? Well, what is your plan for yourself? That is your answer! The Supreme Isness that is the beauty of the flora, that is the clothing on your back, the sheen in your hair, the twinkle in your eye, the beauty of your skin—what is His **only** desire for you? That you be happy. And "happy" is not a mere word of a good wish for another; it is a state of being. When you are in a state of being of joy and happiness, you are in a state of God.

In a state of joy, you are pleased with all things about you, and life and wisdom and creativity flows from you. In a state of joy, there is no such thing as hate. You can never hate anyone when you are happy; nor can you be remorseful, nor can you be

"No man ever had a thought that didn't come to pass. If an ideal exists in the heart of Man and in his Soul and in his God-self, it will come to pass.

The ideal of Christus—God expressing completely, unified, uniquely singular in Man—must no longer be an ideal but a realized, factual existence, for [in] all that you are, there is nothing greater than what you be in your perfect, aligned, complete being."

guilty, nor insecure, nor fearful, nor angry, nor lacking, nor needing. In a state such as that you find Utopia.

When God Is Realized In Your Totality You Become A Christ—A Herald Of Peace

Who are you? You are God-Man called "Christus"--God in the embodiment of Man on this plane. [You] be the one Ideal, [the] singular, purposeful, first Ideal that brought forth itself from the Foundation of Life. Your mother and father did not create your Soul or Spirit. You are as old as they are [for] no one was created any younger than anyone else: all were created at the same moment.

The creations that followed the Gods which you are, they are happening every day. The Father is busily becoming every ideal that every Son of His is thinking. Now, no man ever had a thought that didn't come to pass. If an ideal exists in the heart of Man and in his Soul and in his God-self, it will come to pass. The ideal of Christus--God expressing completely, unified, uniquely singular in Man--must no longer be an ideal but a realized, factual existence, for [in] all that you are, there is nothing greater than what you be in your perfect, aligned, complete being.

When you begin to see the principle and the truth and the value of your citizenship amongst **all things** and realize that God sublime liveth with you; that you **be** the true Son; that you be **all** that the Father is and that all that the Father has, hath given unto you the trueness in heirship to His Kingdom; that all that have pained your heart and given unto you sorrow you can now correct--[then] love is born innately. And through your love, God is expressing Himself in a more perfect principle and cycle. Then Christ is known, Christ is born, Christ walks amongst men; the Messiah is here.

He who loves beyond the meager temples of Man into founding the God within Man, he be a Messiah, he be a Christ; he sees and recognizes a broader spanse of God living in greater elements, and his dominion lies before him. When he hath accomplished and come unto his inherited understanding, he is, indeed, a Prince among men, a King, a God, a Messiah, a Christ; he is a Savior. [When] he hath been all these things unto himself, then can [he] so deliver [them] unto his beloved brothren, for [then] God is understood and seen [in him], and when it is seen, it hath become.

When you realize that you are the Christus, what it means is that you have realized that you are God, supreme ruler of your kingdom. [Then] there is not negative or positive: there is only the God-Force, the understanding, the ongoingness of it.

"The Christ is you! The greatest thing that that which is termed religious orders or the Church did to un-enlighten this plane is that they took God outside of Man, put Him outside, far, far away. They separated Man from his divinity in order to enslave him. You have been a product of that."

When each entity realizes that the Father be not singular but be **all** peoples and begins to indeed live that reality throughout their existence, then that which is termed the prophesied "second coming" is at hand; it has already begun.

There are many upon your plane, beloved, that are possesssed with the idea that there is one singular God coming for them all, perhaps to save them from themselves. What He wishes to do with them I do not know! I know of no such entity, but I know of all entities. "God realized" is realized in all peoples. There is no savior, there is no teacher, there is no law, there is no kingdom that shall save you from you for none have the right to do so.

There be not **one** Christ; there be **all** Christs, **all** Saviors, **all** Lords--and only of their own beings, of their own kingdoms, of their [own] understandings. The Christus be not one messiah but shall be all messiahs. To [say] that there be one savior, that there be one Christus, is to say unto all the masses that all the mass be less than one greater. As I see it and know it and have learned it and have **become** it in the totality of my being, there be no entity, **none**, who be exalted amongst his beloved brothren or his fellow man.

The Christ is **you**! The greatest thing that that which is termed religious orders or the Church did to **un**enlighten this plane is that they took God outside of Man, put Him outside, far, far away. They separated Man from his divinity in order to enslave him. You have been a product of that.

Believe you are God, you are the Christ. And those who fervently condemn you for believing that you be God, they indeed have a great learning to come unto. They who wait hourly for "His Coming" and [wait] impatiently to torture all who do not believe as they do, they will never see it come to pass. And behold, indeed, he who be pious amongst his beloved brothren and condemn them unto a life of devilry, woe unto him, for he shall perish of his own undoing and his own judgement and his own belief; it is **he** who will be riddled with devils and doubts.

The Christ Is Known Only By Living It

Now, Christ is all your brothren. He is wonderfully alive. He sits upon the throne of your being and builds your kingdom in justness and honor. And [He] sees Himself always in all others; be it man or woman, be it colors or creeds, it matters not--He is the same everywhere.

What constitutes Christ in any man is **knowing** that he is [Christ]. When that knowing, that perfected attitude, indeed that perfect moment comes into being, then he becomes that which he knows he is. And that [knowing] is in "the doing of"--the action

"I will teach you to love yourself so grandly that no matter what color stands before you, what nation, what creed, what religion, you can find God in them as you have found it in you and [can] love them as evenly as you have learned to love yourself. That is complete Godhood. That is the Divine Father expressing in His beloved Self."

and the thought all culminated into one perfect alignment, that the thought be the word, indeed the word be the action. You cannot say to men, "I am the Christ," until it is known. It is known by living it; that is the only way.

Now, [there] comes a Great Light unto your heavens at the close of your time as you count it. It is the Great Light signaling that which is termed the Advent of the Age of God and the Age of Spirit. That Age, indeed, is within the next moment of your breath. And all who live upon that Age are only that which **live** God within them expressing outwardly. That is the Christ within Man; that is Man the limited entity realizing God the Unlimited Entity. And it shall only be them, indeed, that shall be drawn to this plane. None can come nigh again unto it lest they be of the same thinking.

The More You Become Your Christ The Greater Your Paradise Of Emotion

All who are gathered in this audience, beloved of my being, indeed wonderful of my being, you be the Son. And the Father, He is the Wind, He is the Element, He is Life.

And who be you in all of your miseries? You have placated yourself upon a plane, engaged in illusions through limited thought; have passed judgements, lived in judgement; have created terror, lived in terror; have created miseries unto your being and live in miseries.

The Christ, the God, the Son indeed--the higher you come unto Him and His realization, the greater you are taken from this plane into that which is termed the Heaven of Understanding, that which is termed the Paradise of Emotion that lacks, in its entirety, sorrow and misery, hatred and bitterness and war. Those be illusionary emotions that are cloistered upon this plane that Man exists upon.

I Will Teach You How To Love Yourself Into Your Godhood

Unto you this day in your time, I am a teacher extraordinaire, servant unto your being, lover unto your being. I will teach you how to Become. I will teach you how to feel and to take with you the truest treasure of this plane--Emotion. I will teach you how to think "unlimitedness." I will teach you how to **be** unlimitedness. And, grandest of all, [I will teach you] how to be God, that you rise above the murk and the mire that has insisted upon you staying here and perishing.

"There have been a small host of Masters appear here on your plane [for] eons in your time to teach you this same teaching: that God is one and the same with you and that the Kingdom of Heaven is within your kingdom. But you do not listen so good. Instead of applying the teaching, you end up worshiping. There shall be no worship here—only learning."

I love you evenly and will teach you to love yourself so grandly that no matter what color stands before you, what nation, what creed, what religion, you can find God in them as you have found it in you and [can] love them as evenly as you have learned to love yourself. That is complete Godhood. That is the Divine Father expressing in His beloved Self.

I will teach you how to do that. And in loving yourself, you will learn freedom: you will not grow old, you will not whither, you will not die. You will learn to love yourself as the wondrous entity that you are. Then you who have led yourself so eloquently can be a light unto the world--only because you are an Ideal for someone else to learn to love themselves, remarkably so.

I Will Not Have You Worship Me!

I have no following. None! If they follow I send them away. I am no religion: that is limited beliefs designed to corrupt! I am what I am: Supreme Lord God of my Being. I will not have you worship me nor make me the Ideal. Only **you** can be your Ideal. Only **you** deserve worship for yourself by loving what you are.

There are many "teachers" on your plane that enhance themselves while having that which follows them worship them. I am not this way. You never become God when you worship the feet of another. And you never become God when you insist your savior is in another rather than in yourself.

You are to learn. You are to learn by an enigma that has no body for you to grasp or hold on to and no temple that you can lie in [for] hours and worship in. Your perfect "temple" is your body. You perfect and most exquisite "garden" lies within your Soul. And you, who be immortal, **you** are your own savior.

There have been a small host of Masters appear here on your plane [for] eons in your time to teach you this same teaching: that God is one and the same with you and that the Kingdom of Heaven is within your kingdom. But you do not listen so good. Instead of applying the teaching, you end up worshiping. There shall be no worship here--only learning.

I am not the enigma that you see--daughtren of my being. I am my own being. I have chosen for you this form of expression for [a] singular purpose. What we love about another is not how they look or how they dress or how rich their purses be but rather what be their "collective being" that shows us **our** being, for they are mirrors unto ourselves. When you look at me, you see a woman but hear a man. God is both man and woman; He is neither. Thus, that which you see of Ramtha The Enlightened One will be what you **feel** of me--the greatest teacher of all.

I have chosen to speak to you through my daughter that you see me as imageless, for beauty is imageless--there is no Ideal for it. And the most important thing you will hear this day is not me and my enigma but what is being spoken and is coming about within your own wondrous being.

When You Know You Are God You Are In The Kingdom Of Heaven

Unto you there is nothing greater. Know you this to be a truth! Whatever is in the Unseen, 'tis not greater than that which you be, for seen and unseen are the same--it is still God! And you are not the "lowerarchy" or the hierarchy--you simply are. There is no entity that has ever lived nor shall ever experience that has ever been greater than any of you here. And there has never been one that has ever lived that has ever been **less** than any of you here. For how can God the Father have degrees of greatness? He doesn't! God, the Entity, is an **Isness,** not a perfection.

Now, thus that which you be, be my beloved brothren. The only difference between that which you be and that which I be is that I **know** that I am God and you do not! Knowingness determines Destiny; that is the only thing that does. Knowingness determines what you term Future; nothing else does. And when you are the greatest to the pinnacle of truth expressing--which is God, the Unlimited Master--then that which you be and the destiny to which you have created has always been called "The Kingdom of Heaven," indeed.

So who be You? You be God, my beloved brothren, that which is termed my equality. That which is termed the Self of my being is you. When you learn to think as I think, you will become the Lord God of your Totality. And that which you know, you shall know as I know. And [then] you shall never die, but you shall ascend into the heavens as a brilliant light--a much more natural way than dying to the world and decaying.

My Only Desire For You Is To See You Become Your Christus

Everyone has their own truth. Everyone believes certain ways. [And] who is wrong? None! Everyone who believes in whatever they believe in is precisely correct for them. Thus, all of you who believe, who have your own aspect of divinity, are precisely correct, for the belief is for you who have created it to be a part of.

I will not take [your belief] from you: it is not my desire to do so. It is my desire to teach you that which you need to know; to help you to Become; to send you on splendid journeys to where you curse me, hate me, despise me—only to see you Become. And no matter what you do, I will never stop loving you.

Love The God That You Are Above Anyone Else

And what shall you do when this day is finished? You are not one of you to be a preacher. Not one of you! For the only thing you can teach is what you truly live; anything other is hypocrisy here. No one is qualified to be a preacher here, for no one knows what the Kingdom of Heaven is, looks like, feels like. None!

But when this day is finished, go and live your splendid lives according to your feelings; not the opinions of your neighborens, your parents, your husbandman, your wife, your lover—whatever it be—but by how **you** feel. When you go by the feelings within you called Joy, your path will take many curves over many mountains and into many plush valleys. But you will have done precisely what a God does for the rarest treasure of all—Joy.

Live your "light" by your feelings. Bless and love the God you are above anyone else for you can never know anyone else: all you know is yourself.

Love Others In Freedom As God Has Loved You

By living in joy and how you wish to [be], condemn no man for how he lives. Love others in freedom—let them be as the Father has let you be. And [then] the light that emanates from your wondrous being will be a Light unto the World; indeed it will, for you who shine forth, shine forth from within, not outward. And "within" is by being who you are—unrestricted joy, declarative of the God you are, greatness humbly expressed.

Those that witness your "birth", your life—they will be in wonderment. When you are a Light unto the World is when the Father within you—unlimited Joy—shines forth that [you] can condemn no thing. And if they hack you to bits, to pieces, it would never be cause for you to despise them or to hate them or deny them, because they are God also and you will live again! When you are a Light unto the World, you are True Christ, you are True God—however you choose to live it.

"We are changing your consciousness here on your plane and we are preparing your humanity for a mass intimidation. And we shall intimidate the integrity of Cloistered Man and allow him to see something great and brilliant that it will cause him to think, to open up and to allow that which is termed Knowledge and Love to flow forth.

You are a part of the intimidation. But the greater intimidation to come will be in your heavens, and we are already working on it. Then that which is being taught here in this wondrous and illustrious audience will be the same [as] you will be able to see with your own eyes."

Preach to no one. Be yourself. Love yourself. That is all that is asked. This plane is weary of preachers, philosophers, and hypocrisy. It is desirous of Sovereignty—Individuality. And that is what I will teach you.

As God Walketh, So Shall You Walk

We are here this day in your time for a greater learning. It is not a new learning, to be sure, for it has always been. And it has always been constant, [although] its undercurrent and overcurrent have not always been seen. But this "new/old" teaching, as it is termed, will give unto your kingdom the immortality, the foreverness in being, the prize of your being.

You are what you think you are. And if you be the greatest amongst men to your own being, so shall you be. Yet, by the same token, if by being the greatest to all other men, you can be the humblest and love them and see yourself and the Father's Face in each of them, then you are God Sublime—the Prophesied One.

As you become more of Life and of the God that you are, all the veils that your Father be in will be opened up to you that you can be a traveler unto Him. It is one of the rewards of simply knowing who you are; it has always been there and it will always be there. Partake of it freely.

Never lose sight of the Love and the Beautiful Entity that you are. And remember, as God walketh, so you walk; as God thinketh, so you will think.

We Are Preparing Humanity For A Mass Intimidation

Now, we are changing your consciousness here on your plane. And we are preparing your humanity for a mass intimidation. It is necessary for your altered Egos, which means altered God. And we shall intimidate the integrity of Cloistered Man and allow him to see something great and brilliant that it will cause him to think, to open up and to allow that which is termed Knowledge and Love to flow forth.

You are a part of the intimidation. But the greater intimidation to come will be in your heavens, and we are already working on it. Then that which is being taught here in this wondrous and illustrious audience will be the same [as] you will be able to see with your own eyes. Why is all of this [being] done? Because you are loved, and your consciousness adds to the whole of consciousness everywhere. Everywhere! Think what you think only affects you in this realm? Consciousness is termed

Space—what you think is empty, yet [it is] powerful enough to hold up your planet. Space is Density. It is that which is termed God: it is called "consciousness." When yours is lifted, everyone's is lifted. Everyone.

For eons Man [has been] born only to live in a "vapor of time," to grow old and die. [But] there is much, much more. And by having you realize this, you add to the whole of humanity in all places indeed, as you soon will see.

Let Us Begin . . .

This day in your time, I am the lover of this God, the lover of the Christus that you are, the lover of Man that you are, the lover of the brother [that] you be unto me. Unto each of you do I serve and teach this day. [And] all the things given unto you in speech, so shall I manifest for the glory of the Father within you, that all things come to pass to give unto you greater realization of Life and to show you the measure called "unlimitedness." So be it. And so it shall be.

Let us begin. . . .

PART ONE

UNDERSTAND YOUR HERITAGE, YOUR KINGDOM YOUR DESTINY

CHAPTER ONE

YOU ARE THE GIFT OF LOVE—THE GIVER OF LIFE

"To understand love is to reach out and grasp it, possess it, and lose it, only to find that it was in you all along. And thus, entity, is the perilous adventure of Man."

"The Father is Ongoing, Contemplative Thought—Life. In order for Thought, or Life, to continue on, it must have a purpose in continuing. The purpose is you.

You became a part of the Father [in order] to continue His expansion in the Ongoingness. For the purpose of going onward, the Father gave [to] you—the once startling, beautiful, perfect part of Him—the only thing that ever is and ever will be: the totality of God. You became the one perfect movement that did not have another ideal to make it come to be. You broke away and stood still, and from your thoughts, the Father moved into that which is termed Forever."

YOU ARE THE GIFT OF LOVE—THE GIVER OF LIFE

I wish to speak upon a word that few understand and all grapple, as it were, to secure. I do believe the word is called Love. Wondrous word! Why [speak] I [of] Love unto you. [For] all here have been perplexed by the word. You have been damned by the word. You have been enslaved by the word. You have been enamoured by the word. You have been intrigued by the word. You **live** by the word. It is time you understand what it means.

What be Love? To [understand] Love [in its] highest regard, we [must] go to the Father that is the Life-going essence, the Continuum of All Things.

You Were Birthed From God's Love To Continue His Expansion Into Forever

In your beginning of your beginnings, all [was] Thought. Thought, the Ultimate Creator, is the Father, the Primal Cause, the Foundation of All Life. There is no thing that exists outside of Thought that is other than what God is. All that is, is the Father. The Father is the Life Force, a wondrous element that is the basis of all that is.

When the Father contemplated within His thoughts, contemplated the thought that He was in, He expanded Himself, [for] anytime contemplative thought [is] applied, the reasoning essence comes forth and that "expands" the thought--the thought will become "more." [Thus], the Father contemplated Himself to an existence to be "more" in His existence.

The very essence of Thought, the very purpose of Thought, is Love. Love be, indeed, that which gave unto the Father His existence to comprehend Himself [in order] to expand Himself into a complete expansion. If the Father [had desired] to keep His ideal expanded form [the same] as He was, then He would not have expanded [Himself]. How could He have expanded Himself if that which He expanded out of Himself was only [to be] an extension of Himself [that] did not have a unique form of Himself?

When the Father contemplated His Most Divine and Perfect Self, you became--all became--that which He expanded: an illustrious part of the expanded, contemplative Thought, realized in a wondrous moment. You became when the Thought became "more." Thus, the make-up of what you be is the same as the Father for you came from Him.

"The Son is the perfect and only thing that is ever the complete duplicate [of] the Source itself. You, the Son, are the only thing that is perfect of the Father. All else are ideals given by the Son and put together through the Father."

The Father is Ongoing, Contemplative Thought--Life. It is ongoing [and] does not stand still, no more than your own thoughts can stand still. In order for Thought, or Life, to continue on, it must have a purpose in continuing. The purpose is **you.** You became a part of the Father [in order] to continue His expansion in the Ongoingness. Thus, [through you], the Father became an Ongoingness into Forever, which has no count, which has no measure, which has no time, for Forever is in a moment, yet the moment is infinity.

For the purpose of going onward, the Father gave [to] you--the once startling, beautiful, perfect part of Him--the only thing that ever is and ever will be: the totality of God that is the totality of the Source--[and] that is **you.** You became the one perfect movement that did not have another ideal to make it come to be. You broke away and stood still, and from your thoughts, the Father moved into that which is termed Forever.

You Are The Son: The Only Thing Perfectly Of God

When you became the expanded part of the Father and you became a reality, you [became] what is termed the Son of the Father, Son of the Living God, Son of the Cause. When you are speaking that is "all for one and one for all," the "allness" is that which is termed the Perfect Brotherhood [that] is condensed and brought into one singular movement called the Father.

The Son is the perfect and only thing that is ever the complete duplicate [of] the Source itself. You, the Son, are the only thing that is perfect of the Father. All else are ideals **given** by the Son and put together through the Father.

Such [things] as your plantum, your fine carpets, your white walls, they came forth from that which is termed an ideal. And who is the giver of the ideal? The Son--he is the giver of the ideal. And where get he the substance to put forth the ideal from? The substance is God--Life.

God's Love Gave You Free Will: The Creative Essence That Is Love

Now, no thought [i.e., entity] of itself can be separate of itself lest it have that which is termed individualized form, or what is termed the action called "free will." Free Will is the essence of the Life Force that was given to each God, to each Son, that he may be the unique totality of himself.

The essence called Free Will is Love; that is the vital bloodstream of the Thought to all of you. Free will gave to you a separateness yet a oneness with the Father [so] that your

"The only reality is that there is no reality. Love is the giver of the option to exercise all realities in whatever illusion state you wish."

thinking, your perfect thought processes, as they are so termed, could have a unique creative flow all their own. The [creative] Flow is called Love. The Will is called Love.

Love, in its ultimate form, is the ongoingness of Life that the Father has permitted Himself to be in regard to His Beloved Sons. Love's purest form is the Will that the Father gave to His Children--Gods that we be--that the gratification of that will enhance and become more [so that] wisdom will be incurred.

Love is the purest form of the Life-blood of all elements, [elements] that are composed through the love of [the] Gods [that we are], through ideal form, [and] created from the substance called God into Life. **That** is Love! And we take Love to the lowest form here and imitate the God that we are moment to moment through our creativeness, [for] each moment that you create, you are [bringing forth] Love from your being. [Creativity] is the act of the personified being of bringing Love forward into an absolute flow, and a flow is not bound by laws and reason, [but] it is a wild, free-movement, creative form that will live on into forever.

Love Is The Giver of All Realities

Your connection [with], your life force [from] the Father is called Love. To define the essence called Love, you must define it as this: It is a wild, free-movement, action-essence that is Life caught up in unlimitedness and [not] restricted by time or impatience.

Love, in the truest purest measure, has no restrictions. It loves unequivocally, it forgives unequivocally. It can love in complete freedom, and it is necessary for life. Love knows no logic nor reason and creates its own set of values because it is a "free essence." It is the "glue" that holds all things together. It is the essence that binds us to all essences. It is the wonderful "peacemaker."

Now, what of Love and reality. The only reality is that there is no reality. Love is the giver of the option to exercise all realities in whatever illusion state you wish.

Love Is The Freedom To Create From God However You Choose

You are the expanded part of the Father. The Father, though separate from us, [is] yet one and the same with us: He is the Ongoingness while you are the singular. [He] gave unto you Himself [so] that you can be all that you desire to be in your contemplative thought. He is the basis of the fulfiller of your dreams. And who is the dreammaker? You are the dreammakers. But what are dreams made of? [Thought], God, Life.

You can take of the Father and create from Him any one thing you wish. Be it great or vile, be it ugly or beautiful, be it wonderful or sad, it matters not, for the Attitude of man is as wild and free as man's Love is. Thus, any thought that you have in your ongoingness, the Father will supplement through His body. And whatever thought and ideal you desire, whatever it is, He can give to you freely.

Now, to show you the Father's love, let me show you an example. We will take a very vile-looking snake [that] is detested by humanity. The creature of himself [has a] long, wondrous body, for he has many muscles and many bones; his skeleton seems to go forever. He moves very swiftly and has a very big head. He has fangs that can puncture you and bit you [as] his only defense and he can bring down a man [great in] size within moments after [using them]; yet any man could hack the snake to bits [or] step on him and crush his head. The snake expresses perfectly [and] is an ideal of a God who created him for the purpose of extended life on a life chain.

Now, let us take two Gods. One [has] a scientific mind, and he'll say the snake is a wonderful machine; it can do this, it can do that; the color of its skin is wonderful; it moves very swiftly; it is beautiful [and] it expresses perfectly. Now, that is the attitude of "fault removingness" of [this] one God.

Another [God] will come up and say the snake is hideous, it is vile, it is an awful creature: it can kill man, its bite is dangerous [and it] is a terrible creature. The attitude of this God has condemned the snake.

The Father sees [all] things as perfect: all things of themselves are ultimately pure. [It is] each entity's attitude toward it [that] makes it a beautiful or a vile, ugly thing. You see?

How great is the love of the Father, [who] be the totality of life substance that the snake is, [to] give you--the most perfect of all that He is--the right to cast your opinions and wills upon the snake however you choose? The love of the Life Source for you is [so] great that the Father has the capacity to become any one thing in the ongoingness of Life that His beloved Son desires through Thought. It will be anything you wish It to be. It will alter Itself in any way you wish to alter It. It will become vile and ugly and vulgar or [become] to the heights of beauty--however you wish It be. Yet in the process of altering and changing and condemning and whatever else man does, the Father remains perfect for us. And that is a wondrous thing, is it not?: that the Father could become all things, destructive [or] great, simply through the whims of thought of his wondrous Son.

That is called Love!

You can do with the Father what you will for His love is steadfast; He is with you no matter what. However you see something, no matter how vile it becomes [to you], it is still God. That promise is unshakeable, for the Father of Himself is pure energy and knows no "objectness." It is only we Gods, who have the ability to contemplate thought, [that] judge a pure thing "evil" through our own creativeness.

The love that is between you and this Source has no condition. If the Father had restrictions upon His wondrous Source, His wondrous Life that your ideals can come from, then you would not have any individuality, for anything that you would think would be censored by a law of the Law of God. Thus, you would not be compelled to be a free-thinking or free-willed entity.

You Are Always Perfect In The Sight Of God

When you became the separate parts of the Father, your first and most wondrous bodies were pure "light synthesis," wonderful light balance. And your first reckoning when you looked upon the Father was perfection, Perfect Thought. When you look upon the Father in the simplest of His forms, there is no alteredness, there is no incompleteness, there is no limitedness: He is pure and ongoing and wonderful.

And when the Father looked upon you, what He saw in the brilliance of your light was Himself, and [in your light synthesis], He has held you always in Perfect Thought. There is where our gift of Free Will, our gift of Love, was given--our covenant was made with Him. Always, whatever you would do, wherever you would venture unto Him, you would always be perfect unto Him. If He looked at you any less than that, then you could not have the ability or the will to exchange altered thoughts or limited thoughts or limited measures, [for] it would not be yours to do. Neither could you have the free will of free-moving thought to [even] have the conception of anything limited. We are perfect entities. Perfect. Why? Through the movement called Freedom and the ability called Love.

The Father's love is unending. He will let you do whatever you desire to do for He knows that you are perfect and [that] no thing can ever take you from Him. The Father has created no thing superior to Himself to remove your life force--ever. So He lets you play out your illusions and your games and your intentions and your sorrows and your pityness and your worries and your happiness to whatever degree you choose to do so. You will always be. When [your] life is spent [there will] be yet another, in however way you wish to express.

There Is Nothing Greater Than Loving Yourself

For you to advance into [Life], you do so through the mastery called Love. And how does mastery through Love become? First [by] recognizing the importance of who you be. For centuries [you have] been taught that you are some spawn of a mistake, that you are outside of the providence of God and all of His wonderment. You are not **outside** of [His] Kingdom; you **are** the Kingdom, you are the God, you are the Life Force, you are the Principle and Primal Understanding, you are the Good. You are the Great "**Is.**"

When you begin to love yourself and care for who you be and the quality of your existence, and care about your illusions or disillusionments, you begin to gain them into a moment that is spent in what is called happiness. Then you begin to advance.

Love of one's Self--there is nothing greater. When you truly love yourself, that light, that united force, that happiness, that jolliness, that mirthful being extends itself unto all humanity. It is difficult to hate anyone, it is difficult to beseige anyone, it is difficult to hurt anyone when you are in a state of Love. When love abounds within your wondrous being, then the world and all of its displeasures becomes beautiful, Life becomes meaningful [and] takes on Joy--and Joy, through the exuberance of your being, declares your being pure.

You can accelerate your being to its heights through Love and Joy. The more you spend all moments in the acts of becoming happy, joyful, loving yourself, the closer and greater you come into greater planes [of being]. [And] when you go from [this plane] to greater planes, you leave behind bitterness and hate and war, diseasements, sorrow, pity, sadness, for they are not of other worlds to come--they are of this world. And the way that you get closer unto that which is termed the Seven Heavens is through that which is termed Joy and Love.

You Master Love Of Self By Thinking "Love" and "Joy"

To be pursuant in life, you must learn the simpleness of loving your being, **all** of your being, [and learn] to treasure it, be at wonderment with it, be at peace with it.

There are many of you that are slaves to time. You are slaves to sorrow. You are slaves to bitterness. You are slaves to hatred. You are slaves to all of those things that have no reckoning value with Love. And there are those who who cry out that they have not found love's sweet hour; that they have not embellished upon Life the fullest of their beings; that they are incomplete. I tell you this: There is no lesser God than any of you: all are equal. Thus, what shall be made available to one is made available to all through the love of the Father, the Life-Force of All Things.

If one has found happiness and joy, he has found God. And yet his neighbor may be in a state of embroilment into that which is termed "enslaved immateriality"--the slave to treacherous thoughts, sorrow, hatred, war, diseasements--and he may say, "Oh, beloved brothren, I am weary in my heart and in my Soul for I have found no love in my life. I have none to call my own or none to warm me when it is cold and embittered outside my window. What have I done to bring on such a curse?"

How did he do it? He let the mundane things that are created through an ideal enrapture his Soul and blind him to the reality of [their being] illusions, [blind him] to what Life is. And he has overlooked Love in the simplest manner for he has reasoned it out of his life: he hath no time for it. He hath no time for his beauty, no time for his Soul, no time for his existence or his bed, for he is busy with his illusions and being unhappy, enslaved, embroiled, entrapped and hurt.

Who is right here? Is the happy entity right? Is the embroiled entity right? They are both right! But I will say this to you: The one who shall gain when [this] life is finished and it is no more is the one who has gained his moments joyfully and found peace. If one thing made him not peaceful, he cut it off from himself. If any action did not make him peaceful, he took it from himself. [And] all the things that were worth happiness, they were treasured in small chests within him.

And of the sorrowful entity, what of those things that caused sadness? They were worn like armour, [like] restful beads, ankle bands, human earrings, [for] he was proud in his unhappiness. [And] the more that he wore them, the more [unhappy] he got. And when he passes from this plane, he knows not what the value of Life is.

What is it that you shall love about yourself that will count in what is termed the continual? Ponder this for but a moment: If I were to take your body away and yet leave your personality, your Ego-self there, what would we see? Nothing, for you are a compensation of the Thought that is immortalized in the Soul [and] has given life to the Spirit. [We] would see nothing, but your thought is still there.

So what is it you must love about yourself? Indeed, you [must] love the body for it is an outward expression of the inward mind. [But] what is it that makes the inward mind happy? Love! And can you see love? Can you taste joy? Can you see happiness? You see the outward **manifestations** of them, but if the truth be heard, you do not see [them].

"To master Love and Joy in this existence, [in] this life form and this body, is not a terrible mastery; it is a wondrous one. And it is mastered through the action of thought—by thinking 'Love, Joy.'"

So what is it that you need to take care of? The unseen essence called Thought. Collectively, thoughts make up your attitude. When you die—and most of you will because you do not believe in ascension—and you leave your body to the world, you are still going to be, but you are going to be in another world where it is "thought." And those that climb in calibre in this other world do so through happiness and joy, [through] love [and] eagerness of heart. That is a truth.

To master Love and Joy in this existence, [in] this life form and this body, is not a terrible mastery; it is a wondrous one. And it is mastered through the action of thought—by **thinking** "love," "joy."

And how do you love others once you have established love within yourself? Well, how does the Father love **you**? Does He love you possessively? Does He govern your thoughts? Does He tell you how you are going to be? Nay, He will not do that, for He loves you in complete freedom to do as you will, for your will is His will: that is the covenant between God and His Children, God and His Sons, God and Himself. That is a truth.

So how be you to love others? Unequivocally, and in absolute freedom. Love one another. Love in freedom and you will love yourself.

Love Gives You The Freedom To Live

Love is not only copulation. Love is the deepest respect an entity can have for himself and others. Love is the ability to honor a bum as well as a king. Love gives the ability to love beauty in all thoughts. Love endows us with divinity. It is the unlimited essence that lifts our totality in the receivership of all good.

Love is the premise of Life. Love is that which permits Life to be. It is the virtue that hath created all other virtues. And when man tires of jealousy and war and hate and bitterness and separateness—when he has done all of those things, he will come back to the essence called Love that binds him to his perfect thought and to his perfect reality. Love is the permitive nature in all of us that permits life to be unbounded.

It is the nature of our beings to have Love. It is the nature of our beings to try to express it. It is the nature of our beings to try to become it, for in becoming it, it brings us closer to the reality of who God be in His love for us.

What you have suffered in your existence, you have suffered in many [lives]. You must learn to love your freedom by freeing yourself from your chains, for when you are free entities, there is nothing that can ever enslave you again, for freedom begins in

**"Love
Is the immortal essence
That allows us to be forever,
For Love
Is the arms of God.
It is the thing that holds us
Into eternity.
It never dies—it never dies!
It only becomes richer,
Freer,
And deeper.
To be utterly God,
You must know how to utterly love
And be loved in return."**

the Soul.

Freedom? All freed men have thought that is ever-active and is never still, that is wild, evolving, moving. As long as you have the ability to have thought, through the love of that thought and the purposeful being of that thought, you will go into your infinity of "freedment."

It was reason and remorse that caused your death in the first place. It is reason and remorse that have caused your age and taken away your youth and valor. It is reason and remorse that [has] caused your trauma. It is Love that will set you free.

You Learn Of Love By Allowing Yourself To Be

To find yourself, you do that by looking within and allowing what is there to be. To be! You will never lead until you stop following, and you can only stop following when you start listening to your own thoughts and your own ideas and your own genius [and] your own purposeful good and put them into play, into Life, into Now. Then you have become a leader. And leaders, in that which is termed the God sense, they are masterful entities [that] are governed through Love. They could not be creators if they weren't.

Learn to be leaders. Become involved in the Now, the Moment, the wondrous Now that uses your tomorrows to come as a result of all your yesterdays that must be lived now. When you exhibit one act of freedom, it will open unto you another pinnacle existence that has been far removed from anything you have ever lived.

You learn Love by "being." That is Love. You must become Love in order to know what it means.

Ponder these words I have given unto you. Ponder your relationship unto the Source and be a perfect reflectant on it. Ponder the creative thoughts and how they come. Ponder your life and how you live it. Are you being governed by time and enslaved by it? Are you enslaved by your society? If you do not have joy, speak from the Lord God of your Being and ask why, know why; I assure you the answer will manifest itself for you. When you have mastered the "why," then there is no more lacking and no more illusion. Then you can begin to live your life in a more purposeful being. So be it.

CHAPTER TWO

YOU ARE A DIVINE ESSENCE—ENTRAPPED IN MATTER

"When the Gods [which you are] began to experience this plane [they created and came] into a 'lower' level of frequency, a 'lower' level of vibration, what occurred was that soon, into your millenniums, they began to be 'locked' into it. For their major concerns were no longer the purity of their being or the divinity of their being, but how they would survive."

"The God within Man is the God that possesses Man of himself. That is the light embodiment that surrounds the body as you know it. Within the embodiment of light, the Mind of God exists; [your] divinity is there, it is assured."

YOU ARE A DIVINE ESSENCE—ENTRAPPED IN MATTER

The Lord God of your being is made up of that which is termed Spirit, Soul and Ego.

Your Spirit: The God Of Your Being

[Your] Spirit was born first of the expanded, contemplative Thought of the Father. The Father is, in the beginnings of all beginnings, Thought. He is the Great Void. He is the Great Space. If you take the Great Space and the Great Void and refine it into a "knowingness," it is pure Thought.

When the Father contemplated Himself and turned His Thought inward unto His Being, He expanded Himself. And the principle born thereof became Light. The expanded parts of Thought will always be Light: thought appears as a burst of light. It is the light that holds the perfect image [of thought] that creates the manifested form in a lower diversion [i.e., mass or matter].

[Of] the Light Field of the expanded parts of the Father, all became. All Gods were created at the same moment: Expanded Father became Expanded Son.

The Light is the Spirit of our beings: it is the God of our beings. It is the original embodiment that we hold, and still to this day in your time you possess the original Spirit, the original God-self, the original embodiment of light that you once were in the totality of your glory.

The Spirit **is** God--in singular form. The Father is the Plural: He is the Substance of All Things. The expanded portions of Him, called His Beloved Son, is Him. Thus, **all** who be, be God. The greatest reckoning, the greatest truth, the greatest awareness, the greatest isness, the greatest awesome power of all that is, all in one, is the totality of the Spirit of each man.

The God within Man is the God that possesses Man of himself. That is the light embodiment that surrounds the body as you know it. Within the embodiment of light, the Mind of God exists; [your] divinity is there, it is assured.

[The Spirit] connects up with that which is termed the Ongoing Thought, or the Premise of the Father, that is the Basis of All Life. Thus, the God of your being is aware, at any one moment in time, collectively of all there is. It hath the capacity for the understanding of all that is and is in a state of pure knowingness of all the moments that are, for the God of your being is aware of the God of All [and is at] understandment and at onement with it continuously.

Your Soul: The Lord Of Your Being

The Particle Light Entities could not manifest thought of their own being: the thought would pass through them. [So], in order for the Light Entity Principles to be that which is termed the ultimate creator of the Mass of the Father, they had to have the ability to captivate the Ongoing Thought and put it into that which is termed a "stillness," what is termed Memory. When this was made available as a conception [by] the creative force of the God, the Soul of the God was born.

In order for a God of Light Being that is in the continuous flow [of Thought] to create; in order for him to take the substance of the continuous flow and create an image; in order [for him] to contemplate the thought to expand it into what he calls "creation," he must have the ability to captivate the thought and hold it still. That is the reason and the purposeful good for the Soul.

For instance, [in order for] a God [to] create a flower, in order for the flower to occur, the thought of the flower must emerge. The thought of the flower is taken from the flow [of Ongoing Thought] which the God, or Light of your being, is at onement with. Thus, the thought of the flower is held perfect in the Soul as an image. Then the God can contemplate upon the image of his thought and give to it color, give to it reason, give to it height, give to it substance, create it as a whole however long he wishes to and whatever moment he wishes to. By holding the thought perfectly still, he may paint its picture perfectly.

Without the Soul, Thought cannot occupy itself within the being. Thus, the Soul, the holder of all truth, the holder of all recognized knowledge, the possessor of all thoughts, was created specifically for that: to hold the Ongoingness still.

The Soul, called the Lord of the being, is a separate unit from the Spirit, for the Spirit houses the body with light and supports the mass therein. The Soul lies within the mass [and] is housed near the fourth seal in a cavity under a shield of bone.

The Soul hath the ability to captivate the essence, the flow of Thought—which is God the Father, the Supreme Creator—and hold the thought completely still into Manifested Emotion. The Soul is thus the recorder of all thoughts.

The Soul, because it records all thoughts as Emotion, has the ability for forever memory. The Soul, because of its ability to store all thoughts within its being, allows the creature of Light Being to have emotional experiences—which allows the entity to come back into the Principle of Thought.

The Soul is [itself] without emotion. It is without, indeed, an attitude. It is merely a storehouse or memory bank, as you would term it appropriately, for all thoughts encountered by the God that is in line with All Spirit.

Memory does not have size; it is an essence. Your memory is not in your subconscious; it is in your Soul. The Soul remembers **everything.** That which is "knowingness" is locked within the Soul. That which is termed talent is locked within the Soul as experience.

When you feel emotional, you are feeling a thought that has bombarded the emotional structure [or] light structure of your being. The memory that the Soul houses in it from eons past are recorded as feelings. You only have to feel to have the visual effect come into view.

Not only is the Soul the carrier of all information, it is the "doer" of the bodily movement. It is called the Lord of the being, for it is the governor of the body. When death passes within the body, the Soul is called forward and houses itself back into a light structure, that the Spirit computes and gains the data of thought and consciousness and continues to expand the living being called Man.

The Ego: Your Unique Personality-Self

When the Soul and Spirit came together, it [formed] within its being a Personality-Self that was unique from all other Gods. No two Gods ever created the same for no two ever grasped from the same point of thinking the same thought and contemplated upon it the same.

Thus, the Soul was the reason [a] collective identity [came] forth. The Spirit gave unto the Soul all the knowledge. [The Soul] held it steadfast; [the Spirit] contemplated it. And through the collectiveness of the Soul and Spirit, an identity began to emerge.

The Body: Your Kingdom

The embodiment of Man was created, after all other things were created, specifically for the purpose that the Gods could express in a lower form of Thought: [Thought] manifested into what is termed gross matter or that which is termed the "solidity in mass."

All mass is a solidifying of light matter. Gods of light matter had no embodiment to solidify themselves upon the plane of Terra, or what you call Earth, to be a part of the kingdom [of gross matter] that they had created in this universe from their creative Soul-Self.

The embodiment of Man, or the "image" of Man, was created through Thought. [It was] the perfect embodiment [for] a God, [for it] could hold the Soul and be enveloped by that which is termed the mind of the God [to allow Him] to experience his kingdom [of matter] that he had created.

It was not **one** God that created this plane! It was many Gods that created this plane. Of all the populace that live on this plane in the Now, that inhabit all seven planes in all five hundred and thirty-three dimensions of each plane and all ninety-nine universes surrounding the one universe--of all of the totality of all that is, if you divide that number by two, you will come up with the precise number of Gods that were created and that took part in the initial part of creation as you know it.

Thus, all Gods created all things on this earth. The mass of the earth, or that from which they created, and the life which they had to create from, is the one God [called] Father Divine, the Principle Cause, the Source.

The embodiment came forth through much experimentation. And only man was created first, and he was not even created with a loin. The loin was inside him [that he may] give birth to himself in what you would call later the process of cloning. Man became the embodiment [so] that the Gods could experience this plane.

The Altered Ego: The Child Of Fear

When the Gods began to experience this plane [and came] into a "lower" level of frequency, a "lower" level of vibration, what occurred was that soon, into your millenniums, they began to be "locked" into it. For their major concerns were no longer the purity of their being or the divinity of their being but how they would survive.

Pure Gods were like little children: they were unknowledgeable of hate, they were unknowledgeable of limitation, they were unknowledgeable of war; they were unknowledgeable of even death. They were like little children for they did not know any of these things, for none of these things existed in the Mind of the Totality [from] which they derived.

All of these "atrocities of limitation" did they experience upon this plane in the lowest form. It was through the experience of emotion--for the Soul records the emotion of images and the thought of emotions--that collectively brought together what is termed the altered Ego.

When [the embodiment of] Man was entered upon this plane [by the] Gods, the "tree of knowledge," the altered Ego was born. How was it born? [By] the Spirit of the God bringing forth images and [the images] being conducively displayed within the embodiment which [the God] had to maintain.

The altered Ego was born through the mind of Man as set principles accepted for survival. The altered Ego is collective attitudes displayed as a certain programming. It was the programming for survival, wrought by fear, that created the altered Ego.

Upon the death of the embodiment, the Ego, [being altered by fear], found it could not return unto the Plane of Antrium, which is called the Plane of Pure Gods, but could return only unto an altered state of awareness; that it was only through an altered state of awareness did it "become."

Thus, born again and again into the embodiment form, the Ego, of itself, intensified. It intensified, and the more it became, the easier it was to have forgotten the greatest divine purpose.

Thus, the mind of Man is the Ego: the "culminated thought-synthesis" that was wrought by the divine Spirit and stored by the Soul into collective emotion: a set principle, a unique being.

The Interrelationship Of Spirit, Soul And Ego

How do they even now work in coexistence in your embodiment? The giver of all the thoughts that you possess daily in your time, nightly in your time, each moment in your time, are a gift of the Spirit, or the God of your being.

The Soul supplies the storehouse of thought. The collective Ego, that has been set into precedence eons ago in your time, disperses [the thoughts], alters them, rejects them--does whatever it decides to do--because it is driven through survival, through fear. Thus, it will not accept an extreme ideal that is not admissable on this plane [without] evidence [of its] being a reality: it will dismiss it. The Soul will thus record the emotion of that dismissal as being "ignorance."

The more that the Ego of your being lives [in an altered state], the more limited and the more cloistered your view on life will become because of survival driven through by fear. Even now, the fear of rejection, the fear of being different, locks away the God-given thought-synthesis that is there always in the pure state of knowingness that elevates Man always.

How do they work in harmony with one another? The Soul, called the Lord of the body, [or] the Lord of the being (the

Spirit being called the God of the being and the Ego called being) is in a state of total receivership; thus it records the information admissable unto its being.

The "programmers" or givers of astute information to the Soul are the altered Ego and the Divine Spirit. Whatever [they] give unto the Soul, the Soul will manifest in the bodily form [i.e., matter], and its grossest kingdom of manifestation will always be the body. Always.

Because the altered Ego lives at all times in a state of total fear [for its] survival, [with] the ultimate culmination of fear being death, the altered Ego is always putting forth unto the Soul the refinement of death. And what it fears it will eventually become.

From the moment you are born, you grow old that you may die and perish. That is the survival synthesis that your Soul has [been] programmed under. Thus the Soul, the Lord of your being, has provided your body into a perpetual state of dying, [for] all things that are reckoned in thought and accepted through the altered Ego will become a reality through the [Lord] of your being.

Coexistence? Without your Soul, you would not be, for you could not occupy Thought. And if you could not occupy Thought, you would not have an Ego at all. And if you did not have an Ego at all, you would be pure God--the ultimate of your being. Ultimate. Pure Being would be the Mass of God rather than the unique Son that you are.

*

Know you what a Soul is? Hmm. Most don't. They only know they have one--or everyone is supposed to. And if someone else has it, they must certainly have it--if they don't, they'll get one! I shall explain to you:

[When] Thought, or that which is termed the Isness of God, passed through Light, an emotion was [created], but the emotion was fleeting to the Light Entities. So the Soul was created [so] that it could captivate Thought (that flees through light) and give forth another frequency to be captivated forever.

The Soul was created inside each Light Principle [so] that it could gather that which is termed the River of Love, or that which is termed Life, from God the Father who issues forth Thought.

The Soul records every physical emotion [i.e., feeling] within that which is termed the embodiment. Every thought that you [have] ever engaged upon throughout all eternity is lodged within your Soul. Through that which is termed its emotional structure, it runs the physical body. The Soul is what allows you to slumber and allows the body in its respiratory systems, circulatory systems, digestive systems [and] electrical fields to continue when the consciousness is far away.

The Soul is the Lord of the body. It does programming unto the body given to it by either your Spirit or your Ego. And whatever thought you allow to flow through the wondrous organ called the brain is experienced through that which is termed the central nervous system as a "rush," as you appropriately call it, [and] the Soul records that as an emotion. That which is termed the Ego or Intellect formulates a word to call it "feelings."

Whatever you have ever thought, you have in your Soul. The experience of everything you have ever done is [registered] in your Soul [as] Emotion. That is the storehouse of Knowledge. If you did not possess the Soul you would only be Light; you would be energy without memory, energy without creative values, energy and only an "isness."

[illegible]

[illegible]

[illegible]

CHAPTER THREE

YOU ARE AMNESIACS OF A GREATER UNDERSTANDING

"You are all creators, image-makers. You are all Christs in your limited understanding of acceptance."

"You are the amnesiacs of a greater understanding. Who else designed this magnificent place for you to inhabit? Only you did this, for are you not the supreme creatures of intellect and intelligence? Indeed you are. You did not evolve into that; you always were that."

YOU ARE THE AMNESIACS OF A GREATER UNDERSTANDING

I am Ramtha the Enlightened One, indeed, servant unto the Isness of the Force I AM that be termed the Giver of All Life, that be the basis of all that is.

Thought be indeed the giver of all that is. And the power that is the giver of all that is has been called the Mother-Father Principle of All Life; indeed, for it is. It gives forth of itself to become all things, that the substance that makes up the creativity of all things be that which is termed God Almighty or Life--splendid, silent, perfect, indeed ongoing extension that will never dim but only become greater.

Unto the Father, indeed unto the Force, the Life Source, the I AM Totality, the Isness of All That Is, indeed am I a servant unto this hour.

The Christus: The Genius Of Creativity

And who be what is termed the "creator" that takes the Ideal Thought, manifests it, elongates it, divides it, subsequents it into what is termed another collective creativity? It is the Christus who is the creator of all magnificent Images that are, in their basic form, the Totality of God.

The Christus, the image-maker of all splendid life into the forms that separate it from the mass, gives uniqueness to the character form [of] all that is. [The Christus] is the Son of the Principle Cause, is the singular motivated unit of that which is termed God the Powerful, God the Source Giver, indeed the Force-maker, indeed the Principle Understanding of All Matter. He is the Son of the All That Is. The Christus be the one who brings together thought collectively to bring forth the image of the thought into the matter that the Father is.

Without the Father and the Son, there is no thing, for the Father gives Life, but the Son gives the creative form from which all things of Life come forth. With the Son and the Father together, All is. And with the alignment of the All That Is, you thus have a spectacular platform of existence that is multifaceted upon several planes of understanding, indeed upon several heavens of being, indeed upon several thought frequencies of understanding. Without the two there is indeed nothing; there is no thing; there is not even the word to bring forth that which would be, for nothing would be.

The Father, of Himself, is pure energy mass. But He has no form. He has no beauty for He is All-Beautiful. He has no beauty for there is no part of Him subsequently to ever give

"You are amnesiacs. You are the true Christs. You are the ones that made the spectacular light that you see in your heavens, that brought forth the genius to put forth a million universes in a single, tiny cell. You are the ones that brought forth color, design, texture, smell, together in dimensional forms of vibratory understanding. You are the magnificent creatures, indeed, of a magnificent Father that is truly everything that is."

credence [to], to ever give alignment [with] or perfect reflection of another part of His Being. Thus, the Father simply is. He is pure energy, bound with emotion and motion, but colorless, imageless, indeed vast space.

The Son, His prize being, the apple of His eye, is the master handyworker here. He takes from the void, indeed the mass, the pure energy, and creates vividness from it, design, eloquent being, the wonderment of that which is termed Forever. The Sons have brought forth into the looms of life that which is termed color, that which is termed texture, that which is termed smell, that which is termed, indeed, Being, that which is termed Totality.

The Son would not be if the Father was not. Thus, with the two perfectly aligned, Life is boundless. Even a singular cell has its own universe, its own universe within universes. Did you know that your cell, or your molecular structure, has that which is termed the atom rotation within it; that it rotates around its own central life force, or its sun; and that each particum that goes around the central spark also has its [own] universe; that a single cell can have a million dimensions, for it hath a million particums of life within its tiny structure?

Who is the genius of all this creativity? It is the splendid Son, the Christ, the God Know That I AM Realized with the freedom of what is called thought perspective [who] created millions of universes within a tiny cell [and] universes in grand number and display amongst a galaxy that truly hath no end.

Unto the Christus, who be the Image-maker of the Force, who hath given a spectacular array of "beingness" to the glorification of his Father, who hath painted a masterpiece in the Illusion of Time for all here to be a part of--unto He, the true Lawgiver, the Dispenser of True Beauty, the True Isness, the Crowned King of God's Kingdom, I am a servant unto.

You Are Amnesiacs Of A Greater Understanding

And who be you? You are amnesiacs, for you **are** this Christ! You struggle to be an image of your own Self by [bringing] forth creativity upon this plane in very limited measure and form. All of you are artisans, whether it be upon canvas or [through] stylus and paper; whether it be [in] business transactions or clothing or color or word manufacturing. You are all Creators, Image-makers. You are all Christs in your limited understanding of acceptance.

You are amnesiacs. You are the true Christs. You are indeed the ones that made the spectacular light that you see in your heavens, that brought forth the genius to put forth a million universes in a single, tiny cell. You are the ones that brought forth color, design, texture, smell, together in dimensional forms

"What do you [do] to get back to the vastness of creativity and to the knowingness of having your Father aligned perfectly with you? By allowing yourself to know that you truly are [the Christ], that that be a truth, to know that that be the reality of Isness. That is all it takes. Knowing allows you, God of your being, to be the Christ of your being, to be the Great Creator."

of vibratory understanding. You are the magnificent creatures, indeed, of a magnificent Father that is truly everything that is.

What do you [do] to get back to the vastness of creativity and to the knowingness of having your Father aligned perfectly with you? By **allowing** yourself to know that you truly are [the Christ], that that be a truth, to know that that be the reality of Isness. That is all it takes. The "knowing" is also a stroke of the brush upon the canvas. The knowing adds glitter to a picture without it. Knowing allows you, God of your being, to be the Christ of your being, to be the Great Creator.

You all have that which is termed the River of Thought. You all have the Ego which sets yourself into purposeful being, that gives unto each of you the right to create. Each of you have the Ego to collectively divide a pure thought into a form of emotion [so] that it [may] come to pass for you. You all possess this. You have this "divine fire" right within you all the time.

You are the amnesiacs of a greater understanding. You have limited and inhibited your greatest potential of being [the] God that you are. Who else designed this magnificent place for you to inhabit? Only you did this, for are you not the supreme creatures of intellect and intelligence? Indeed you are. You did not **evolve** into that; you always were that.

What Shall I Teach You? How To Be Gods!

Who are you? You are the ones that can put a cloud in front of the sky. You are the ones that can put a cloud in front of the sun. And you are the ones that can sustain life. You are the creator of this magnificent portrait of God I AM through the perfect image-maker, the continuation into the refinement of Life Isness. That is what you are.

Unto you, I am a teacher, servant indeed, lover of the totality of your being. That which I have given unto you, indeed have I given unto myself. And [from] that which I have given unto myself, indeed have I found the answers and the wisdom. To love you is very easy, for I love myself and the totality of the God I am, for I am a lover of the Father, the virtual Source of all that is.

What shall I teach you, indeed? Not to be magicians, [but] how to be Gods, and how to become [that] simply: how to think unrestricted; how to be in a totality of absolute freedom, always. For each one of you that becomes these things, then this beloved place of splendor of the imagery of your creativity shall sustain a greater extension of life and will allow the thinking of this plane to be virtually illuminated; that babes born unto ignorant mothers will teach their mothers; that babes born unto warlords will bring peace to the family; that babes born to the simpleton will teach him love.

When you add to the consciousness of this wondrous plane, you add to the life that it shall draw to it. And each time life is drawn to it, or another God enters therein, it must enter according to the "consciousness level." If you have improved the consciousness level by the virtues of becoming that which you are in the splendid array of your being, then you add to the qualities of the entities entering upon the plane.

The treasures of heaven are in a palm turned upward. For all that is issuing forth from the palm is love and peace and happiness and God-Life forever. Each entity that enters from this day forth upon this plane shall enter and shall teach their parents. And they shall be the Heralds of Peace, the true troubadors of a miraculous age coming forth.

Add to this plane by Becoming. Everytime that you Become, the plane becomes greater and closer unto a Divine Seventh.

CHAPTER FOUR

YOU ARE NO LESS THAN THE BLOSSOMS

"Death is a great illusion. You always have been and you always will be."

"Master, with feelings that are different and unique and beautiful and a being that is purposeful within its innocent self, where did you accumulate all of your knowingness, your feelings, your uniqueness? Think you evolved to become what you are in one life that is only a breath in Eternity?

Everything that you are you have accumulated over the vastness of time of living time after time after time and gathering from each life experience the emotional values and wisdom that have helped to formulate the character and the unique and beautiful thing called you. You are much too priceless, you are much too beautiful to have allowed your beauty only a moment's seige upon the eternalness of Life."

YOU ARE NO LESS THAN THE BLOSSOMS

Are you any less than the flowers? Indeed. What is their life? They are born of a pregnant bud and burst into full bloom from a warming sun. Their wonderful essence and aroma fills the air with a maddening sickness that is called "fever" and causes all things to be rejoiceful. They help the birds in their flight, the insects in their vigil, and man in his delight and quest for love.

And so the wonderful flower sets a seed for itself to come again. And when the bloom falls off and the fruit bursts forth, Ah! that is termed "wisdom"; that is the product of life. And when the fruit is consumed and the leaves fall, and the spice and harvest of autumn is on the land, the tree begins to shiver with an eastward wind, begins to loose its wonderful leaves and stands blatantly bare.

And when the great white silence comes and fills the boughs of the trees with thickening, glistening brilliance, and all is cold and barren, where be the blossom? It is in the memory. It is in the wisdom. It is in the growth of last spring, and it is coming forth again, for when the season has turned and winter is gone, the buds come again, and behold, there is another blossom.

Why think you are any less than the blossoms? You think that you only live in spring, produce your fruit in summer, drop your leaves in your autumn, and die in your winter? You think that is all for you?

If the promise of life is enriched in a singular blossom, then are you not greater than a great blossom? Is not your life more important? Indeed, it is, for as these continue to bloom every spring, so will you live every life.

What a story your blossoms could tell of all the seasons you've seen!

*

Master, I will tell you, [and] I wish you never to forget this: **Life Never Ends**!

It is a truth you can mutilate a body. You can hack its head off and disembowel it and do every wretched thing you can to it. But you never destroy life! That is immutable; it is immanent. And those who go for the folly of war, or enslave in attack, or beseige their neighbors, they are doing a great folly, for they never destroy the person. Ever! EVER!

Death is a great illusion. Everyone here has died in wars. Everyone here has been betrayed. Everyone! And yet they still are. 'Tis a game! I laugh. No one can betray me. No one, indeed, can betray you! For what should they betray you to?

I tell you, the moment life ebbs from your body you are in another embodiment of your Spirit--what gave credence to the value of flesh. You always have been and you always will be. Unfortunately, the flesh is vulnerable because we make it that way. But that which is the prize which lives within it no one ever destroys--it can never be! Remember that.

And learn to have pity on murderers and enslavers and slayers, for they have a terrible working through of emotion that they have to deal with when their conquest is finished--and that often takes millenniums. The slain has a body within the next moment; the slayer never forgets!

*

Death is an unnatural state of being, for the body is created by the attitude, the possessor of the body. But you who think in the silentness behind your eyes always live. And what you go into is what you came from and there decide what you wish to do upon the next adventure--for that is what this all is.

This [life] is a **dream**, a **great** dream, a facade, if you will. It is "thought playing matter," and it creates deep realities that bound the emotion to this plane if not dealt with.

*

When you pass from this embodiment you are pure emotion. Are you not pure emotion when you remove all of this! Aye? What is it that is making all of this work? What is making the mouth work, the eyes work, the ears work, the body work? It is this wondrous energy behind this "mask" that is pulling all the little strings, as it were. It is the energy that we love in another: that wonderful Personality-Self. But could you identify it if you removed the body? You would not even see it--not with **this** eye!

When you pass without the body, you are passing into a state of pure emotion--**pure** emotion. That means you no longer have the aches and the pains of the body, or the hunger of the body, or whatever. You are simply emotion, which means that everything is amplified and intensified.

What is loved about you is not the body; it is the "unseen essence" that makes [the body] work. That never dies! Try to destroy your thought. You cannot do it. Try to destroy light. You can concentrate it, amplify it, but you cannot destroy it--and **that**, entity, is the physiological make-up of the true Self!

You never die; you never will.

*

The peace that passeth all understanding occurs before death. It comes with passing from one element unto another. [In] death, merely the body passes and the entity is free of all the instincts of the "infernal" body, of all of that which is termed pain of the body, and it becomes a free Soul-Self.

There is a saying that is associated with your religion: "Behold, in the cradle of God there is no more pain and no more tears and no more sorrow and, indeed, no more agony." [It is a truth] because that which you become is pure light, still retaining that which is termed the auric body and Soul. That which is termed the physical body that associates all of these things is no longer, and the entity is in Utopia; it **is** "in the Cradle of God."

*

The death of the body is like slumber. The Spirit calls forth the Soul, which is the child of the Spirit. The Soul travels up the last of the "seals" through a "tunnel." The light at the end, indeed, is the invisible dimension to which it shall be longing to. And the body expires. It takes but a moment and is painless.

Then the entity is aware as it has never been aware. It can see all the levels below it, around it and through it, for it has become a pure Light Principle. And in that Kingdom, it no longer suffers the pain or agony of the body; it does not suffer sorrow of the body; it does not suffer disappointment—it only "is." That is called Utopia, or what Yeshua ben Joseph [i.e., Jesus] spoke of as being "Paradise."

Death should not be feared, for it is not the "ending of," only the continuation of that which you be.

CHAPTER FIVE

YOUR LIFE IS AN EMOTIONAL ADVENTURE

TO REALIZE YOUR DIVINITY

"This is an audience of that which is termed, indeed, Knowledge, deep, profound, Isness Knowledge that gives unto you, indeed, Answers unto that which is termed the perplexity called Life.

In this audience shall you learn that which is termed a grander understanding of your existence, the reason for your existence in this 'level' of learning, and what use that which is termed the Divine Body is for."

"And who is God amongst you all? He be sublime Life that has given unto you the foundations of your being. God be All Life. [And as] you are not outside the jurisdiction of Life and how it is seen, thus we must conclude that you be God!

But how be you God? You do not express as the [rain] or a calm day or a vivid storm when it rolls. You are not a great oak who knows not its time to perish. You are not the beautiful bird whose song is unique amongst its friends, that wings its way into an elusive sky, into a wind it does not see.

You are not birds, to be sure. You are not clouds. What are you? You are the thing that has realized them. Who realizes life? Not the subjects of life for they are busy participating in it. Who, then, is the realizer of life? It is the one who created it who realizes it.

You are God explicit, God sublime, God the Supreme, God formed in such imagery that his own species is assured in the beauty and the likeness of what He hath patterned.

You are God who hath manifested himself as Man."

YOUR LIFE IS AN EMOTIONAL ADVENTURE

TO REALIZE YOUR DIVINITY

Introduction

I am Ramtha The Enlightened One, indeed, servant unto that which is termed the Source, Explicit Life; unto that which is termed the Christus, the Creator in Life; unto that which is termed Man, the Creator of Creation; indeed, unto you, God.

This is an audience of that which is termed, indeed, Knowledge, deep, profound, Isness Knowledge that gives unto you, indeed, Answers unto that which is termed the perplexity called Life.

In this audience shall you learn that which is termed a grander understanding of your existence, the reason for your existence in **this** "level" of learning, and what use that which is termed the Divine Body is for. Thus we begin this hour, as you term it, in this wondrous audience, to learn, indeed, a bit about that which is termed "Whys" [and] to give forth that which is termed Answers.

[What] you will hear, you will contemplate, and your mechanical scribes will play it over and over and over and over, endlessly--tireless, wretched creatures they are! And you will listen and listen, and listen and listen. And lo, indeed, shall you contemplate more and more and more, and you will say, "Ah, 'tis true! This is how this and that indeed occur." But for certain, [you will] not be sure the reason **why** it occurs that way until you experience it.

That which is termed the interchange of what is called experience makes what you will hear this day in your time, in your calibre of understanding, a knowingness--a knowingness of that which is termed a steadfast "isness" that simply **is.** [Then] there is not a question, indeed, as to the reality of it--it simply is. It is not that which is termed the dry morsel of a mundane philosophy; it is that which is termed a profound reality.

Knowingness, indeed, is not only being able to have the capacity to repeat [what you hear] verbatim--after listening to it over and over and over--but experiencing it, indeed, [so] that it becomes a part of your reality. Knowingness is **feeling** that which you hear: experiencing it conclusively in the totality of your being.

"In order to understand 'created form,' or life, that was now beginning to expel consciousness [on] this plane, you, [the Gods], the Light Principles, [the thought], took on an embodiment and refined it [so] that you could interact [in] its size, its greatness, with all life that had been created."

God the Father, the Source, is not that which is termed a **word**! It is an Isness; It is a Complete Ongoingness. The word, indeed, poorly exemplifies that which is termed the exalted value of God. To know what the Presence is, is to be it, experience it, taste it, become it, indeed, in your ongoingness of Life! Then it is not "God" the word, but it is, indeed, that which is termed a "feeling-isness of experienced value." Philosophy, indeed learning, is **nothing** until you have lived it.

All of you here, indeed, are experts in hearing. All of you! You are experts in repeating. All of you! [But] heaven forbid if you should repeat it as you hear it, for that would lack imagination. So you change it and add to it and make it a bit more . . ."isness" as you repeat it. I find it entertaining. But few of you know how to **live** [what you "know"]. Few! And more than few, most of you refuse because you **fear** to live it; and in that, [you are] allowing the credence of fear its own principle of modified life to occur every moment. In the act of refusal, you are really living an altered vision, an alteredness of what could become an All-Consciousness.

When you begin to understand the words that you repeat [by] experiencing [them], then experience upon experience, measure to measure, adds to the quality of your learning. And little by little, ever so slyly, you are Becoming. That is how I teach!

This hour we will teach the Knowledge of Isness—the "Why." [So] that you feel everything that you hear, you shall experience a measure of it in reality that the knowledge adds to the quality of your profound and beauteous being [and] becomes a steadfast Knowingness. Thus, when you learn "how it is," the "how" can indeed be practically applied into this kingdom called Life into any measure you wish to apply it.

Let us begin with feelings.

The Embodiment Called "Man" Was Created To Provide An Emotional Interlude With Matter

The creators, the Gods, they have created all life here, everything, from the beginning of what is called plant life, into that which is termed animal life as you know it, into the kingdoms divided called fishes and insectuals, lizards, and all of that.

Creatures were devised by the Gods for the expression of feeling, the expression of creative life, creative life that was mobile [and] that could [itself] express. The flower was created by a group of Gods: color was introduced, aroma was added, [and] various degrees of the flower were then brought unto different designs. And everyone did not labor but simply **became** what they desired to create.

"You not a flesh entity. You are a culmination of electrums that are cultivated as feeling-attitudes [for] expression.

What you are, endearing entities, 'tis not that which you inhabit but what you feel. You are known by your emotions, not your body."

The Essence of all living things has within it, indeed, the secret of a spark of life from its creator—You!

The Gods created the embodiment [of Man] for the express purpose of having a "vehicle" that had a complete sense of "modus operandi," if you will, to interlude itself with Mass.

In order for a thought to smell the flower, to hold the flower, to wear the flower, in order for a thought to grow the flower, the thought must have a vehicle to do it with. [Of itself], the thought passes through the flower: it cannot embrace the flower because it **is** the flower; it lacks the sensitivity of its own origin to embrace the flower. In order [for] the creator to know that the [rose] is explicit, is beautiful, in order to experience its vividness, [he] must have [a vehicle that] vibrates at the same tone as the rose vibrates.

In order to understand "created form," or life, that was now beginning to expel consciousness [on] this plane, you, [the Gods], the Light Principles, [the thought], took on an embodiment and refined it [so] that you could interact [in] its size, its greatness, with all life that had been created.

The body was created [that the Gods could] have the sensation of the "unseen" [i.e., feelings] experienced through the "seen" [i.e., the body]. In other words, the reason and only reason that Man, the embodiment, was created was to **feel** that of the lower kingdom called "gross matter." That was the **only** reason: to experience life that the Gods had created in a much lower form.

The body was created to house a most complex, explicit, electrical system of light variables that make up and constitute the true Self-entity. You are **this** big! You are not this big; you are **this** big! In the **smallness** of your being [is] composed everything that you have ever been since you evolved from your beloved Father.

You, the God Principle, are not a flesh entity. You are a culmination of electrums that are cultivated as feeling-attitudes [for] expression. What you are, endearing entities, 'tis not that which you inhabit but what you **feel.** You are known by your emotions, not your body.

The only reality that exists in any of you is your Spirit, which is the "great light" of your being [that] is **this** small, [and] the Soul of your being, that records everything and allows you to have credence and a reality of thought. Your body is a chosen, refined vehicle for expressing and [for] feeling upon the "first level" of Life.

[The embodiment] you [now] possess is a refined version, if you will, of a very humble creature in your beginnings. The creature was Man-like, a humanoid, but did not possess the swiftness of feet [and] thus was continuously made a meal of by

"When you forgot [your divinity] and became Vulnerable Man, [your] quest has been to find you, through heavenly heavens, through burning fires of hell, through dogma, religion, conquering war, dissension—anything to know what you look like!

As creation has 'gone into a slack,' if you will, the becoming is now into 'Self,' [the creator of] all of this [plane]."

the animals about. [As] the understanding of Man began to grow—as his survival necessitated it—the entity of the body perfected itself over ten and a half million years in your counting here on your Earth. It took that long for you to become what you are this moment.

[Thus], the creator of the flower became an embodiment that he may embrace the flower. By embracing the flower, the created value [i.e., the flower] stood forth Self, God I AM: "This I created, and from this splendid ideal I shall create more and more and more. And I shall **feel** [my creations], for feeling is the **prize** of my creation." It certainly is, [for] a God does not know it is a living God until it creates "itself," that that which it creates mirrors back to itself its creative genius.

You Are "Lost" In Matter And Have Forgotten Your Divinity

Once the [the Gods], the creators, had learned what it was like to feel all the plant life, to see all the animals, to taste aqueous substance, to see the wind, to lie in the sand, what was the next creation? More! Kingdoms, cities, societies, creeds, religions, histories, [for] the God within Man is a **compulsive** creator, compulsive because his life depends upon it, for he and life are one and the same thing.

As Man began to create, as a creative principle began out here [in matter], entities were **driven** to experience [their creations] that they may derive the treasure of this reality in here, [in feelings, in emotion.]

[As] life became an onward, ongoing, [creative] principle, Man began to forget his Divine Self and became "Vulnerable Man," [forgetting] why he was here [was] to be a part of his kingdom. Now he has forgotten the Divine Fire within him [and] has become entrapped in an embodiment, for he thinks that to be the **only** reality there is. And because he **thinks** that is the only reality, it **is** the only reality there is!

Now Your Quest Is Not To Create But To "Become," To Go Back To The Source Of Your Reality

When you forgot who you were and became Vulnerable Man, [your] quest has been to find you, through heavenly heavens, through burning fires of hell, through dogma, religion, conquering war, dissension—anything to know what you look like!

As creation has "gone into a slack," if you will, the becoming is now into "Self," [the creator of] all of this. Who set the stars into the heavens with a backdrop called Forever? And who was

"In this life, everything that you do, you are doing for the fulfillment in [your being], a "knowingness" in [your being].

All things have already been created. You are continually on the path of this life experiencing that creativity to learn of the greatest mystery of all—You! You do everything to experience You.

Now your quest is not to create. It is to 'become,' to go back unto the source of your reality."

so clever as to design the brightest star but never to overshine the smallest one? And who created the change in the leaves, in the seasons? Who did all these wondrous things? You! Why? To feel. To understand.

Everything that you do, you do for feeling. **Everything!** There is not **one thing** that you do that does not equate emotion to you. You are an emotional, powerful entity that has the ability to feel. It is **feelings** that created the universe! It is **feelings,** entity, that created the rose! It is **feelings,** indeed, that created all there is! And it is feelings experienced in your being [that] teaches you what you are in the sum total of your Personality-Self.

Without feeling you will never know who you are. Without feeling, you are not! Feeling is the prize of every action; it always has been, it always will be. In feeling, you ascertain your Self to the depths of your Self and to the heights of your Self.

In this life that you are living, in this moment, you are living it to the degree of feeling to learn by, to become, to identify Self. Not to identify a flower any longer: that has already been identified. Or an animal any longer: that has already been set into precedence. Not energy any longer: that is already beginning to be known through "light source" and "thought." Thus, what is the "last frontier," as it were, of creative value? You!

In this life, everything that you do, you are doing for the fulfillment in [your being], a "knowingness" in [your being]. All things have already been created. You are continually on the path of this life experiencing that creativity to learn of the greatest mystery of all--You! You do everything to experience You.

Now your quest is not to **create;** it is to "become," to go back unto the source of your reality. You have already fulfilled within your Soul the ability to create; you do it every moment you think. Every moment you speak, you are creating, because the value of **feeling** is being created.

The reason that you are here and have chosen to come back here is because you **want** to--and that is a feeling; and because of Life, which allows you to experience everything that you are lacking; and [for you] to understand the identity called "Self," which equates "God."

None of you are here because of "karma." There is no such thing. That is a restrictive law the **no one** ever fulfills. You are here for the destiny to live, to experience, in **this** illusion, a mass that will equate to you a feeling--[a feeling] that brings you closer to the understanding of Self fulfilled and the collective mode called "emotion." That is the reason you are here.

Creator, you have created your sorrow. All of you have! You have created your depression. All of you have! You have

"You do not ever love another entity. You never have. In loving another entity, you only love the entity for what you can identify as Self seen openly within the other entity.

The reason you are incapable of loving another entity is because you are not the other entity! You love the other entity for what they, in their unique experience of life, express that you, in your life, can identify with. They mirror back to you 'Self.' That is love! That is the love of Self, the beginning of breaking down the mystery of what you are.

Love is feeling. Love is identity. Love brings you closer to the greatest mystery of all. You!"

created your lessness. All of you have! You have created your joy. All of you have! You have created **every moment** you have in this life, and from that creation, you are continuously obtaining feelings which give you credence that you are created value that is powerful!

To understand yourself, you must understand the "whole," you must understand the "platform" which the whole lives upon. That is why you have chosen to become this color [or] this profession. That is why you look this way or that way, and you live here and you live there, and you are expressing this and you are expressing that--for you are all taking turns with what you are with one another in order to understand the emotions of one another.

Loving Another Is Loving Yourself: The Beginning Of Unraveling The Mystery of Self

You--the greatest mystery of all mysteries. Why is Self the greatest mystery? [For] the greatest desire of all desires is the desire to know Self--what you look like, what you appear at a distance, how well you are in your learning, and where you stand in respect to the "whole," if you will.

Why is love so important to you? Love, it is an unseen essence, yet it is the most forceful, moving essence of feeling there is. And why? Because it helps you to identify what you are.

The reason love is wanted and needed so greatly is it is the one essence that permits you to see who you are and what you are and to be profoundly moved by the **great** entity that you are without restriction. The reason that love blooms and prospers is [because] it is the grandest feeling of all because it is the ability to find out who you are by seeing yourself from another's perspective; indeed, by seeing yourself from another "value."

Love! You do not ever **love** another entity. You never have. In loving another entity, you only love the entity for what you can identify as Self seen openly within the other entity. **That** is love! That is the love of Self, the beginning of breaking down the mystery of what you are.

The reason you are incapable of loving another entity is because you are **not** the other entity! You love the other entity for what they, in their unique experience of life, express that you, in your life, can identify with. They mirror back to you "Self." Whatever you find abhorring, ugly, despising in another entity, it is because **you** possess it! Whatever you find beautiful, lovely, understanding, sweet in another entity, that is because of **you.**

"When you love another, you love your Self, you embrace your Self, you become passionate with Self. When you are in joy with your Self, you are embracing God within your being and you are becoming a knowing force that is awesome in its power.

Every feeling you experience, every feeling, brings you closer to the identity of the enigma called Self. Every feeling."

You can never identify in another what you have **never** known in yourself. You can only see beauty in another, kindness in another, understanding in another, compassion in another if, in essence, you **are** that. You never **know** that until a "mirror" has been put in front of you that **is** you in all of your actions that says unto you, "Ah, 'tis beautiful, 'tis wonderful, 'tis magical. I feel such a grand way and I do not know why." Because for the first time Self is getting a good look at itself. That is why Self loves so intently.

You, my esteemed and beloved brothren, cannot split yourself into a half and send one half of yourself off to watch the other half so you get a better understanding of yourself. You cannot do that [for] you are explicitly an "isness", a "totality." Yet that which you perceive and see in another will represent you yourself every moment.

In love, you will see all of these things of Self and will experience a complete myriad of feelings--from the most cloistered of limitation, jealousy, possessiveness, doubt, anger, hurt [to] ecstasy, passion, indeed life. For love that is seen in another entity will bring out the full spectrum of all feelings [so] that you can identify who you are through your emotional understanding.

Thus, Love is the love of Self, not another. And when lovers embrace, they do not embrace one another; they embrace Self. And when lovers intertwine, they are intertwining with Self. When they are emotional with one another, they are being emotional with Self. Deep and profound and magical love occurs when another blooms the very essence that you are within your being. Then the mystery of Self becomes explained, understood.

Love teaches us humbleness. It humbles the arrogant, the pompous, indeed the insidious entity who insists upon looking to life in a most sterile mode. It brings the most reasonable entities to a most unreasonable state. It creates havoc, only to bring about peace, knowingness.

Love, **indeed,** is a wild, free-moving essence that is neither controlled by time nor age nor color nor religion nor creed. It is a **God Essence** that exhibits itself in all things, and wherever felt it brings about an alignment of unlimitedness within the being. Love is feeling. Love is identity. Love brings you closer to the greatest mystery of all. You!

When you love another you love your Self, you embrace your Self, you become passionate with Self. When you are in joy with your Self, you are embracing God within **your** being, the principle that is **this** large, and you are becoming a knowing force that is awesome in its power. Every feeling you experience, **every feeling,** brings you closer to the identity of the enigma called Self. Every Feeling.

"The reason that you do what you do is because you are driven to do it [for] the completion within the Soul that allows an identity with Self to occur; that is the reason. The experience is what is called "wisdom" in the Soul.

When the Soul, that is the greatest 'scribe' of all, closes its books, that there is no more that can be obtained from this plane of matter [for] you know who and what you are, you go on to a greater adventure. And the adventure is to wherever you wish to create it—wherever! That is simply how it is."

You Are Driven To Experience Feelings To Complete Your Identity

So what is the greatest mystery? You! You are doing all this for You, for the reason of feeling: that is why everything was created. The reason you love, marry, have that which is termed relationships is for what the entity can do for you to bring you into an emotional fire that you can learn from, [for] it brings you closer to an identity. This life provides a platform in which to have an interaction of mass with other creatures of humanoid understanding to allow feeling upon feeling to mount to be declarative of a personality that you can understand yourself in.

You are here, in this life, to experience everything in your illusion to bring about creative feelings to allow you to know who you are. That is the way it is! You are not here to be a great conqueror. You are not here to be a great healer (we have enough of them!). You are not here to be a minister or a politician. Your destiny has not been ordained eons ago, for eons ago had no conception of this moment, only of that moment. You are here to live this moment, to take from it every feeling, that every feeling will equate what you are behind the wondrous masks that all of your wear.

The reason that you do what you do is because you are **driven** to do it [for] the completion within the Soul that allows an identity with Self to occur; that is the reason. [And] the experience is what is called "wisdom" in the Soul. And when the Soul, that is the greatest "scribe" of all, closes its books, that there is no more that can be obtained from **this** plane of matter, [for] you know who and what you are, you go on to a greater adventure. And the adventure is to wherever you wish to create it--wherever! That is simply how it is.

Feelings Are The Keys To Creation, Completion And The Kingdom Of Heaven

The key to creation is feelings. Everything is created from that standpoint. Everything has **emerged** from that standpoint. And the prize of creation is the feeling one gets [from] the created value called "completion": identity of Self.

In order to manifest your desires completely and openly [so] that you have **all** that you desire to complete yourself in this life, in this interchange of transient illusion, desire from the Lord God of your Being and **become** your desire within your being--become [the feeling], the "fire" that is fulfilling. [Then]

"How do you complete yourself? By knowing you are God, [that you are an] imageless, faceless, indeed awesome, ongoing power that hath no design but whose only purpose is 'to be,' and for the sake of being, gathers unto its being all calibre of experiences to complete itself, to become a completed entity.

[You complete your identity] when you remove the images that you consistently think your Self [to be] and become an 'isness,' the 'God within,' which is the totality of all-encompassing feelings."

that which is termed the Aqueous Substance--the Father, the Platform of Life--will compose into your life, or **this** illusion, a situation of manifested occurrence that will bring to you the same electrum of feeling in [your being]. That is how you become a "magician." That is how God stands forth [and] creates from this principle and this pivoting of understanding all of its life that it wishes to have.

Do **not** visualize the image of what you want; it will never come that way. Whatever you want, **feel** what it [would feel] like [to have it]. The Source will [then] provide the actions nigh in a moment [so] that that feeling can be matched. That is how you become the Lawgiver. That is how you create your destiny. That is how you create whatever you desire, whatever you want to complete whatever is needed within your Soul totality.

The "keys" to the Kingdom of Heaven is [to learn] that the reason you are living this life is for feelings [and] that whatever created this value, [this life], can create [whatever you desire] in a moment by [your] becoming it in superb feelings. When you infinitely learn that the Kingdom of Heaven, the Treasure of Heaven, **is** Emotion, is Feeling, then you will also infinitely learn that the same feeling that created [your life now] can create **anything** you wish now.

You are still beggars. You are beggars! You continuously fight the will of others and their decision to accept you. You beg for the pence that buys you more bread. You labor in the most remorseful way to obtain life to feed the body so that it may continue to have the capacity to feel.

Stop being beggars. Indeed! Cease it! Speak from the Lord God of your Totality and **feel** what it is you want. Feel, until you become **all** of it! The Aqueous Substance will bring you what you want [so] that it fulfills and matches the feeling [within your being].

The Kingdom of Heaven is Feelings, Emotion. To have all you want and to cease your begging is to become what you wish within your being. The outward, material, lowest plane of all, will manifest [it] for you that you may add [it] to the treasure of this kingdom here [so] that it may equate and match the value of the "kingdom within," which shall live on into Eternity.

You Complete Your Identity When You Know You Are God

How do you complete yourself? By **knowing** you are God, [that you are an] imageless, faceless, indeed awesome, ongoing power that hath no design but whose only purpose is "to be," and for the sake of being, gathers unto its being all calibre of experiences to complete itself, to become a completed entity.

"Self's greatest knowingness is when Self demonstrates to Self its awesome power, its awesome creativeness, its awesome ability to change an 'absolute' into an uncertainty.

When Self knows it is God, then it can alter life in frequency values [and] become whatever it wishes to become, whatever moment it wishes to become it in. That knowingness is now!"

[You complete your identity] when you remove the images that you consistently think your Self [to be] and become an "isness," the "God within," which is the totality of all-encompassing feelings.

Self's greatest knowingness is when Self demonstrates to Self its awesome power, its awesome creativeness, its awesome ability to **change** an "absolute" into an uncertainty. When Self **knows** it is God, then it can alter life in frequency values [and] become whatever it wishes to become, whatever moment it wishes to become it in.

You have the power to raise the body vibrations [and] to take the body wherever the thought wishes to go. When you [can] take [your thought] to be a part of the laughter of a child in five hundred years to come, that is when you know you are God. That knowingness is now!

Loving Yourself Gives You The Power To Complete Your Identity

All of you don't really know what you look like, but you are a great ball of light, so brilliant in its core that the color is uncertain; that the corona outside of the fireball is the greatest rose color you have ever seen, and from the corona, the rays that extend outward are golden rods of light. So awesome is the power of this light that it has the ability to take thought and create with an emotion whatever lowered value it pleases to.

And where are the eyes in this fireball? There are no eyes. There is only Absolute Knowingness that is the true principle of everything that is. That is what you look like!

Why is it important to love that which you are? For there is not another like you. In loving you, it brings into harmony and perfect alignment You--your kingdom, your power, your ability to manifest. Never, ever, not love you! Love! Enjoy the fire that is within you, for that fire in **immortal**, forever!

The fire that you possess created the rose, the bird, the stars in your heaven, the eightieth universe and solar systems within and without. And without life, you can experience none of these things. Without life, children, you cannot have little playhouses in which to arrange, become depressed over, oppressed over, worried over, happy over, miserable over in your little game.

Without life and the toys that are here, you would not be able to play [in order] to gain, for life is the greatest treasure of all, the greatest reality of all. This illusion, it is nothing; it is a game for imaginative adventure to gain a new reality called Self.

You are not woman or man. You are God, a **Great** entity who is playing a game to experience a feeling. And when you are tired in your body and this mode of entrapment, you will fulfill Self and get on the back of the wind and be gone from this place to yet another--simply!

CHAPTER SIX

YOUR PURPOSE, YOUR DESTINY, IS TO LIVE AND BE

"The reason that you are here is not to become famous or to become poor. The reason that you are here is to become. To become what? Yourself! And to do what once you have become that? To create in this life whatever you choose.

Your purpose here, your destiny, is to live, and in that living, to be."

"When everyone gets beyond this plane of thinking that they must do this and they must do that and their destiny is this and that, and gets down just to the business of being—living explicitly in the Now, the Moment—then they will find a grander happiness, a greater freedom, a greater pleasure and laughter than they have ever known before—a release into life, into how it should truly be lived!"

YOUR PURPOSE, YOUR DESTINY, IS TO LIVE AND BE

No one has a purpose when they come here, as if they were struck by some divine lightning! Your purpose is to live. Anything other than that will be an extension of your beauty and a contribution to the overall reasoning of life. When you realize that living is the most important thing--that is where you gain your "points," if you will--and that you are here because you desire to be here, you want to be here, that you, of your own being, entity, found it a pleasurable place to return to, then everything else will be taken care of.

You see, entity, in this audience we no longer have someone to blame our miseries upon, or perhaps our edict into this plane upon. You are responsible for your own beauty, your own wonderful life, your own being--and its about time that that was the way it was!

When everyone gets beyond this plane of thinking that they must do this and they must do that and their destiny is this and that, and gets down just to the business of **being**--living explicitly in the Now, the Moment--then they will find a grander happiness, a greater freedom, a greater pleasure and laughter than they have ever known before--a release into life, into how it should truly be lived!

No one sent you, entity, for there is no one that can ever send you or make you do anything other than you! You are the one that decided to come here; you are the one that wished to be a participant on this plane again, simple as that!

And regarding what you [think you] are "supposed" to do here, [that] cannot be done without **living** first. Your first and foremost reason for being here is to live! The most glorious thing you can achieve in this life is living through it. Is it not a truth? What would be a grandiose king if he did not first have life to become one? That was not his "purpose"; he only did that because he decided it would be a good thing to do. The most important thing was that he got to the point that he could live to become one!

*

The reason that you are here is not to become famous or to become poor. The reason that you are here is to become. To become what? Yourself! And to do **what** once you have become that? To create in this life whatever you choose. Your purpose here, your destiny, is to live, and in that living, to be.

"There is no greater priority than fulfilling you. Your purpose is to be. All things other than being are only frivolous attitudes that are being fulfilled through desires, and they are no thing without the purpose of 'being.'

The greatest purpose is to be and to live. From that, you have the ability to create all else and all things."

All of this is an illusion. Everyone thinks that it is the reality; it is not. It is the Illusion. This is all created to evoke emotion within the Soul. It is the emotion that is unseen that transcends death and matter. In life, you do everything here for emotion and feeling, and the ultimate feeling is Joy.

*

There is no greater priority than fulfilling you. Your purpose is to be. All things other than being are only frivolous attitudes that are being fulfilled through desires, and they are no thing without the purpose of "being." The greatest purpose is to be and to live. From that, you have the ability to create all else and all things.

The purpose is You--the highest purpose of all, the greatest destiny of all. And once you find out, entity, that you are **worth** it all, then from that worth and that power and that genius, you can put forth your light unto the world into any labor, to any fulfillment that pleases you, at any moment that pleases you. The purpose is You!

If purpose is to remain with you for eternity and give you a "reason" (for always we must find reasons for things for being) then let the reason be, entity, for the one thing that will carry you through eternity--and that is called "emotional love."

Emotional love for yourself, entity, will survive eternity while the purpose of being a labor will only end in this life for the replacement of another. Labors are not forever things; they are illusions, entity. What will count, entity? What will be with you for always? Whatever [you] can add unto you that will perfect you in the light synthesis of all-knowingness--[and] that is making **you** the greatest you can in You--the most discriminating eyes there are. That will last forever.

That is your purpose--**to Be**!

*

Why do you think everyone comes back [to this plane]? Do you think they are **made** to come back, [that] they are kicked from whatever plane they are on back into an embodiment [to] struggle through the birth canal [to] become what they call completely helpless? There **is** a ceasing to this. It is called desire.

No one ever made you come back to this place. Ever! There is no entity forcing you to. Everyone has come back here because they wanted to. And karma has nothing to do with it, for the laws of karma do not exist save in the hearts of Man. **Want** is the determining factor. And it **is** a great decision to come back here. But most have forgotten they are greater than

"The way one finishes his life here is [that] he lives it and loves it and becomes a part of the simple things. And [he] rids himself of ideals that are intimidating, limiting and are in grossness to the nature of humanity and begins to live the freedom of himself, and loves himself, and ceases to compare himself."

this place and they think that there is nothing else; so they come back over and over and over.

If you don't **want** to return here, don't! You do not have to. Ever! The Valleys of the Kingdom of Heaven are even more immense than anything upon this plane, and **it** is the emerald of this universe! The sun and the golden light [there] enraptures all things, and there is no darkness. And the music of all things living together in perfect harmony are exquisite and beyond words.

If you do not wish to come back here, do not come back. The way one finishes his life here is [that] he lives it and loves it and becomes a part of the simple things. And [he] rids himself of ideals that are intimidating, limiting and are in grossness to the nature of humanity and begins to live the freedom of himself, and loves himself, and ceases to compare himself.

You live to be like an image. And fear of age catches you up by the throat, entity. And oftentimes you have despised yourself for you do not wish to lose your youth and your beauty, and yet you feel insecure that you are. And that is, entity, a terrible thing, but that is all made in the mind that makes the body what it is. When you release that and give that away and begin to love the **eternal being** and live for the Ideal, however that is within your being, then you become one with the flora and one with the birds—indeed one with all things. Then you can say, "I have finished this experience. I have loved all life that is here. And because I have, I am ready for a new adventure. I am ready for a far-off kingdom and a new understanding and a whole different being." And that will come.

This life, regardless of all the things that have occurred in your history of Mankind, really is quite superb. Unfortunately, those who dwell in cities and dwell amidst and into the thickness of consciousness think that this is a miserable, wretched place to live. But they have never had the guts within their being to pack meager belongings and go into the wilderness and live one with God and get away [from] ideals and threats of old-age and intimidation and hurt and selfishness and all of that. Then, when they do, they find that life is quite splendid; it is nothing as the consciousness of Man sees it in reality. It is an ongoing, unlimited, beautiful thing.

You have not seen that facet of experience for you are flung into a supportive role, a laboring role, a competitive role, an idealistic role, a suffering role, a neurotic role; and no matter how hard you try, you seem to get worse. And that is only one minute particum of what life is if you dare ever go see the other parts of it.

"Everyone thinks that they must have an excuse for being here. And so they want to know their destiny, and I tell them "Life!" and they are most perplexed and unhappy, for they are waiting for a very elaborate plan that they will arise above a great mount and be draped in gold and have birds singing around their head and they shall be the salvation of Mankind."

I never came back, entity, for I ascended with the wind and took everything with me that was me. And so the totality of the I AM belongs within the uttermost parts of my being, and I am a free entity. That is because I transcended all the things I had done in my experience; I forgave myself and got on with the business of knowing who God was. And so can you.

Everyone is here because they wanted to be here. Everyone thinks that they must have an excuse for being here. "Ah, alas," they ask me, "I know I have a destiny here, a purpose. I know there is a reason I am supposed to be here. There must be an excuse for my existence, otherwise I am not enjoying the whole lot of the thing!" And so they want to know their destiny, and I tell them "Life!" and they are most perplexed and unhappy, for they are waiting for a very elaborate plan that they will arise above a great mount and be draped in gold and have birds singing around their head and they shall be the salvation of Mankind.

The reason you are here is to live. But you have not broken away from the things that cling you to this world. And you have not walked on a glacier, and you have not hidden under a rock bridge, and you have not peered out of a poor paned window at winter and seen a redbird sitting there, brilliant against the snow.

Nor have you been in deep caverns or been into the deep. Nor have you been on explorations where no man has ever been before--and there are plenty of those places. And you haven't slept in a great pyramid all alone, and you haven't gone through tombs deciphering who you were and trying to read your scratchings of the wall that someday you were hoping you might come back and make out what they were (and all they said is, "Remember me.").

And you haven't walked in the desert and sat and watched the snake in his quest for food, oftentimes being out-slyed by the entities around him and thus going hungry. And you have not watched great fish jump and tried to wonder where they went to next or followed a deer into a dappled wood.

You have not done many things that are electrifying and thrilling and wonderful--and not **one** of them ever said you looked good! The tree never notices your beauty, and the deer doesn't care at all, and the snake ignores you because you smell bad. You see, so they [don't] judge you at all; they simply allow you to be, so you can be whatever you want to be.

This is a facet of life that you have not seen that you need to see, [that] will break down your neurosis and your fears and your traps and your imprisonments and your wonderings and your unhappinesses. And [there will be] moments you wish to explode; except you [would] want somebody to see you explode; and yet you would be intimidated if they did! That is your nature. But there is nothing wrong with that. You just have not given yourself an option to live here, and you have been hardpressed and hard put to it to be an ideal that is so fleeting.

When you have done all those things, then, my beloved entity, you leave this plane in a blaze of glory; you see a great star and a light appear from its zenith. And that is how you would leave. That is how I left!

I am a lover of this plane. I trod its valleys often, entity. I blow in the trees. I become part of the laughter of children, for I know what Life is. So I have not missed out on the values here; I know them quite well. But far greater, I know the sufferings of that which I love--my beloved brothers. And I have the answers, but they are of little use unless applied.

PART TWO

LOVE YOURSELF INTO LIFE, INTO JOY
INTO GOD

CHAPTER SEVEN

CALL BACK YOUR KINGDOM

"Man does not become the Immortal Essence until he realizes that that which he be indeed be Divine [and that] Divinity becomes a prescribed emotion within the structure of the Soul. For Man to become the Immortal, for Man to become that which is termed God, he must call forth his Godhood unto himself, unto his own being."

"It only takes one Christ, one sublime God to Know that He is to change what is called history and permit a future.

It only takes one Christ to add a new star unto your heavens, to create a new planet in your sphere.

It only takes one Christ indeed to evolve and evoke a new species of created form.

It only takes one Christ to set a loftier truth far above [Mankind] that is accessible by all.

And it only takes one Christ to be the Ideal that all can see within themselves.

If you be that Christ then great is your destiny, great is your life. It is easy to achieve and more difficult not to become. Becoming you in the greatness of your being is evoking the God from within to come outward that you can become all of these things in precedented form.

Only one Christ, standing forth as Reverent and True Light, can rearrange all ninety-nine and one universes. That is how powerful they are. It ebbs you on to complete [yourself], yet you never will. And that is good. That permits Foreverness."

CALL BACK YOUR KINGDOM

I am Ramtha The Enlightened One, indeed, servant unto the Source evolving into that which is termed the Force, becoming that which is termed the Element, becoming Spirit Divine, being that which is termed the Mother-Father Principle of all Life: the Isness of the principle "God Almighty." Unto the Source, the life, the beauty, the basis of All Being, am I a servant and lover unto.

I am Ramtha The Enlightened One, indeed, servant unto the Christus. The Christus be the product of the Source, [be] the Image of that which is termed God Almighty. The Christus be the Son of the Father. It be the culmination of all that the Father be in a singular movement.

The Son be God in all that He is in that which is termed the "Christ understanding of the beauty of Man." Christ be the Son of All That Is. It is the receiver of all that the Father be, conclusively. [As] the Father progresses, [as] the Father accumulates, [as] the Father accomplishes, [so] the Son readily accomplishes, for whatever the Father be, the Son is. The Son is the Given Life Spark unto the movement of Man.

Man be, of his Ego-self, limited into the lower forms to which he hath evolved himself into being. The Christus be the Giver of All Forms; thus, Christ born in Man, realized in Man, is God realized in the totality of Man. Then Man be not enslaved to the consequence of his being; he be evolved into the purest motive form of All That Is. [Then] Man be the recipient of the Kingdom of Heaven--which be the Kingdom of God in all life domains ongoing each moment explicitly into the moments to come. Then Man be the inherited Son of the Mass; Man be the Dominion of All Dominions; He be the Herald of Peace, the King of Kings, the Savior, the Lord, the Justifier, the Lawgiver, indeed the Creator.

And who be you? There are some still asking that. Most wondrous entities, illustrious brothren, **God be you**! You be the Core of All Thought. You be the Ball of Light Continuum of the Movement of the Core of the Mind of God come forth in a rally, in an Ocean of Life that spurs itself into the Allness of Forever. You be "light synthesis" who now be a part of the kingdom you have created for your being. Travelers? Nay. Participants in Life? Nay. **God,** indeed! Wanderers into your illusions, wanderers into your beings, into your thoughts.

You who have been at the mercy of thinking that you are less than your own creations, you who be at the mercy of thinking that you are less than your own collective attitude and [who]

"There is not under heaven, in heaven, above heaven, of heaven, any one creature, thing, consciousness, entity, that can make one God; only the one that is. You do that yourself. No one else can do that for you, for you are a willful God that must proclaim it for Self in order for it to be."

regard yourself as a no thing, you **are** the glistening God standing forth above the Ocean of Thought into Life Ongoing, becoming the radium of all life there is. What Holier Movement, more Divine Movement? God is **never** outside of you; indeed It **is** you!

Illustrious, beauteous brothren, you **are** the principle life of all things, God Supreme of all things. Yet in your advent upon this plane, [you] have been caught upon this Plane of Ensnarement [and] struggle arduously to find your belongings, your destiny. "Where be I and where be I going indeed? And what purposeful meaning have I when I am in the bounds of my despair and at the hands of my own undoing?" Indeed, that is how the Soul cries out, that is how the broken spirit is!

In [his search for his belongings], Man has brought forth to acclaim himself, to teach [and] to assimilate himself with Gods outside of him, for he who be perilous indeed think not that he be **amongst** the Gods but be the bastards of them! Thus Man, in finding his destiny, finding his purposeful meaning in life, hath created Gods, religion, enslavement, governmental rule, indeed separateness of being, in order to find himself!

But Life hath continued on. Oblivious to the scream of the lost entity, it hath continued on. And the winds come and blow. And the clouds, they are pushed further into the horizon to where they are no more. And the scream, it is carried upon the wind like a gentle wave and is caught up in the sphere and becomes the beauty of the cry of a nightbird.

Thus, where be Man desolate? He be an entrapped God that hath entrapped himself in forgetting himself.

You, **each** of you, you be indeed a sublime ruler. Your thought has always connected you to All That Is, hath permitted you the basis in which to become. You be, indeed, the Becoming, the Now, the Answer, the Ongoing, the Giver, the Thought, the Light--the Purposeful Being!

Call back the wind unto you for you have **believed** it to flee you and it will bring back unto you your voice and exalt you, for you who believed the wind to pass you by have called forth it back and it shall return, for it believes and knows and understands that the superiority of your being hath now been acclaimed! [Then] God rears up his Great Head indeed, no longer humbled and feebled and despairing and without and at the mercy of illusionary understandings of your own creativity. Indeed, it is a new day, a new mind, a new creation!

Then all that is here to be experienced shall be experienced with great zeal, for each particum of life will you now see as a particum indeed of your own existence. And for that, indeed, shall you experience and revel.

"Thus who hath been you? You hath been the Great, the Almighty, the Awesome, the Purposeful Correctiveness that hath become, in your own creation, the entrapment of the lowerness of your creation and have forgotten who you are!

Let no man tell you that you are less than God! Believe not that He be outside of your supremacy, for that hath caused the lessening. Be you Him. Know you are Him, sublimely Him, sovereign of your own reality, of your own purposeful being, thus your own kingdom, your own dominion. And thus you are freed men, not unto any audience, not unto any rule save your own."

Then behold unto you, the illusion of negativity, [of] limited, cloistered thought are no more! And one by one, the dawning of realization, the gaining of knowledge by having the illusions removed, comes forth and God becomes greater. Then Man is **realized** in his superior form of what he was created for!

And behold, as [your] life is executed in meaning, the simplicity of God and how you see It all shall bring together a conclusive "I AMness," the reality of **purposeful being.** [And] the reality indeed shall come forth into all that you experience around you. And you will become lighter and greater and more beautiful, and you will transcend this Plane of Materiality unto your own being, above the Wave and the Core of the Mind of God into Light.

And [then] you shall be freed of the Antichrist of your being by **believing** that you are. And you will come unto, indeed, your Godhood and your greatness!

And behold, you will look at all things as separate yet [be] one with them, for the "separate oneness" means you are aligned but no longer enslaved to that alignment.

When you indeed realize this, one by one, you will see the results around you. And one by one, your beloved brothren shall remove their illusions and begin to see God rear up the proud and beauteous head and [they will] become Supreme Rulers, Supreme Lawgivers of their own domain.

And what [are] they then? They are indeed the Givers of Life Known and they come again and breathe upon the air and bring forth the Winds of Change upon the plane, that the Winds bring forth change of thought understanding and remove the stagnation of limitation; that all may breathe a new day, a new life, a new understanding, a new knowledge.

Thus who hath been you? You hath been the Great, the Almighty, the Awesome, the Purposeful Correctiveness that hath become, in your own creation, the entrapment of the lowerness of your creation and have forgotten who you are!

Let no man tell you that you are less than God! Believe not that He be outside of your supremacy, for that hath caused the lessening. Be you Him. Know you are Him, sublimely Him, sovereign of your **own** reality, of your **own** purposeful being, thus your own kingdom, your own dominion. And thus you are freed men, not unto any audience, not unto any rule save your own.

Unto you, individualized entities, your worth is without word, it is without count, it is without measure! All that is, that ever has been, that ever shall be conclusively in the moments of infinity that advance themselves into the purity of the moments unborn, are you; and you have, in all of that, the dominion, the principle being of All That Is.

"Man, created specifically for Emotion, has long forgotten the Christus within him as he became indeed a surviving creature, prone to [the elements], prone indeed to fears. [When the] Gods developed the character 'Man,' they evolved themselves into Matter to such degrees [that] they lost their divinity; they lost it because they forgot the priority of Self and became a frightful creature that fears the dark rather than being the Lord of it.

Of you and your worth, it is only as great as you **realize** it and will only **be** as great as you **know** it to be! Thus, unto you, I am divinely aware of who you be and [I] love and serve and hold you in the highest regard and salute you as being that which I am in my being.

Call Forth Your Christ

That which is termed the Christus, what be that? [It be] God, the Sublime Thought, manifesting into Matter to create Man the Divine, the instrument through which the divine Soul, indeed the divine Mind, could express through. The Christus came forth to become Man for the explicit reason of experiencing Matter: the finished product, as it were, of an ideal or creation.

Man, created specifically for Emotion, has long forgotten the Christus within him as he became indeed a surviving creature, prone to [the elements], prone indeed to fears. [When the] Gods developed the character "Man," they evolved themselves into Matter to such degrees [that] they lost their divinity; they lost it because they forgot the priority of Self and became a frightful creature that fears the dark rather than being the Lord of it.

Man does not become the Immortal Essence until he realizes that that which he be indeed be Divine [and that] Divinity becomes a prescribed emotion within the structure of the Soul. For Man to become the Immortal, for Man to become that which is termed God, he must call forth his Godhood unto himself, unto his own being.

Christus is God **seen** and **realized** in humanity. Christus is God-Man: Man realizing that he is God, the Unlimited Principle.

*

The Christus is the resurrection of seven great "seals" [within the embodiment]. The seven seals that are in the body are called ductless glands. In order to make a body functional from the Supreme Thought, the body must engage in a very thorough, scientific process through [its] glands, [which have] existed [within the body] ever since the body was conceived.

Each gland stands for a plane of limitation. This plane you are existing upon now is one of seven. There is nothing lower than this plane: this is the beginning to go back into your Godhood. The seal that is aligned with this plane is the first seal; it is your reproductive area, a very powerful area, for without it, man's copulation does not exist, [and] thus the lineage of man does not exist.

"To bring forth the Christus, as it is termed, indeed, is not the anointment of anyone. It be not ritualistic. It be, indeed, an act of "isness" that occurs. It is the realization that there is a greater part of you that lies dormant within your being."

In raising forth the Christus, we align the body by touching the glands; and as we touch the glands, they begin to bloom like a flower, a lotus blossom, and slowly the vibration grows from the pit of your being to the height of your knowingness.

Everything here, including your embodiment, is a product of Thought. The brain on your being does not create thought; it does not create thinking; it does not create ideals. It is a "receptor," as it is termed. If it does not create thought, then whence does thought come from? It comes from outside of your being and is caught up in your "auric field." The thought is [then] transmuted into a propellant and enters into the function [part] of the brain that is geared for that frequency [of thought].

The thought is then transferred into that which is called the pineal system that allows the thought to travel through central nervous system as a spark, and it engages the entire embodiment in every cellular structure; [thus], the thought encompasses the body with the feeling [and] becomes a reality in the bodily movement through emotion.

Without your brain or the glands that govern it, the body would not be a [vehicle] that could be mobile for the Spirit that inhabits it. Thus, through that which is termed the selected glands--and there are seven of them--the body can function through that which is called the enigma of thought, wonderfully well. Of these seven "seals," as they are so termed, or "chakras" as you have heard them to be, the body becomes an operative and functional unit.

The seventh seal is aligned with the seventh heaven. It is the greatest premise of reality there is. The seventh seal is the pituitary [gland]. It is located within the center of that which is termed the forehead. It is shaped like a delicate pear, and when it opens, it is the gland that stimulates the brain for greater thought. Entities that are limited in their thought have a small portion of that which is termed their receiver or brain that is operative; thus they only receive the limited thought through limited consciousness.

When we open the seventh seal, it opens and expands and flows that which is termed a hormone flow throughout the brain, [which] activates a greater portion of the brain [to receive] greater thought frequencies. As that part is activated, then thought of a higher level can come into the body for the experience of feelings.

To bring forth the Christus, as it is termed, indeed, is not the anointment of anyone. It be not ritualistic. It be, indeed, an act of "isness" that occurs. It is the realization that there is a greater part of you that lies dormant within your being. We merely touch the seven seals, beginning with the first all the way into the seventh, and draw forth energy throughout the

"I will teach you to speak as a Master speaks. Whatever he says, so it is, and it occurs and it becomes. When [the Christus is brought forth], all things [that] are said and spoken, the Soul records it herein and it shall never be forgotten; [thus] you will never again lose sight of who you be, for the Christ within you will not let you."

embodiment. The seventh seal will open gently and will feel subtle unto the being. But as one experiences the opening of this, he experiences what is called a "rush," or what you would term an accelerated "high"; that is the term I have heard here that fits quite well. That is when you have the rush of Unlimited Thought coming into the body for [which] there are no words, only emotion and feelings. [Then] you know all that is and yet you can explain none of it, for that which is unexplained is Unlimited Thought.

We open this [the seventh seal or pituitary] up to allow that which is termed the greater divinity of Self to emerge, to allow the Spirit that encompasses the entirety of the body to feed the body a greater spirit of understanding--knowledge, as it were, "knowingness." Thus God comes forth in the anointment of the Christus; it is when you realize that you are God expressing in the body called human--or mankind as it is so-called here.

These seals, once they are opened, allow you to perceive Unlimited Thought in a greater dimension, a greater feeling. And what shall follow, indeed, will be emotion: you will feel; you will be confused; you will know and yet you don't know. And all the experiences from this moment will linger for quite a while when this is [done], for once that portion of the brain [i.e., pituitary] is activated, the entity can experience greater thought, greater genius, indeed greater creativity.

Why be that important? In order for you to come from limitation, indeed, come from a life that is only a struggle for existence into a Utopia, you must have another frame of thought, indeed, another being, another compassion, another feeling, and this allows that to occur.

And you will go through "fire" when it is [done]. The "fire," indeed, is the Christus come forth in the a realization of God, [and] that will replace in your life those things that have inhibited you--whatever they be and whoever they be--and allow, in that which is termed that "space," a greatness to come to you that will uplift you and support you.

You are not alone in this life. In the Unseen, there is greater love for you and care for you than you know. They assist you, indeed, and help you to realize who be you--and I am one of them!

Now. [Bringing forth] the Christus takes but a moment, and in that moment the body is touched and the seals will respond. And when [that] is [done], I give unto you a proclamation, a proclamation you repeat from the depths of your being, for the proclamation says, adamantly, "I am God and I call forth all that is mine and all my knowingness."

I will teach you to speak as a Master speaks. Whatever he says, so it is, and it occurs and it becomes. When [the Christus is brought forth], all things [that] are said and spoken, the Soul records it herein and it shall never be forgotten; [thus] you will never again lose sight of who you be, for the Christ within you will not let you.

I do not make you God or crown you Christus. There is not under heaven, in heaven, above heaven, of heaven, any one creature, thing, consciousness, entity, that can make one God; only the one that is. You do that yourself. No one else can do that for you, for you are a willful God that must proclaim it for Self in order for it to be.

This speech, it is very small, but it is spoken as a Master speaks. And all that is spoken, it will come to pass for the glory of God that lives within you and in all peoples. And that is what we do this hour. Why? Because you are loved; and when given an opportunity to be greater than that which you are, you will excel in it, and that is known, for that is in the nature of Man; that is the God within his being. And when you become, you will become a "light" to other peoples, simply because the love within your being will present an ideal for others to live by. You will not teach them; you only have to live: that is the answer; that is all that you need.

And once you see [that] whatever you think happens before you, then you will become a Manifesting God. All you have to do is **feel** what it is you want, and the feeling of the desire will manifest before you and will become a reality.

Then what happens to war and jealousies and hatred and bitterness and insecurities? They exist no further, for when you have the capacity to manifest directly for yourself whatever you want, then you will never have to take from another or theive from another or be enslaved by another; you can be who you are and have everything that you want—**by feeling it**. It is a truth. And by this action, you are allowed to do that. And what shall become of it is called "the Kingdom of Heaven," [for] a God lives and is and becomes whatever he desires to become. And you shall be the [example] that what is spoken here is a sovereign truth.

The Soul, indeed the Lord of your being, awaits the next emotion, the next command that it may materialize the reality of that thought for you in this kingdom. Words, they are only that which is termed the created sound frequency to describe that which is termed emotion. Emotion is what gives reality to thought.

[When] Masters speak [they] waste no word, [and] that which they utter **is** what is within; it is a declarative command. [They] choose words that represent the emotions [within] and call them forth and align them, that the word will bring forth a direct command back into God, the Source, and manifest what [they] have just spoken.

I give unto you that which is termed a proclamation, what you would call speech. I give it forth to you. Let it ring out from the Lord God of your Totality, for it is the language of Masters and how they call forth that which is termed their kingdom, indeed their power, indeed that which is termed the life flow within them.

It is very short, but within it, all that you ever want shall be spoken. Speak each word and contemplate what you are speaking and **feeling.** 'Tis the feeling that will manifest [what you desire] for you thus to understand what the Kingdom of Heaven is.

Speak it. Let it ring forth from your being. Then you have crowned yourself that which is termed the recognized Christ, indeed the God, indeed that which is termed the Understanding of the I AM. When you have said this commandment, you have placed that which is termed the Crown of Christ upon your own head: you are acknowledging to Self the sublime divinity that you are.

> **"From the Lord God of my Being, I call forth my Christ into Life, into Light, into Now. So be it!**
>
> **From the Lord God of my Being, I call forth my Kingdom. Come forth! Now! So be it!**
>
> **From the Lord God of my Being, I call forth my Power. Come forth! Now! So be it!**
>
> **Beloved Father, Divine Source, Wondrous Life, that which you are, I be also!**
>
> **Beloved Father, behold unto you that which I be, sublime reflection, God I AM! So be it!**
>
> **I am the Lord God of my Totality, Ruler of Destiny, indeed Life, indeed Joy. That Which Is, All That Is, come forth! So be it!**
>
> **I am the Lord God of my Being, Now and Forever!**
>
> **So Be It!"**

And what can any man be other than what he says he is. Thus that which has been spoken, it **is,** for how is your destiny created? By what you **perceive** yourself to be: that is called the Kingdom of Heaven. Thus, all is yours. All! Partake of it however you choose, indeed, and however much you want.

You, God, watch how you speak, for every word utter you indeed comes to pass, for it is only mocking that which is termed the creative emotion: that **is** coming to pass. Speak as a God. Let every word uttered from your kingdom come back to you in one hundred years **joyfully**, for, I assure you, it will!

CHAPTER EIGHT

BECOME UNLIMITED: COME TO BE

"I beckon unto you, you are the Lord of Hosts. You are the Prince of Peace. Learn to live it, that the immaculate entity that presides within you is the immaculate entity now seen.

Love yourself enough to live, to live in the moment, to exalt all that are."

"To become Unlimited is to be without fear, without guilt, without hate, without bitterness. To become Unlimited means you can love no matter what you see before you. That is becoming God!"

CAST YOUR LIMITATIONS TO THE WIND AND SIMPLY BE!

To become Unlimited is to be without fear, without guilt, without hate, without bitterness. To become Unlimited means you can love no matter what you see before you. That is becoming God!

In order to become that, you must master and regress yourself by overcoming all the things [which] you have so sternly learned to limit yourself by--taking them away and removing their illusions; going beyond that which is termed "accepted theory," going beyond that, for life is ever-changing every moment; it always will be; it is refining itself every moment.

Unthink all your limitations. Cast them to the wind and simply be! The God within you will bring you feelings you have no words for. Any feeling that can be described on this plane is **of** this plane and not of the higher realms. The feelings I am speaking of have no words. None! You cannot even begin to utter them.

In a state of being, you will have all of those feelings. And when you are in the midst of the "fire" and their emotions and you weep and want to understand but seemingly cannot, a great change is happening: In a state of being, you are Becoming, [becoming] a God who can see beyond limitations; who can look at anyone gathered within his sphere and know everything there is to know about them because he has learned to love himself and them that he can now see what he would not permit himself to see before: now it is all seen and known and visible. You can call forth anything that you desire and it will manifest before you. And you will be a man of little words and great emotion.

Then you can walk out into any city and stand in the center of its marketplace and close your beautiful eyes and roll them to within yourself and illuminate yourself, that your great light has taken the entire encompassing view of the marketplace. And in that moment, everyone will have a grand thought, everyone will. Everyone!

And when you walk, they will look at you in utter amazement. And you will know what God knows. And you will love how God loves. And you will be able to teach them, in an equality.

"Becoming is unfolding in measure from limitation into Unlimitedness, are unfolding to a feeling that can go beyond the senses of the body, indeed go beyond the limitations of the flesh and traverse with greater civilizations in Light, Principle of Thought."

BECOME AN ALL-FEELING CHARACTER OF DIVINE PROVIDENCE

Let us talk of Becoming. What shall you become unto? What have you been that you may thus become? Who were you? Where did you issue forth from? What is the reason for the issuing? And if you are to become, what be it shall you become that is so different from where you came from?

Becoming is becoming without the regulation of laws, superstition, dogma, into an essence of freedom, unto an expressive value that is able to express through the totality of the individualized [Self] without limitation.

[The] Gods became Man in limitation, for they became all that they were in their isness into a small portion of knowingness, constricted in distance and reach and fervor of feeling. Yet, within that same strike, were they able to immerse themselves with mass and be a part of creation, and feel, and taste, and touch, and hear, and speak, and become glorious with their wonderful painting of universal creativity. Thus, the Gods, the explicit creature of All That Is, became singular, individualized, limited entities on this plane.

Becoming is unfolding in measure from limitation into Unlimitedness. Coming into unlimitedness is unraveling Self for the divine preview of what you are in all understandings.

What are you? Your bodies, they are [a] wonderful collection of work; but the principle of your "essence" body is as far and as vast and as deep and as high as the value of Thought can take you. You are a Light Principle! You are unfolding to a feeling that can go beyond the senses of the body, indeed go beyond the limitations of the flesh and traverse with greater civilizations in Light, Principle of Thought.

The adventures of the body have been great; they will continue to be. [But] the exploration of [the] Truth of Self is an ongoingness [which] excels each moment you roll your eyes inward and begin to feel the hearth of your being, begin to perceive the infiniteness of your beauty, and begin to know that there is more than that which is termed the collection of molecular structure that equates flesh and blood and bones.

We have taught of Becoming for nigh a good spell in your counting. Of becoming what? What [are] you [to] become in the "opening up?" A **feeling** entity: an entity that goes beyond the bodily feeling into emotional feeling.

"[In Becoming] one gets in touch with his own premise, his own intelligence, his own purposeful being, his own good, and begins to feel it."

Emotion is not **born** of the body. It is explicitly **explained** in the body through outward spasms of the body convulsion. Emotion is born of gratified thought felt in the conclusiveness of the entity and **expressed** in the body.

You do not become God until you become the epitomy of emotion: to **feel** profoundly. Feeling allows Divinity to occur back within Man; his Godhood replaced, his Capstone replaced, his uniqueness in becoming.

You become from a measure of likeness, from law and restriction, into feeling. Love, deep love; joy, deep sorrow; deep feelings of a weeping Soul that knows not why it weeps; [feelings] of tenderness, gentleness, compassion (what this plane would term "humility") is brought on in Becoming. To go back unto that which is termed the Isness, you cannot! To ongo unto Its peak of Being, you can. You are becoming **in the moment** by feeling.

Everything that all here have done, have struggled for, have designed, experienced, has been for the virtue called Emotion, feelings. You have lived as the product of society, of changes of consciousness; you have been the duplicate of the conscious "ideal." All of you! Your society has dictated what the ideals of feeling should be, and all strive to be it so they are accepted! Unfortunately, the ideal is [a] very limited, wretched entity [that] is prone to ailments and sickness and neurosis and all things that inhibit the becoming of the individualized Self. In Becoming, there is no ideal except what is felt deep within the individual Self.

[In Becoming] one gets in touch with his own premise, his own intelligence, his own purposeful being, his own good, and begins to feel it. And in the "breaking away," as it were, from what is called the "normal society"--its laws, its regulations, its petty ideals--comes a "war," a difficulty within the time of becoming. And all will experience it.

In Feelings That Gratify You Are You The Receiver Of The Virtue Of God

What shall you become? The body [will] continue to elevate itself and refine itself, will continue to become more valid and more useful to the great creative mind that sits within it. But it is the mind of collective value that is becoming more unlimited--and not through "intellectual fervor," but through emotion, deep emotion, profound Isness.

God is reality, all that life is. But what life is, in the semblance of its ideal, is an illusion. The pulsing of the illusion

"No one enters the Gates of Heaven lest he have love within his being, joy within his being—feelings! For what are the Gates of Heaven, indeed? They are made up of the Isness, and all that prevail within is Emotion."

is the emotion called feelings that God's Kingdom is made up of. The tree pulsates; the grasses pulsate; indeed the clouds pulsate; the waters pulsate; the flower in its budding bloom pulsates in color, in hue and aroma. 'Tis these things that are cloaked in illusion but allow the true value of God and emotion to become prevalent and clear.

To Become, you do not restrict yourself from love and joy and feelings, deep profound feelings; you allow them to come forth. For in feelings that gratify you, elevate you, give you purposeful value, you are the stigma [i.e., receiver] of that which is termed the Virtue of God.

Feelings Are The Gates To Heaven

Becoming? The body will continue to become, but that which is within it will become an all-knowing, all-feeling character of divine providence, divine beauty. Words often shall not describe [the] feelings; only emotion will--emotion that hath no value for a word but simply is. Then quiet becomes prevalent, as it is in the heavens; peace becomes prevalent. You become one with **all** great things that are ongoing and silent. Does the sun speak? No. Does a great star speak? No. A smaller? No. The moon? No! Does the tree speak? The plant? The bloom? What speaks? God, within His **infinite** Isness, is quiet within Himself.

As you become, the joy will overtake you, for the revelation of divine beauty seen within you shall become clear. Your beauty shall become profound, the limitations of arrogance shall dissipate from Self, and Self shall become a feeling creature of Isness--what it really is! You will begin to lose words to explain: feelings will immerse and overtake and overcome [you]. And the body [will] begin to feel [a] "liftness" within itself because the grandest vibration is taking place within and cannot be uttered without.

Joy exudes life. It draws life from all principle understandings. In joy and peace, you have not to utter a word but simply to feel. Feelings, indeed, is the language of all things. All of you shall experience the heights and the widths and the depths and the breadths of love and joy and feelings--without words; of electrical emotions that electrify and explicate the being into another dimension. All will learn this--you **must** learn this--in order to become out of your body a traveling entity that can immerse himself, indeed, on other realms of realities.

No one enters the Gates of Heaven lest he have love within his being, joy within his being--feelings! For what are the Gates of Heaven, indeed? They are made up of the Isness, and all that prevail within is Emotion.

In order to become, you must **feel** the becoming. Becoming is "becoming to feel"--to love, to look upon lightly no matter what it is you see and be at peace with it. [Becoming is] to remove fear and exalt Self; to live in the virtue of Now; to be glad at a sunrise and a sunset; to laugh with a child [and] to hold it in your arms; to see the blooming of flowers; to smell the seasons as they come and go; to be part of the wonderful enigma called Life; to transmute the feelings back into the Godhood of Realization.

Be happy with that which you are. Fruitfully live **in the moment**! Feel. Become the rose. Become a lilly in the field. Become a trout in the stream. Become a great leaf who has changed its color. Become a tree and how deep the roots grow. Become the child in laughter and the wind upon the water and the suppleness of a new bloom and the hopefulness of fruit. Become all of these things. **Feel** them! **Know** them! Become the Isness and love what you are and be a light unto yourself. Then, entities, you shall see the Kingdom of Heaven for all this it is: **Emotion.**

Those who fall in love when the moon turns to purple or when the wind blows through their hair or when a twig falls to the ground or a bird takes flight know about emotion. Thus they know about the enrichment of the God that they are and the virtue which they have obtained to know that.

Learn to feel, to touch, to examine, to be. Bless the Lord God of your being and the Father that is the Magnificence of All Magnificence and behold the splendor that you shall feel. Then you perceive a life called Utopia, which is the Promised Land coming into full vista and full view. All the mysteries, they become resolved. All the superstitions, they are done away with. All the dogma and doom and destruction, they are no more. [Then] God reigns supreme over all that He is, and He **is** Life, the Ongoingness, the Isness, that no one takes away. That is how it is!

Love Yourself Enough To Live

Torment yourself no more. Do not be abusive to yourself any longer. Relinquish guilt. Do not live in a hurry. Slow down and live in the moment. Do not live by rules; live by feelings. Do not obtain through that which is termed acknowledged laws; create them, be free of them.

Be! Stop being another's ideal; be your own. Have peace with your body; torment it no more. Starve it not into little unnotice; love it, nourish it, it is a tender thing. And be liken unto no one else except what you are within your unique, individualized Self.

In the [time] to come, **feel.** I will be with all of you. I will show you the greatest, the most beautiful thing and you will weep over it. I will bring you to your knees that you know what humbleness is. I will exalt you beyond the clouds that you can see better. And I will teach you how to feel, if through fire, if through gentleness, that your lessons to come are no longer the spoken word, but the felt movement. And all here shall feel it. All! And in the [time to come], you will be anew. And what was missing before will be complete; what [you] have been out of touch with shall be felt.

All of you, you are great lights. I have seen all your tribulations and all of your doubts. In [the time] to come, you will grow and bloom more, greater than you ever have before, for feelings is the "fertilizer" of all growing. And all of you will begin to see visions and have dreams of splendid nature. You will dream of one thing, and lo, it shall occur in the next moment. You shall perceive in one moment, and the next moment it is! Your knowingness shall become absolute.

And the wind shall be part of all of you and uplift you. It is time for your uplifting! All the world will know of you. All of it! And all the world, indeed, will succor after you to be a part of your knowingness. All of it! And lo, kings, indeed, shall come to your doorstep, and humble entities shall come to your doorstep for you to give them the Knowledge of Life. Then you have fed them the grandest of all things.

I beckon unto you, you are the Lord of Hosts. You are the Prince of Peace. Learn to live it, that the immaculate entity that presides within you is the immaculate entity now seen, not the duality that causes confusion.

Love yourself enough to live, to live in the moment, to exalt all that are.

BECOME LIKE A LITTLE CHILD AGAIN

[Note: The following is from a story told by Ramtha to a four year-old child attending his audience.]

> Once, in a moment called time, there was a Grand God who traveled about the land speaking to all who sought His wisdom. One day, there gathered an audience to listen to the Grand God speak of love, of life, of truth. And in the audience that day was a little child, holding the hand of his mother. And the Grand God smiled as he looked upon the child,

Lord,
Will you do me the honor of sitting with me?

And the little child came forth in quick steps of excitement to sit upon the robed expanse of his lap. And the Grand God eyed the child;

You are beautiful!
Are you what is called "a little child?"

The child nodded his head, drew up his shoulders, and giggled "Yes." The Grand God paused a moment and then inquisited unto the child,

Little means you are not grown up, aye?

The child nodded his head and frowned "Yes." And then the Grand God spoke unto the child:

I will tell you, little child,

Once there was greatness—
thunder in the sky,
and lightning in the sky,
and a wind that blew a warm rain
over a land that was as small as you.

And the gentle wind
that blew the gentle rain over the land
nourished all the little things therein.

And that which created the thunder
and the lightning
and the great wind
and the warm rain
was a God littler than you.

And when the warm rain went over the land
and nourished everything there
all the elements rejoiced,
for everything had exercised itself in being good.

The God that created all of these things
was littler than you.
And all of his children
were as small as you.
And they were all called Gods also.

And the wondrous thing of what they had created
  is that they loved it all!
They did not know that which is termed evil
  or wrong
  or ugly
  or fear.

And when they became upon this place
  just as you, a little God,
  someone told them that they were not perfect.

And they began to get scared
  and frightened,
  and wondered
    of all the things they had never experienced before.

And that made them grow very tall.
It made them grow tall to protect themselves.
And they became giants.

When they became giants,
  one tried to be taller than the other,
  larger than the other.
And they began to war with one another.
And the littler Gods ran and hid in fear
  for they could not understand all of these things.

And soon life became such a turbulence
  upon the little place they had created
  that they decided to leave it
  and go back to their first home.

And the little Gods watched
  with great curiosity
  as their brothers that had grown very large
  became very hateful
    and spiteful
    and angry.

They looked out the window, so to speak
  and watched them,
  and could not understand.
And they began to weep.

And soon the Father of these little Gods came
  and said unto them,
  "Why weep you?"

And they said,
"We know not why
they feel the way they feel,
and cannot feel the way they feel;
and they will love us not because we are small."

And the Great God, the Father,
looked upon them
and pondered for a moment
and said unto them:

"Do you love your brothers because they are large
and because they are still expressing
those things that you know not?"

And the little Gods said,
"Indeed we still love them.
What else is there?"

The Great God said,
"Indeed!
What else is there."

So he placed the little Gods
and called them The Overlords of the Universe
and put them in a great force around Terra,
which is called your Earth,
which was the little place of the Gods.

And the Great Voice said unto them
that they would keep balance
and that they would be a constant reminder
to their brothers
that had grown so tall
and become so limited,
what purity really was.

Beloved child,
there are cities of Gods
that protect the entire universe,
and they are smaller than you.
And yet, they can hold the Sun in their hands
and the stars upon the tips of their fingers,
and their laughter brings harmony thoughout the world.

I find you most beautiful
because you are like a little God
who is more powerful than the bigger Gods.

Look at your little hand.
I have made it very powerful.

When you feel bad,
put your hand upon your being
and it will be well.

When someone else feels bad,
put your hand upon them
and they will be well.

And when you forget that you are wonderful
and beautiful
and perfect,
Look into your hand.
It will remind you of the story of the Gods
that protect all the others,
and how small and wonderful they are
and how powerful they are.

And when you forget to love
Look into your hands.
It will remind you of it.

And the Grand God raised his eyes to gaze upon all those who had gathered,

Look at all of them.
For them to become
what they are here to become
they must learn to think as you think.

Never be in a hurry to grow up.
Be the age that you are
for as long as you want to be it.

Continue to be the magnificent God that you are
just as you are.
For all of these that have grown up
and are weary in their life
are trying to become
just like you again.

Be happy with who you are
And be a little child
for a long, long time.

You were born a knowing God
like all of them have been.
And they are brought up
to have it reasoned out of them.

I will teach them how to be
like a little child again.
So be it.

"[Becoming] is reversing back to the original God-self or the child or the purity within Self. That is when the 'miracles' start occuring. Little by little the layers come off, and the innocence that lies within is Divine God, Divine Master, pure Spirit, pure genius, uninhibited abilities. That is what you become."

In the process of Becoming, [there is a] whole shift of the balance of knowingness within your embodiment and Spirit, a merging or coming together, a realization.

Everyone suffers a duality; they are suffering [from] the illusions they have built up around them. [From the time] you were a little child onward, you have built layers of yourself for protection. You have built layers of yourself to perceive the world how the world wishes to be perceived so that you could be accepted. The pure individualized Self underneath [these layers] is lost from childhood on because [there] is a continuous up-building; and it is always built from within outward.

[Becoming] is a reversal of that process. It is removing all of these outward things, stigmas of the Soul, until they are removed down to the finite part, the child again, for, in essence, that is what a child is: the Purity of Spirit.

Once this is done, there are several things that happen. The body begins to become younger again; the thought process is unlimited and more joyful; and things can be seen in a clearer perspective and in more depth than they have ever been seen before.

Becoming is not a maturity of that which is termed the intellect. Quite the reverse. It is the innocence of the intellect that allows it to become an unlimited thinking process.

[Becoming] is reversing back to the original God-self or the child or the purity within Self. That is when the "miracles" start occuring. Little by little the layers come off, and the innocence that lies within is Divine God, Divine Master, pure Spirit, pure genius, uninhibited abilities. That is what you become.

*

The simplicity of God, master, is in the line. The simplicity of the Father is so blatantly open and the truth so obvious that even the simpleton can see it. Children are blessed, say everyone, with abundance of unlimited thinking, or the talent to perceive truth. That is because they are simple and see blatantly what is before them, evenly.

To live, to be, to be the Everlasting Thought, to see no end to it, to perceive and know brilliance, is only a moment away. All [you have] to do is want it. Wanting does not mean that you sit upon that which is termed your rear end and contemplate want! It means Becoming, that that which is termed the Ideal is **actively** imparted in daily thought. 'Tis living it; it is that simple.

If God were to be the least complex, the simplest of His creative forms would never understand Him.

CHAPTER NINE

CREATE THE PATH OF JOY

"The most sought after and the fewest secured accomodation in life is happiness. Everyone wants it. Unfortunately, not everyone knows how to get it. If they only knew they already had it."

"Everyone sits upon their rears and contemplates Infinity and God and take it all very serious. Actually, they are very boring! The Father is very jolly, and the more you laugh and the more happy you are, the closer you come to becoming God. Those that do this in pious seriousness are very much further from the Source than those that laugh with the Source."

IN A STATE OF JOY, YOU ARE IN A STATE OF GOD

When one attunes himself unto the voice, the volume, as it were, of the Father, what does he hear? Many presume it to be music for they love music. Many presume Him to have a loud, demanding voice [for] that is what they love; that makes them happy. And others perceive him to say no thing for they love no things in speech.

But the truth is that the roar of the Father is all life forms vibrating in harmonious tune to one another, and it equates itself as if the sound of laughter that rings in the high pitches of its joy to the rolling thunder of gathering itself up for another wave. And if the Father hath such mannerisms in his personable Being, then we must quickly understand that all things have that also.

If you listen carefully you will hear the music of the Father, the laughter of the Father. It is most joyous. I have not once heard Him weep.

*

God, indeed, is not a loathsome entity. It is not a serious entity. It is not a brooding entity. It is not a boring entity nor is it a restrictive entity. It is Rolling Thunder. It is Magical. It is Movement. It is Contemplative. It is Compulsive. It is Evolving. It is Laughter and Joy.

The greatest heights that any of you shall reach--that which is termed the pinnacle of your own truth--is in the midst of joy and laughter and the loving of this wondrous life. When all of you have learned to do that, you will have reached the top of your isness and from there you may see many more pinnacles and greater valleys and many more places than you can see at present.

Do not be afraid to be your God or dare to be unlimited in your thinking, to dare to think beyond the restrictive thought or [to] live it, for [there] awaits a greater kingdom than you can even imagine. [And] what shall bring you to this place is laughter and joy.

What is joy? Joy is not simply a state of happiness. It is a state of Becoming. It is the **ultimate**, if you will, of Becoming. In a state of Joy you are in the "flow" of what God is. And in there, there is not room for hate or self-doubt, for war or jealousies or bitterness or differences. In a state of joy [you] are caught in a charisma of God-action. That is how the Father

"It is not a point of physical ideal or transfiguration that declares you have 'become.' What declares your becoming is sheer joy."

is: It is Joy at all times.

*

This plane enjoys a meagerness of happiness. [And] if happiness be the ultimate desire of the Father for you, would it not be readily concluded that anything "higher," that goes further into a more complete state, unto God, will have more joy than this plane has? Of course. That is pure reasoning, pure reasoning.

The closer you are to God, the more exhilerated you are. The closer you come to realizing who He is, who you be, the more exhilerated you become. In evolving into Him, step by step through the perilous [plane] of materiality, you [always] are getting better: never do you retire, never do you recede, never do you lose a joy of life--never. The joy becomes more permanent.

Now, what are things that are not of joy? They are called despair, sorrow. They are called worry, concern. They are called fear. If these things are the robbers of happiness, then God is the giver of them, for Man, in his own limited understanding, has created them from Pure Joy. Do you know that they must come from Pure Joy in order to exist, for how can you hate, despise and be sorrowful about anything if you were not once happy about it?

Once you go into [the Father], into the basis of Pure Thought, [you find] its basis is Happiness, its basis is Joy. And the further you get into that, the less do you become of an altered, limited understanding that would impure you, that would take from you, that would alter joy. Thus sorrow and despair and war and diseasements become no more, for man's limited thinking becomes no more. Thus, we go back to the purer sense of understanding and joy.

The Father is the Totality of Joy. Do you think that all the cellular structures or molecular understandings of all the composites of various and wondrous unknown things could exist side by side in the minuteness of form unless they were happy? [Since] unhappiness separates us, fear separates us, war separates us, sorrow separates us--if that were true of the cells and in the science of life that is in the faction "gross matter," they would [be separate], not together. Then all of this abundance that seemingly does not laugh and seemingly does not purport to have joy, would never be--would never be--for they could not correlate themselves into an understanding of coexistence.

So, the Father, in His refined Essence, is Complete Joy. And the wonderful "cosmic glue" that holds that [Essence] together is called Love. [Thus], the further we go into the Father, through His "cosmic glue," the happier we are going to become and the more expansive we are going to be.

*

Entities that are seeking God think that It is a most serious and arduous and foreboding thing. That is very boring! The boredom of sadness and pious attitude, I assure you, does not bring you to the glory of the "Father within."

When the Father burns within you--when that which is termed the Self is awakened within you--there will be joy and laughter, for [you are] free to express without the condemnation of anyone.

God is a happy entity. And know you this: The one desire God the Father has for anyone here or ever wants for them [is] to be happy. To be happy! And that joy, master, is whatever happiness means to that individual, for the happier you become with your beauteous Self, the greater you come to the likeness and alignment with the Father.

*

To live this life openly and completely is to understand God. And the reality called "God" cannot be understood unless it is coming from the viewpoint of the emotion which all of you feel about your [life] adventures.

Every emotion determines reality. The less you become judgemental upon your precious being, the greater the emotion and the greater the prize of Reality will come to you. Then you will come to the only thing the Father has ever desired for **any** of you: Joy.

What is joy? Joy is the freedom of movement without interruption. It is the freedom of expression without judgement. It is the freedom of **being** without guilt. Joy is sublime movement of Self--**allowed.**

When you are in a state of joy, you can hate no one. In a state of joy, you love all things. In a state of joy, life becomes the fervor and intensity of a dawn when the sky becomes rose and the clouds are tinged in the most beauteous of fiery red, and birds are whistling in trees and the whole heaven is set afire in a blaze [of] intense color.

[In joy], you cease [to] age and will live forever, for life is no longer a drudgery but a victorious experience that you hunger for more of. When joy is apparent, you are at one in your kingdom with Self.

*

I am Ramtha, The Enlightened One, indeed, lover of God Almighty, the Supreme Principle Cause, Supreme Understanding, Supreme Thought, Supreme God, Supreme Happiness. I am indeed in service to those elements, [to those] things that comprise the enigma that I be.

In order to serve happiness, I must seek happiness out. And in my "world," as it were, finding happiness is a wonderment, for **all** things are there. To serve happiness means this: serving it means loving it; serving it means worshipping it; serving it means **being** it.

In all of God's attitudes of perpetual emotion and expression of ideals, happiness indeed is one that all should seek as the fulfillment of their Godself to the depths of their being.

What be happiness, indeed? Happiness is that I am indeed of the I AM. Happiness is that the Christus that I be, whom I also serve, is the one perfect creative element that is the totality of the Source that has performed itself into singular motion, meaning: I am not an ideal that hath been projected and then is consumed into life by the Aqueous Substance; I am not an after-thought of another's creative form; I am the form of myself, purest extension of the Source, God Almighty, Expanded Thought. And for you, happiness is knowing that what I proclaim I am, thus the truth must follow that you be that also.

In happiness--sublime element, wondrous mode of attitude--learning to be what you truly are in the simplest of your print, to the simplest of your form, to the simplest of your thought, is magnanimous, for in your simplest form, beloved brothren, you are the Perfect God, singularly evolved. That is happiness!

You see the flower in all of its beauty and color and array and aroma. It denotes its happiness from the seed. And the seed denotes its happiness from the creator of the seed. And the creator of the seed denotes its happiness within itself, for itself is the Source. Unlike the flower, you are the unique, wondrous forms that are original. The flower is of **your** creativity, thus taking the Source through you to the flower. You are the Living Cause, the Living Purpose, the Living Ideal, the Living Thought.

Now, there are [those who] "bridge" themselves to a perpetual Cause or a God or some divine deity. They bridge themselves there, meaning they think themselves [to be] as the flower. And as long as they think themselves to be as the flower, indeed they must die, bring forth their seed [so] that they may live again and again and again--usually in the same bed.

As long as you "bridge" yourself to the Source, as long as you use ritualistic practices, historical ideal forms called "dogma," you will never quite reach the Source. The Source will always be out of reach to you as it has been unto Mankind from the beginning

"You look for others to make you happy? They never will. You look for things to make you happy? They never will. As long as you seek happiness in objects outside the purest principle of what you are, you will find it only in temporal forms and fleeting moments—"nows" that never seem long enough."

of his beginnings through the great vortex of superstition, hatred and bitterness that Mankind created amongst himself. Thus Man had to find bridges to bridge him [to] his divinity.

I do not teach this. And though I be an outlandish teacher of great propriety and wondrous movement and a different truth, I am, in the simplest of my truth, God, and need no bridge that I have to cross to get [to Him]. That is my happiness. That is why I serve the Source. That is why I love the Source. That is why I understand the Source, for I understand me.

A man may look at the flower and find happiness, for it delights his nostrils and tantalizes his exuberant mode for color and form. That may bring him happiness for it reminds him, in the innermost parts of his being, of a touch of creativity that perhaps he had his hand in. But then, he must remember that it was built by another God, so he must bridge [that] God to congratulate him on such a wondrous form, [and thus] the happiness is rather lost. That is the way it is with you and how you live.

You seek happiness in different forms, modes, symbols, [and] that happiness gives you a small supplement. But what are you trying to do? Why are you reaching **outside** of your kingdom to make you happy? You look for others to make you happy? They never will. You look for things to make you happy? They never will. As long as you seek happiness in objects outside the purest principle of what you are, you will find it only in temporal forms and fleeting moments--"nows" that never seem long enough.

Thus, where does man find his happiness? Where will you find yours? Not in your entanglements or your embitterness or your confusion. You will find it when you, in the simplest of your thoughts, dare to contemplate that you are the original Source who is the giver of all inanimate objects, inanimate thought. It is **you** who give the projectile of happiness acceptance [and] creativity to any one thing you set your hand to.

So who must you find and succor to that will give to you unfleeting happiness, that will not give unto you sorrow and will not betray you? The flower? The flower will wilt and perish. By serving you--serving **you**--and [by] a complete reversal of your thinking into loving yourself. That is where your happiness is! That is your God. That is Life. That is the Source.

Once the steadfastness and the beauty of your being have been established by you, then it is quite simple to obtain happiness in all other things about you. For how can one who is steadfast in the movement of his wondrous Self, loves his wondrous Self and is pleased with his wondrous Self find fault in anything outside of his wondrous Self when fault lies not within him?

"The experience of joy, complete joy, will not be experienced outside of your being with a spouse or a lover or siblings or a career or labor. Those are only excuses for it!

True joy emerges from deep within one's Self, from the realization of one's Self. The wonderful elation called Joy, beloved entity, is the wondrous adventure of knowing who you are. What purpose you are is that you are. You are an adventure, entity, into your own being."

To go back to the Source means to go back to you, in to you, around you, through you, by you. There you will find happiness, for you will not let yourself down.

And if someone wishes to give unto you a sorrowful understanding or tries to betray you, let them. But do not fall prey to the emotion, for it is not the body they wish to betray but the emotion of you. Once they bring down the happiness of your character into sadness, then they have won, for is that not the ultimate death? Is that not the ultimate snobbery? Is that not the ultimate conquering--not of life, but of attitude?

When you are happy in yourself and others are projecting gloom and doom, do not fall prey to what they are doing. Be happy in spite of them and for them. When they are tired of it, they will see [that] all the time they have gathered their face like a prune into wrinkles and worry, you have the sweetness of youth about your countenance and a joy and exuberance of life that is beyond words. Then maybe they will look into your eyes to find a truth and a happiness. [Then] you can look at them and say unto them, "Be the God that you are."

You have wondrous sayings upon your plane about happiness, and it has pleased me greatly to see these things. Happiness is many things. But let us say what happiness is in its purest form and purest sphere. If happiness is a flower, then happiness in its greater form is the thing that made the flower, which is God, the giver of all good. When you find happiness, love is always there. When you find happiness, peace is restored. When you find happiness, God is seen--and that is a true measure.

Thus, I am Ramtha the Enlightened One, servant unto God Almighty, the Source, the Principle Cause, the Element, the Life Force, the Exuberance of Happiness. And I am a servant unto the Christus: the one, pure, perfect Son; the [one] conceivable singular ideal form of the Father. Unto Him, I serve and love, for He is happiness. And unto you, my illustrious brothren who are so beautiful, happiness is you in learning about you. So be it.

*

You who be Gods and Christs, perfect Sons of a Great Mass, you have the ability to determine for yourself whatever you desire, whatever it is. The greater you create from that which is termed your opinions of life, however they are, the greater the experiments of joy shall occur within your being.

The more you create and find your potential getting grander and grander and grander, and the more you unlimit yourself that the potential can come into play, the happier you will become. For [then] you are getting close to your own knowingness, your own self-esteem, your own trust within the steadfastness of your

"When you accept that which is pressed to you and when you live it in joy, the joy heightens the tomorrow of your destiny and expands it into greater receivership. That is why loving yourself every moment is imperative, for that moment sets the pace, if you will, for the hours to come. Joy begats joy, entity. It is a wondrous diseasement."

own perfect being. That brings joy and happiness, for God is in a perpetual state of joy; He knows no other way to be.

Now, that happiness, indeed, cannot be purchased. It cannot be bargained for. It cannot be served for. It must become only by allowing yourself to Become. When you allow yourself to Become, then you have allowed joy to be the principle emotion within your own perfect directive, indeed your own life. Inasmuch [as] joy be the greatest attainment, it also is accompanied by love, for they are one and the same--they are one and the same! This must be earned by allowing yourself to Become, indeed.

Create only for the mere joy of creating. When you create for joy, you will soon find your own perfect being **living** for joy. And when you live for joy, then you will never do anything in your life to ever inhibit the flow of joy or happiness. You will never sell it, you will never serve it--and you can never purchase it.

By bringing joy into perfect alignment within your own beautiful existence, my beloved brothren, you have allowed the treasures of a greater heaven to occur, for when you pass this plane, the treasures that you have incurred shall not be of kingdoms that are built from three-dimensional matter to be sustained by three-dimensional forms. You will [have] built the form to the Form of Joy, which shall build in itself an enrichment within your totality which shall be your treasure in that which is termed the Heavens to Come. And in that, joy has a solidity in form upon the vibration [of] whatever plane you shall be aligned. And that joy shall be waiting for you when you pass this plane to give unto you yet a greater ability and advantage to create there, in greater form and measure, what you have created here. And for what purpose? To obtain the joy from it.

Never grow anything unless you grow it for the joy of it. Never labor for anything lest you labor for the joy of it. And neither purchase anything lest you have purchased it for the joy. When you do [these things] with joy within your heart and within your mind, then it is not what you have purchased, labored for, or grown [that is the treasure]; it is the emotional gratification secured from that one effective movment. That adds up into a totality that will gain you the essence of greater lives to come.

Now, each step by step in this divine mastery, my beloved brothren, of procurring in [a state of] joy, brings you closer to that perfect alignment that occurred once, many millenniums ago without count, when the Son was born of the perfect Father and the Son created from his beloved Father all that he could collectively create within his perfect vision.

"Each time you obtain joy, through whatever acts, you are getting closer to the totality of your own perfect vision, indeed the totality of your own being: God I AM.

Happiness and joy, my beloved brothren, are the emotions that find Love; and Love leads you to your beloved Father, straightaway. And the path is not narrow; it encompasses all that is. Thus you can never stray off of it. Never! And straight unto your beloved Father shall you go back, illustrious King, indeed Lawgiver, indeed Prince of Peace, the Herald of Life."

Each time you obtain joy, through **whatever** acts, you are getting closer to the totality of your own perfect vision, indeed the totality of your own being: God I AM.

The truest treasures of the world to come are not those of three-dimensional matter; they are the happiness or the despair or the sorrow that is **earned** from matter. Thus happiness and joy, my beloved brothren, are the emotions that find Love; and Love leads you to your beloved Father, straightaway. And the path is not narrow; it encompasses **all** that is. Thus you can never stray off of it. Never! And straight unto your beloved Father shall you go back, illustrious King, indeed Lawgiver, indeed Prince of Peace, the Herald of Life.

What is the mastery of life? It is not one [lived] in abstinence. It is not one in poverty. It is not one in that which is termed pious sorrow. It is one [lived] indeed in jubilant joy, whether that joy takes you to become a pauper or to become a king. Whatever it is--**whatever indeed**--the joy obtained from it is the mastery of life: letting life become all-happiness for you.

When you begin to realize that God I AM be that which is termed your own totality, be that which is termed your Perfect Joy within you, that you are the giver of all you desire and want, [then] happiness can [truly] be reached.

*

On this plane, the consciousness here is more readily to accept fear, more readily to be excited over sorrow and death, gossip, war, jealousies. They are attuned to that accepted consciousness, [and] that brings heightened zeal, anticipation and excitement into their lives. And if they do not have a little bit of that every single day, they are put into a trauma of immense depression. [Many] do [not] even know what happiness is [for] they have never dared to let their thought contemplate it, never dared to let their life be intertwined with it.

How do you become happy and go above this? By contemplating that there is such a mode of existence, by contemplating that there is such a reality of joy.

Did you know [that] each moment your life is without boundaries; it is without height and depth; it simply is, and is awaiting your unique design or alteration upon it. Yet [many] inevitably will choose to worry, ponder, feel insecure, insignificant, unwanted, unbeautiful, undesired and unloved, moment after moment after moment. [But] the same power and the same law [that] makes [those feelings] effective in the moment has also the inalienable ability [to allow you] to become happy, joyful, peaceful, mirthful, jolly, extensive, expansive, being, total, laughter, lovely, beauty--Now! But this plane chooses to think the other way.

"The path to the Kingdom of Heaven is what you declare as Joy. That brings you back into the Mind of God."

What need you to know to make you happy? That there is **nothing** on this plane worth not being happy for. That each moment of your life gives you the opportunity to express happiness, and you have chosen not to.

What can make you happy is only how your attitude is towards it. Thus, if you don't have anything to be happy about, perhaps you should look at you; that is enough to make you happy. And don't ask anyone else what they think! What would they know of happiness when all of their life is governed by the same things that have plagued yours!

You are enough reason to make you happy. You are the giver of the design of happiness. You are the giver of the design of joy, of fulfillment, of pleasure.

CHAPTER TEN

FEAR NO THING

"Whatsoever we are in fear of are we enslaved by."

"Fear is a great whore. It will rob you of happiness. It will rob you of the joy of existence. It will rob you of the moment of love if you permit it.

Fear permits conquering. Fear is an all-encompassing power that preys upon its enemies relentlessly. And until you stand up and become the God of your Being and become greater than Fear, you will continuously be enslaved in it all of your life. No matter where you go or who you are with, it will always be with you.

As long as you are dominated by Fear, you will never know the Kingdom of Heaven, for the Kingdom of Heaven is without Fear. It lives in the joy and hope of life lived in a foreverness of being."

FEAR NO THING

Fear is an illusion. It is a deception made by the cleverest of minds--your own--that deceives you into thinking there is something dreadfully frightening about this place, and that one should at all times hide behind closed doors and never participate in life lest he be slain. What [kind of life] is that!

Fear is an illusion. Man is under fear; God is above it. God hath dominion over fear and all unknown for He **is** the Unknown. You simply have to rise above your fear and deal with it like a conqueror. Only then can you be set free of it. Only then.

The basis of all illusionary fear is death, for [in] all of your lifetimes, for eons in the counting of your Soul-memory, if you didn't do certain things you would die; if you didn't believe a certain way, you would die; if you didn't do this you would die or your children would die or the plague would come and you would die.

The religions taught in some aspect that Man, once he dies, was dead and gone and that was it! And so fear became death; fear was really born out of it. But when enlightenment comes and the planes of the seven emerge within the one and entities can thus be seen from other planes, or [come] I from another understanding to tell you and to reason with you that there is nothing to be frightened of, then **who** could ever have dominion over you if you are not longer frightened of death?

Well, death is a no thing. In the Kingdom of Heaven, nothing ever dies, ever, for how can a thought ever perish? It is always alive and well, for it is the premise that begats the next thought and the next and the next and the next. So nothing ever dies, not even the body dies; it changes form, but where does the form go? It goes back to Thought. So the body is always regenerated through that which is termed the genetic style of Mankind. Man in his loins holds the intricate pattern of his beautiful Self--his clone, if you will; and so his genetics pass it on. And the woman, the same with her delicate egg. But nothing is ever lost.

To overcome your fears is to face them, because you cannot bury a fear anywhere. When you think it is behind you and you are charging up for your greatest quest of glory, in the moment you are to receive your crown and standard, here will come Fear behind you and assail you.

When one realizes that death is an illusionary enigma and can understand [that] that is all that it is and can live in spite of it, they have conquered the base of fear. Then what can life be

"Fear is an amplifier of thought and it will bring to you whatever it is that you fear. Fear is the amplifier of the 'thought-action,' [for] whatever you fear, fear draws it into you a thousandfold. That is why you must learn to fear no thing, for no thing is worth the value of fear."

without fear? Well, it is, indeed, a happy interlude. So for that which come to this audience to learn by, I simply manifest for their fears for them that they look at them, that they deal with them, that they overcome them. [I show them that] the root of fear is the "ending of": the ending of relationships, the ending of labor, the ending of gold--whatever [it is that] means [to them] the "death and dying of." [I show them that] they are a no thing, for **they** have created them.

And they immediately shriek, as it were, in horror and shiver inside and are frightful even to get in their autos. But the fear will come to pass nonetheless. And when we bring it to their doorstep, as it were, I give them the strength to open the door and to see that it is nothing, and teach them how to manifest a kingdom that has no fear.

*

How do you rid your life of fear? By having all the things that you fear become manifest. It is not an awesome thing; there is good reason, for if fear can manifest itself, then it becomes a knowingness. It is the unknowing that we fear, never the known. I will manifest all your fears for you; then you will see what they are and you will never fear them again, for they will now be known [and] you will now have dominion over them.

*

What be the Science of Our Destiny is in reality the Science of Our Thinking. Whatever we contemplate, even the bizarreness of our contemplative thoughts, comes to pass, for the bizarreness of what we think is emitted in emotion, and that emotion will come to pass in our being, always. [So] you see, not just the good thoughts manifest [but] also the negative, the awesome.

Fear is an amplifier of thought and it will bring to you whatever it is that you fear. Fear is the amplifier of the "thought-action," [for] whatever you fear, fear draws it into you a thousandfold. That is why you must learn to fear no thing, for no thing is worth the value of fear.

[If] you wish to perfect yourself, you must understand that truly the greatest refinement should be in your thinking--your thinking! [If] e'er you have a thought [of fear], then take the thought and project it from the Lord God of your Being into the Father. Anything that goes into the Father goes there into perfection and it will be taken from you; it will not be in your life to come.

All here will realize one day that Thought is the Ultimate Destiny, that that is the Ultimate Creator, that that is the Ultimate Life, that that **is** the simplest of what God is.

"To eliminate fear? [Know] there is nothing to be afraid of. Nothing! For the Father, in His Infinite Being—even through His beloved Son—hath created no thing in His Providence, in His Being, in His Personified Self, to ever eliminate Life, for if He did, He would eliminate Himself. And He hath not wrought in His being such a design, and neither has His Son—for all that he has done! Thus, you will live forever!"

Unfortunately, Man all along has overlooked it and always wondered if there is something out there that he hath angered that hath caused the awful things to occur to him. [But] Man himself is the creator of his tomorrows.

[Any] act [that] you have feared is not nearly as awesome as the thought. You see, the thought is more terrible than the act because the thought could never be predicted [as] to when it would come to pass.

And the time between the thought and the action is called "hell."

*

How do you elimate fear? The answer is simple; it is the receiving of it and the acceptability of it that you will find difficult, for you are geared to fear.

How do you elimate fear? By reasoning with yourself in your Soul that there is nothing to be in fear of, for will you ever die? You will never die! You have lived millenniums; you will live millenniums.

The body hath been geared to die, for it has accepted its lot through the Lord of your being, the Soul of your being. For the standard consciousness of your plane is to be born only to die--to be born only to die. [In] that [consciousness], each day you grow older instead of younger. You do not know how to live in the moment! You live continuously either in the past or in the future but never in the moment. If you learned to live in the moment there would be no future or no past; there would be "continuous now" which is "continuous God" recognized.

To eliminate fear? [Know] there is nothing to be afraid of. Nothing! For the Father in His Infinite Being--even **through** His beloved Son--hath created no thing in His Providence, in His Being, in His Personified Self, to ever eliminate Life, for if He did, He would eliminate Himself. And He hath not wrought in His being such a design, and neither has His Son--for all that he has done! Thus, you will live forever!

Speak kindly unto your Soul and have it acknowledge only the good. Tell your Soul, the ultimate recorder of all things, to never acknowledge fear: a direct command by you. Then the Soul will never acknowledge fear; then you will never have fear in your being. Tell your Soul never to acknowledge age; it never will! Tell your Soul to acknowledge life; [then] it will fervently acknowledge life.

As easily as the Soul is susceptible to the programming of contemplative thought given [to it] through the altered Ego, the Soul will listen to a complete being speaking to it, and the Soul, entity, will be the abider of the law. And who is the Lawgiver?

You, the Christus of your being: Supreme Lawgiver, Creator of the Law, Dispenser of the Law; and the Soul carries it out.

Speak to your Soul: you are speaking to yourself. It is a powerful, awesome force. If you learn its secrets simply as I have taught you, you will learn how to gear your life into perpetual life, perpetual happiness, without ever acknowledging fear of failure or criticism. And that is a truth!

The truth I have told you, it is a very simple truth, very practical. There is no intellectual mystery about it. It is open to be viewed by anyone, for God hath not hidden His mysteries from even the simpleton in the street. The simpler you look upon it the grander it will become. Do not complicate it: let it be. Know that you are Forever God, for that has been assured in your Beginning of Beginnings.

*

The Prophecy Of Armageddon

Armageddon, as it were, is a very wrathful prophecy, [and] fear was the basis and the reason for the prophecy.

Your society, you must understand, is motivated by fear. That is the "modus operandi" of your society. That **is** its basic conscious level. [But] I will tell you, your consciousness here is being changed. And I will explain consciousness to you in but a moment, how it works and why you are a part of it.

Everyone lives as though there is no tomorrow. They are living in such a rush, they are idolizing in such a rush, and they are uncertain, for there have been soothsayers and seers who have prophesied doom for the end of this time. Everyone is uncertain about their tomorrow, and everyone wants to grasp a part of the material kingdom before it is over and finished and they can never have it again. That is a truth!

And there are many wondering why they were even born, why could they have not been born some other time [and not] have to be a part of the murk and the mire and the catastrophies that are set in a looming balance to occur. All that are affected are aware of this [the prophecies] in their consciousness, which is the totality of their subconciousness, for everyday in your time, fear is the greatest seller in the marketplace.

All the religions of your world prophesy doom; they prophesy "end"; they prophesy the separation of God and Man, Man being imperfect, never achieving perfection. If a man hears this when he is a child, he will be driven by that ideal--striving for protection, striving for life, striving to "become" in the time left to him. The lot of this plane believe that.

I will tell you, beloved: Those who prophesied doom on this plane did it **outside** of their lifetimes so no one could ever say that it did not come to pass—and also that they wouldn't have to be a part of it—for they despised Mankind in their beings because they despised themselves. But this plane will never end, and [the prophecies] will never be! There is no battle that is ever fought in the "physical" that was not [first] declared in the "mental."

The consciousness [on this plane] is being changed. Is! It is already infiltrating, it is already becoming a part of your totality on this plane. The world will sleekly and beautifully go right into the next time. And it will not fall to pieces and blow up! It will not quake. It will not turn to blood. No bomb will ever blow it up, for the consciousness that feeds the tyrants is becoming elongated, not limited.

You have a light sphere around you: it is called your "auric field." It is the source, as it were, that gathers thought. You are connected into the River of Thought that is everywhere: the consciousness is everywhere. When you go into a city, if you were to see the consciousness, it would be like a bowl over the city: it engulfs the city as a cloud. Everyone that goes into the city, their [auric] lights automatically are in tune to the consciousness of collective thought that is accepted within the city. And soon, they begin to change and they wonder why. [The reason is:] they are part of limited thought.

There is a balance in your universe: like are drawn to like. That is how the great Gods, which you are, manifested so evenly. The science [utilized] was the magnification of their "auric stratum" [which] drew to them everything that was needed for that manifestation to occur. When consciousness is lifted, is elongated, it will draw to it greater consciousness, and greater and greater. And everyone that is in tune with the consciousness will **become** greater and greater.

The thought is being elongated, lifted. There is penetration coming, indeed, from within the earth, on the earth and above the earth, from the entire galaxy. And all soon will not be thinking of passion love for other selves, but for the humility of other selves—the truest love there is, the **truest** love there is. [Since] you are a part of this plane, a part of this consciousness, you will also begin to feel the change [of consciousness].

Fear has been the thing that has separated equality. It has been the thing that has given dictators and tyrants and lords and kings their rule. And it is the thing that has kept the [ruled] underneath them. They keep the fear alive by threats of war. They keep the fear alive by extenuating themselves above others. And they keep the fear alive by not bringing "medicine" to the current focal point of attitude rather than drugs. When

"When fear is removed and everyone knows (and soon will be proven by your scientist) that the body can live forever, and that it is the thought-accepted processes in it that make it grow old and diseased and die—when everyone soon learns that even if the body dies they are forever, what will they fear [then]? Nothing!

And with the same stroke of that understanding, then there will be no more sheep for shepherds to tend, for all will become shepherds, "meek" if you will. For who is to govern a lord other than himself? And what is the use of war when no one fears anything? What accomplishment is there in that? And when everyone is equal, then there will be no one to worship the powerful."

[what is] feared is removed, who is to fear what?

I will tell you what is the basis of fear. Death! That is the raw basis of fear because it is an unknown. [And] that stretches its arm all the way into the Ego, that even the death of the altered Ego, the death of pride, is feared.

When fear is removed and everyone knows (and soon will be proven by your scientist) that the body can live forever, and that it is the thought-accepted processes in it that make it grow old and diseased and die--when everyone soon learns that even if the body dies they are forever, what will they fear [then]? Nothing! And with the same stroke of that understanding, then there will be no more sheep for shepherds to tend, for **all** will become shepherds, "meek" if you will. For who is to govern a lord other than himself? And what is the use of war when no one fears anything? What accomplishment is there in that? And when everyone is equal, then there will be no one to worship the powerful.

Very soon in your time, we are going to have a great sitting on this plane of myself and Overlords that come from a distant place. And we will sit and exhibit our power--for all to see. I have brought animals from death back to life--an amazement! I can bring man back to life, anyone can. And when this is demonstrated, who upon your plane will exert themselves to be greater than anyone else? None! And they that do the demonstrating will show everyone how to do it, in an equality.

And government rule, what is called "republican rule" at the present time, is going back to a more refined republic, which will eventually go back to Self-rule. And there will be no more room for kings or dictators or tyrants--**and that is coming, entity!**

The world has been governed by prophecies of doom for ever so long, and it was created to rule the sovereign of the meek. It will never come to pass. Never! And they who bring such prophecies and fear in writing to the people, they will be at the hands of their own fear and their own prophecy, for whatever they put forth is building their kingdom; whatever word they utter **is** their kingdom, and they will have it all back!

CHAPTER ELEVEN

RELINQUISH GUILT : BECOME LAWLESS

"All that is, is; and the 'isness' has nothing in it—except isness. And everything from that fact, entity, has truth. You go and contemplate it, aye?"

"There is no one that is the jailer in God's Kingdom. There is no one, entity, that is the lynchman in His Kingdom. There is no one that is the tormentor in here. If God be Love, then He is explicitly that and nothing less."

THERE IS NO LYNCHMAN IN GOD'S KINGDOM

[A dialogue with an elderly woman in a wheelchair]

Ramtha: Dear lady, who rides on silver wheels . . .

Woman: I love God but I am afraid of dying.

Ramtha: Why?

Woman: I don't know. I can't . . . reach the bottom of it. I've thought of it and thought of it and thought of it.

Ramtha: Do you believe in hell?

Woman: Yes, I do.

Ramtha: That is why you don't want to die, for you feel that is where you are going.

Woman: Oh, yes . . . I don't **think** I'm going . . . I don't believe God will let me go 'cause I've asked for forgiveness for all I've done.

Ramtha: My lady! My lady! Do you believe that the Father has greater love than you do for your own siblings?

Woman: No.

Ramtha: Do you feel, entity, that He loves as you love?

Woman: Well, I just don't feel like He loves me sometimes. Maybe I feel like maybe I'm not forgiven. But still, I know I am.

Ramtha: What have you done that is so wrong?

Woman: Well . . . several things.

Ramtha: Have those several things, entity, kept you from living?

Woman: No. I have . . . tried to live, and I want to live, and I want to live right.

Ramtha: And what is that?

Woman: That means the Devil won't get me . . . You tell me, please ma'am, what it is.

Ramtha: Would you believe me if I did?

Woman: I will.

Ramtha: What if I told you there is no "hell?"

Woman: I've been taught that there is a hell, though.

Ramtha: But I'm teaching you there isn't! Will you believe me as firmly as you have believed there is?

Woman: Well, I believe you.

Ramtha: Then accept it, for there isn't. Listen to me. There are so many that believe in hell. "Hell" is a term that was used in the Kingdom of Judea to describe a shallow grave. That is what the term means translated. But preachers and priests have determined it to be a place of torment.

Woman: Well, I read my Bible regularly, and it, it puts emphasis on hell.

Ramtha: Who wrote the Bible?

Woman: Different ones.

Ramtha: And who where they? Were they "man?"

Woman: I don't know.

Ramtha: They were! I have looked into the depths of your world, into the center to find a "burning lake of fire" and I found nothing. And I went to the farthest reaches of your universe to find "hell," and it was not there! And I looked same places for Lucifer and could find him nowhere. And alas, when I returned, I found him in the hearts of those who believe in him and "hell." But there is no such place.

Woman: Well, I'm glad you think so.

Ramtha: I **know** so!

Woman: You know, it doesn't look like God would love us so and then the least little thing we did that He would send us to hell to live in burning fire.

Ramtha: That is precisely correct. Will you listen to me? The Father hath created no such place to torment anything, for were you not created by God?

Woman: Yes.

Ramtha: Then if you were created by God, do you not have God in you?

Woman: I have God in me--I love God!

Ramtha: But are you not part of God?

Woman: Am I?

Ramtha: Indeed!

Woman: Well, that means a lot to me.

Ramtha: My lady, what would God make you out of if He didn't make you out of Himself? You **are** Him! Why would He cast Himself into a pit and never love Himself for doing what is called a "wrong" that He Himself invented? He would not do that!

I will tell you: Man has created a God that they could use to control their brothers. Religion was created, lady, to control nations where armies failed, and fear was the tool, entity, that kept them in line. If you take the divinity out of any man, or take the God out of him, then he becomes fearful of everything, even death.

God has not created "hell" or a "devil." He has not created any of those things. That was a creation of Man to torment his brothers. That is a truth! The Father is forever loving--

Woman: God loves all of us. I know it.

Ramtha: Indeed, indeed, for He **is** all of us! And what about all of your "wrongs?" My wondrous lady, you have done nothing wrong. Nothing!

Woman: Why, thank you.

Ramtha: . . . for life has not been altered because of anything you have done; it has been enhanced by it.

Now, your religions, entity, and your belief has caused the annihilation of civilizations for eons. Your Mayans and your Aztecs were obliterated and murdered through the rule of the Church because they did not believe as the Church did. The Holy Wars in your Dark Ages of your world, entity, was fought for the belief of religion and conquest.

And in a place called France, at the time of the greatest point of the Holy Wars, entity, babes were plucked from their mother's arms because they did not believe according to the Church. Women had their eyes burned out with hot irons and their chests branded, and the streets ran with blood--all because of a belief!

And then the Protestants took that which is called "hell fire," "brimstone" and the "devil" and caused their congregations to stay intact by producing fear in the hearts of their little ones, [telling them] that if they did not do certain things and abide by the rules and regulations of the Church, they would burn forever in "hell."

Woman: That's kinda the way I was raised.

Ramtha: My lady, you were raised in an atrocity! Did it ever make you wonder what happened to all of the people that existed before the Bible did?

Woman: No. I just thought maybe hell destroyed them. . . Oh, well, I'm so sorry.

Ramtha: Don't be at all. That is the product of the belief. Now here you are, an old woman. You are not youthful and zestful anymore. And you are worried about dying. And all the ominous teachings that have been programmed into you, entity, are coming to bear upon you: "Is there hell? Will I go there? Have I been so wrong?"

I will tell you straightaway: You will not go there, for there is no place to go to! You will live in a twinkling of a moment when you pass your body. You will be above it, and you will be a pure Light Entity once again.

[Then] you call forth the Kingdom of Heaven to come forth, and great teachers will come, entity, and take you to a place of further learning that you may see for yourself all of these [truths] I am telling you.

And God, the Splendor That Is, hath created no place to punish anyone, for He has been living as long as Thought has been. And the Thought created the "Great Light," and it will go on into eternity.

Yeshua ben Joseph, who you call "Jesus of Nazareth," he was a great God, just as you, but not **the** Son of God, **a** Son of God who became God, just as you [will] become God. He never taught, entity--

Woman: Do you believe Jesus was **a** son of God?

Ramtha: Not **the** Son of God, **a** Son of God. I do not believe it; I **know** it! Just as **you** are a Son of God.

Woman: I haven't been taught that!

Ramtha: Now lady, but he was your brother, not your savior. And he taught everyone that the Kingdom of Heaven was "within" them, and that they and the Father are one. And he spoke **not** of "hell," entity; he spoke of life and its beauty.

Love that which you are and the God that you are and cease reading your insidious book [Bible]! And start knowing within you that the Father lives within you and that you will live forever, for you will, entity. That is the way it is.

And besides, what would the "devil" do with you once he had you?

Woman: I don't want to find out! But thank you.

Ramtha: My lady, what kind of a Father would have created such an entity and such a place and such fear, and made you so helpless against all of them? He is not the God of my being nor do I acknowledge Him! I acknowledge Life--The Supreme Cause.

God is everything, for if there be one thing not God, you must ask yourself **who** created that! Everything **is** the Father, for everything **is** Life.

And the Father knows only Love. He has never judged you or anyone, entity. Ever! He has no ability to alter Himself to become less than Love or Life, for if He did, life as you know it in the next moment would cease for everything.

Woman: Well, God is Love. I knew that!

Ramtha: And is He hate?

Woman: No, I don't think He is.

Ramtha: Who is hate?

Woman: I guess that's a bad one, if there is one.

Ramtha: There isn't one!

Woman: Well, how are we punished then?

Ramtha: You have been punished well enough by doing it yourself. What need is there for punishment? Who is to determine how one should live in life? What is "perfection?" Why are so many people different? Is everyone to live the same? No! And who is to determine what is right and wrong? God doesn't even determine that for He is **both** right and wrong, yet He does not alter Himself to determine it, entity. He is everything!

By believing that you are wrong has caused you to live in your own hell all of your life. To believe that you are going to be punished has caused you enough worry and enough sickness that that hath been your lot—and you have created that yourself!

There is no one that is the jailer in God's Kingdom. There is no one, entity, that is the lynchman in His Kingdom. There is no one that is the tormentor in here. If God be Love, then He is explicitly that and nothing less.

Woman: After you have been taught for so long, how can you feel that there is not a devil?

Ramtha: You know how? By **knowing** there isn't! By the same process that taught you there was.

Woman: Well . . . thank you.

Ramtha: Love yourself, and meet the Father within you. And be at peace with you, my lady, [for] when you leave this plane, you are going to brightly live again.

Woman: Amen.

Ramtha: So be it.

ONLY MAN

Only Man could create a God that did not laugh, that was judgemental, that was embittered, that was for one people and not the other. All of this [biblical] history--unfortunately written by madmen, unfortunately recorded by madmen, and unfortunately worshipped by those who didn't know any better--has set up a status quo that God, the Superlative, Wondrous Cause, has been a vengeful, spiteful, hateful, war-like entity. And, in truth, He has for they have **believed** Him to be that way! And who, in the essence, is He? Them!

That is not my God. I was enough of all of those things to learn what my God is. Thus, the [God] I give to you is Pure Reason, Pure Understanding, the simplicity of Complete Joy that can be taken right down in your scientific understandings to its gross matter of coexistence--and it is all true!

Religious orders from all over your world have played a major role in the enslavement of peoples to return [to] this plane. [Thus], the Second Plane of Existence is the acceptance that God the Father is a singular entity that has judged the world and had [only] **one** perfect Son (which alluded to everyone else that they were "bastards" of a spawning universe) and that [for them] to accept the love of this Divine Father, [they] must equate that they are grossly imperfect and accept the master of this perfect Son. These teachings, as erroneous as they were, convinced many that when they die, they would be in death until that which is termed the Christus came for them.

Upon the Second Plane, [a] plane like this one, know you what is there? Dead peoples! Their wondrous Spirit lies in a catatonic state, for they **believe** and know they are "dead," waiting for the return of Christ, waiting for a "resurrection." Do you know how many have been burned [because of] that [belief]? How many have died for that?

Envision for yourself, entity, a plain greater than the Plain of Sharon [where you] see Light Embodiments in full sleep. [And] they are suspended three feet above the plain with simple aisleways in between, lying as far as the eye can see, lying as wide as the eye can perceive. And they lie there in a dead slumber, for they "believe"; [thus] they are the lawgiver. [And] thus they are "sleeping" through ages. And we try to awaken them into another consciousness, and they refuse to wake up! They are caught in a terrible void. And those that do wake up, where can they go? The only place they realize is this place.

"How atrocious, entity, how abominable [is it] that [religious] organizations have separated Man from the God which he is and made him feel [that] he is the bastard of the universe? [Why] feel guilty [because of] these [teachings] that have held the world in subservience?"

Thus, they return here to work out that belief to make them stronger [so they may] go on.

That is the atrocity of religious orders [that] have taken our Beloved Father and separated us from His providence. That is the erroneous teaching of a God that is governed by Man to rule his brothren and to torment them by an evil creature that they have created within their own Soul.

How atrocious, entity, how abominable [is it] that [religious] organizations have separated Man from the God which he is and made him feel [that] he is the bastard of the universe? [Why] feel guilty [because of] these [teachings] that have held the world in subservience?

The ultimate truth in [my] teachings little by little releases you from the bondage of death, [for that] is where the hypocrisy of religion goes. Have you ever seen one "pious" man ascend from death? Have you?

I am a lover of all peoples, even the hypocrites, even the priests; but their hour of demonstration is coming, entity, and they will utterly fail to fulfill it. They care not for you, entity; they love you not. Do they know who you are and what you are? Do they **love** what you are? No, they do not! They are incapable of doing that [for] they are too busy enslaving others; they cannot be particularly attentive to you.

Their hour is coming. And they will call me "Lucifer" and "Satan," the deceiver of the peoples. And why would they call me that? For I am the direct **lover** of them. And what I do that they would call "miracles" I do for Mankind, who **is** Godkind. I will tell you a truth: The Great Church, who is the Great Whore, does not even believe in Yeshua ben Joseph: they think him to be a myth! That is a truth.

I realize that it is disheartening for some of those who have put such a grandiose affair backing religious dogma to have it shattered by knowing that it doesn't matter anyway. [But] if you put forth pure reasoning to any heretic law, entity, you would find readily that pure reason, pure God, pure understanding, will hold it at bay; it cannot even account for its miserable self.

Priorities? Priorities? Who is more important: God that you are or ridiculous, spiteful, hateful, vindictive, enslaving law? Think, entity, think with what is the "seat" of your being and reason this all out applicably. Think in terms of the sphere of "unlimitedness," of "Godness." Think of the Benevolent Entity that is in all life, and then try to discern the Entity that despises life that you must be in fear of. You will come up with your own answers.

All Christs that have lived spoke, "The Father is within me. The Father and I are one. The Kingdom of Heaven indeed is within me." If it is "within you," entity, what are you doing by giving it to others that are the dogs and hyenas of the plane that would eat the flesh from your bones and then gnaw [them] until the marrow is out of them?

Think about this and ponder your life yet again and how beautiful life is and how beautiful you are. Look within you and see who is there. If you look, entity, you will find a brilliant mirror, and the image you will see is clearly you--emanating, radiating, proverbial beauty before your eyes; the excellence of your being. That is sweet God. That is His Son. That is the Christ that all wish to see. It is a "consciousness understanding reality." That is what we teach here.

The Father is Life! His perfect Son is **you.** Christ, Yeshua ben Joseph, what you call the "Nazarene," he was a Christ and still is. But so be Buddha and Osiris, Isis, Pharoah Ra-ta-bin, Mohammed and all of you!

Ponder that in your days to come. And [ponder] how susceptible Man is to having his divinity taken from him and to accept the erroneous teachings of an all-loving Father that would torment him forever. And then remember the God I have spoken to you about--the one that is the wind upon the water, the color in a trout's side, the fervent smell and aroma of a flower deep in its color, a beautiful woman in her laughter, lovers in their embrace, leaves shivering from trees, pumpkins with frost on them. He is all of those things, and He expresses them in "isness," to which you, entity, are! So be it.

THE LAWS OF GOD AND MAN

The "Law of God" as it is seen in the Book of Books are **many** laws, for every one prophet added unto the laws; never did he diminish them. It is indeed a powerful statement to give unto and to frighten dignitaries that the Law of God says this or it says that, or it restricts this, or you must do that. Thus, [from] the Law of God, people have learned to hate Him, to surrender unto Him, but never to love Him. They have learned to fear Him; they have learned to humble before Him. Children are not to humble before their parents; they are to **be** as their parents!

The "Law of One" is that God, the Source, the Life Force, in enacting and being, [allows] **all** things to express **totally** from His Being **as they will.**

The Law of One is freedom for each and all things to express as they will, as their freedom desires. For what [will] be their "coming home" will be the "positive" and "good" and of God. And when His children return nigh unto Him, and as the Source that is brilliant and beautiful and expansive contemplates the "homecoming" of Himself, it is a great day, a great forever, for His children have come to **be as He is.** And always, in being as He is, is a life of Love.

*

Master, if God's Will were to be **imposed** upon all of the living--and He **is** [all of the living]--then you would not have a will! If God only wanted His Will [to be done], you would not have a will, for then God would not "wrestle" with Himself!

In this understanding [i.e., teaching], God does not have a will, save yours and yours and yours and everyone here. Is the [truth] so narrow that there is only one little, narrow path for all of these "wretched" creatures to get upon?

God is multudious. Every will here **is** His will. He is not the great Overlord; He is the great Inner-Lord! You are never in conflict with Destiny, for it is not preordained. [It is ordained] only by your will. If God has preordained Destiny, you would not need a will. Your very moment is [simply] the reflection of a thought a moment ago.

God is not separate, nor are you separate, but rather you are one and the same. Now, if you are to see the will of the God that is the creation of Man [as] His will versus yours, then you are always in a battle: your will wants to do certain things and feels it must and yet the will of the God of Man tells you [that] you must not! The will of the God of Man is a great enslaver. The God of Man is the Great Deceiver.

What you want to do and must do **is** Divine Providence, Divine Will. Yeshua ben Joseph said, " 'Tis the Father within me that does these things, as it is the Father within all of you. There is not one in this kingdom that is astray, but only if he thinks that God and he are separate from one another."

The God within you **is** your own will. You must do what you must do! Your destiny is preordained by you and no one else! The Father only permits life to occur, that this dream and illusion can occur according to your thinking, feeling, emotional capacity--that determines matter.

Every structure here is the result of a thought. And every molecular structure here is a result of [the] solidifying [of] emotion: that is the Science of God. Thus everything you think manifests; [everything you think creates] your destiny. Every feeling within you is the pearl, the treasure, as it were, that you have gained from this dream, this life, this illusion. That is called Will. That is individualized, and it is also God.

You contemplate this. If you have to be at odds with God, then perhaps you should reconstruct your image of what God is, for I tell you, He is not worth loving if you must fight Him.

*

Master, the splendid thing about God is that He **is** unique. God also, because He is so multudious, is "optional," if you will. He has options or degrees to His Unlimited Truth. Because Man is a creative entity, it would not do him justice to think that he is simply a creator of truth; he must create stipulations to truth that add to his own individuality. You understand?

So God, the Truth, has been Man, the Christ, who in the unique enterprise of that which is termed life, hath taken the parcel "Truth," the great clear gem, and he has created it into the facets which befit him as the originator of truths. You see?

Then what you have is religions, multudious religions, all based on The Truth, when, in essence, **everything** is Truth. How could it be anything else but that? If Man were simply to acknowledge the God within him, he would not be original; so he takes the God within him and puts stipulations to this God. Power is created by taking and passing laws, laws that take away the power of others. That is how it is.

[So] then you have Gods who have options to Truth. To whatever degree you are wishing to align yourself with that truth, you may find any of them to fit whatever you need at the moment. But when you look at all of them, and you are trying to find The Truth, you will realize that all of it is Truth. But [to] what degree do you wish to **become** that truth?

For you who have gone an succored unto all the ministries, they all have something to give. Basically, their giving is, "God exists." From that point of understanding, they have brought forth various degrees of how to get It. "God is" is the greatest of all truths, for you don't have to do anything to get It; you only have to **be** it.

God the Father is lawless. If He had laws, He is limited. Being that He is lawless, He is also unlimited and allows the options to occur. You see?

Now, for any one entity, this is what I should give unto them: Go and learn until you are bored with it or it makes no more sense or it is ridiculous, and then seek the answer until it **feels** right. When it feels right within the Soul, the Soul will rejoice, for it will **know** what The Truth is because [The Truth] is unlimited freedom. You see?

If everyone were to put to papyrus their philosophy (mainly it is philosophy because it hasn't been lived), everyone here would have a different degree of understanding of God and their own way or "path," if you will (a most despicable word—a "path") that someone must follow to find God.

Now, in my audience, there is nothing but God and Options, and whatever your truth is, it **is.** It is not a lie nor is it less. It is a truth, for God is the underlying premise that allows all of this to occur.

*

Guilt [is] a self-created illusion, a self-inflicted wound [that] makes Man subservient of his Lordship. In the Kingdom of God that exists within Man, all things are reality of "possibilities." The illusion occurs when there becomes an alteredness of that reality, and guilt alters the reality of God, or Omnipresent Man, if you will.

Everyone [may] chose to express guilt if they wish to; so it becomes a reality unto them, [for] anything that they ascertain "is" will become; hence [the existence of] that which is termed karma. [But] karma hath no precedence in an ongoing kingdom, for if karma were a reality of law, then [it] would be [ever] so difficult to reach a state of "isness"; no one would, ever, [for] they would be so immersed in indebtness rather than receivership.

Religious law, entity, hath created and made Man wretched rather than being divine. And it hath **invented** guilt to keep allegiance to its own sanctimonious embodiment. If you are taught relentlessly in altered laws, master, then that law becomes a reality, and so does the punishment for breaking it. You are conditioned entities [by what you have] accepted through the factor called "belief"; then it has a credence and abilities within your own being.

[But] you must go back to this: God is lawless, and because of that, He is judgeless. Whatever you decide to become, He will become it and manifest Himself in that reality [so] that you may experience it. And He has never judged the action of [the experience]. If you are persistent in becoming God, you too will become lawless and judgeless in the jurisdiction of beliefs and allow the flow of the moment to be eminent within your Divine Self.

The retributions of guilt are numerous. They are whatever you have created as payment for having it. But inasmuch as you have created the belief in the illusion, you can change it—and it only takes a moment.

If karma were, the Father would make no progress in the progression of Life and Self: He would be too busy paying off His indebtness of "incorrect thinking," and then Life would go nowhere. Unfortunately, there are those that believe in karma and they cannot live for fear of having a "terrible thought" and thus having to come back and pay for it. And so they are in continuous payment and fear. That is **not** how the Father exhibits Himself in all precedence. [Karma] is a farce, but a true one. Do you understand?

Only remember this, master: What you think to be **is.** Anytime you believe in **anything**, it becomes a reality of truth within your being. That is why everyone is on the pinnacle of truth no matter what that point of view, if you will, is. **Your** creative reality will always be different from anyone else's; and when they fail utterly to see your reality, it is only because they are so immersed in the blindness of their own. Thus, whatever you know **is.** And if you've known long enough [that] you have been "without" and [that] you have been a "miserable, wretched creature," perhaps it is an appropriate time to be God and think as He. Then you will be free of it all.

I am a despicable creature and despicable teacher to those who inflict the Laws of Religion. They term me "evil." But that is all right. They are correct! I am, indeed, but only because I go against their creations.

*

Multitudes are living under the residue of what is called "self-created karma." Everything they **do** they attribute to karma! [But] that is a very poor explanation for life; it deserves much more than that.

Cause and effect? Indeed [there is], but even that is a limitation, [for] God is ever-expansive—**ever-expansive.** This, your universe, can disassemble itself in a moment—and not that anything **caused** it; it simply wanted to!

Karma does not exist; **Want** does. And Want is very fickle: it can do and be anything any moment that it wishes and change its mind in the midst of being it. That is why there is no karma.

My beloved entity, because of karma everyone thinks that they have come into this life to do something, to pay back something, to make amends for something. That is called imprisonment or enslavement. When you get rid of karma completely, then entities don't feel they have to pay back anything or be responsible or enslaved. They can simply be the power that they are to create and to regenerate themselves and Life. Then the reason they have come here is not to make amends for whoever they did whatever to, but rather because they are here because they want to live—and that adventure unfolds moment to moment to moment.

*

There are no Laws of Karma; that is a man-made law, a religious hypocrisy. There is only Creativity. There is not [a law of] Cause and Effect. There is no Law of Balance. There only is! God hath to regulate nothing of Himself to be.

If the Father were a law-creating entity, then the entity would have denied Himself the freedom of expression that allows Life to perpetuate itself. He also would have denied Himself the Perfection of Isness that transcends the quality of Isness into Omnipresentness, Allness. He would have become a limited Source, an ending. An ending! There are no endings to Forever; and Forever cannot be contemplated, [only] experienced in a singular moment. What law bids into being [an ending to Forever]? None!

There is no Cause and Effect, entity; there only is. Creativity is the Virtue of Man, for through the Virtue of Man does he create from the Father that he is. He creates from His embodiment. He does not cause anything to be effected: there only is!

Man's laws are uniform. They are a "sovereign entity" that dictate the requirements of a society, of a world understanding how to live. Unfortunately, most [laws] are required and created through ruthlessness only to enslave, which they have also done. Man utterly fails to understand the premise of the Father. Man can see nothing as being a lawless state because he, in the terror of his own being, must have [laws] to govern his own being. That is where he does not see the infiniteness or the divineness of himself—God!

When all the Gods were created for worship, they were created for the stigma of enigmatic rules such as karma, such as heaven and hell, such as good-bad, positive-negative, and all that muck! Master, whatsoever you have done a millenia ago you do not have to pay for anytime. The moment you did it was the creative value learned: the creativity of that thought, that became an "absolute" in its creative form, is but the "after-effect" of **already** what was learned.

If Man is ruled by the Laws of Karma ruthlessly, then Man is not a free Spirit, nor is God, which **is** him. And no matter how many lifetimes he lives, he shall never enter into that which is termed "symbolic perfection"—never—because he will be too busy making up for the thought of "regret" he just had a moment ago. That is an enslavement! And the God from [whose] mouth the Laws of Karma spew forth is a negative God that is a no thing, that is an enslaver!

You are a free Soul and Spirit. The Father eminently is you and yet shall become you and will be all things that you desire to transcend upon to eloquate your being into whatever reality you so choose. And any moment you can change your mind. Any moment!

Become lawless. That does not necessitate recklessness or evil or ugliness. It means you are going to live, and that which is termed the "ropesman" will take the rope away from your throat and allow you to breathe.

To be an entity that has the right to enter the Doors of Eternity, you must be unlimited in your understanding and know that the Father that is all things, [that] can be multudious universes inside a single atom, is infinite. And if He that can reach into an atom and unto the universes of universes that possess their own atoms--[if He] hath that depth, then He has no laws; He is only ongoing. Man creates the laws to perpetrate freedom, not to exalt it.

When you contemplate this, contemplate the benevolence of a God who rules with laws and what would be the outcome eventually. And then contemplate the infiniteness of one million universes inside a singular atom and the state of infinity. Then ask yourself who prefer you!

*

If karma were a truth in the understanding of your life, then one has to question that which is called freedom: the freedom of God to express within one entity.

Tomorrow is not a certainty, entity. It only becomes the certainty of reality according to the dreamer. According to karma, Eternity has been laid out for the whole [of everyone] and it doesn't make any difference if they dream a good dream or a bad dream or they do a good deed or a bad deed: they've done so many [bad deeds] before that they [will have to] pay for them in this lifetime and will go on paying for them. That is not the love of God nor is it the freedom of life; that is enslavement, [for] then [you are] but prisoners, prisoners of [limited] thinking. That is [your lot] under the auspices of what is called karma.

Creation is created by the contemplative entity. Everything here became a living object according to the entities that could think. Everyone here dreams in a kingdom to create from the kingdom. And at anytime the entity wishes to re-create the dream he can do so, for he has unlimited power. Karma creates limited power and retribution.

[Murders, accidents, and robberies] are [the result of] contemplated experiences; they are not entrapments. They are created by the creator--You! They are not "forever" things; they are not "forever" circumstances. So they are not "miseries" as a whole. In retrospect, they are great teachings.

You [may] see the slaughter of ten thousand innocents, and you say, "Woe unto such a misery. Why [don't] the angels weep for this atrocity? Why do they sing to the glory of God?" Because, entity, they have not limited themselves in the capacity to believe in the ending of any one thing, for nothing ever ends. And that which is slaughtered are already caught up into "heaven," as you would term it--or the plane of their reality--for a greater learning and more experiences and what I call "adventures." And yet you bury ten thousand bodies and you weep over them and cast the memory there forever. [But] they are ongoing. God does not weep; that is why tomorrow always comes.

Who think you controls your destiny? Religion believes it to be a Sovereign that controls everyone and manipulates everyone. And that is well and good, for [then] the responsibility of life is taken off of your back. But **you** control your destiny. And you only have to learn that that destiny is forever; 'tis ongoing. This "now" is the product of [the] ongoingness that is not the captive of yesterday but is the "now" that was created to dream tomorrow [into existence].

*

Well, master, you are in what is called "a pickle," as it were. If you had a "lower self," a "medium self," and a "higher self," the great desire would be to have balance, for certainly you would go mad in your confusion of trying to discover which one was best for you.

Let me tell you this: There is no such creature as a "lower self" or even a "higher self" at that! There is only **one** Self. Lower is indicative of something less than divine--it is more worldly, it exasperates great emotion, it is ugly, vile, shameful and, unfortunately, natural.

The "higher self" is abstinence, virtue, divineness, greatness, holiness, prudence, and boring! This, in what is called a "spiritual understanding," is the plot that everyone gets themselves caught up in, you see? For they get into becoming "more spiritual," as it were, and they think they must do away with everything that is "natural" to become spiritual. But then you [may] say, "Then where is the separation of spirit and nature?" Is there, indeed, any?

Everyone that wishes to become spiritual, or God Divine or holy or virtuous and all of that, goes through abstinence, and that, somehow, is their torment or "divine torture." Well, that is not how it is!

There is no such thing as "balance." You do not have multudious selves. You have only one Self! Multudious experiences? Indeed! But not selves. Your "lower self," entity,

"Your destiny is moment made. You did not come here with some wondrous karmic plan as everyone would like to have you think. If that was the case, [then] that is pre-ordained life and called enslavement, and the Father has nothing to do with such things. No.

Your destiny is in the moment you understand it. Your destiny is in the moment that you live. When you truly understand that, then you truly understand what joy is.

You have to fulfill nothing. Nothing except to be!"

is really you. Your "higher self" is really you. So who you must get in touch with is you.

Your destiny is moment made. You did not come here with some wondrous karmic plan as everyone would like to have you think. If that was the case, [then] that is preordained life and called enslavement, and the Father has nothing to do with such things. No. Your destiny is in the moment you understand it. Your destiny is in the moment that you live. When you truly understand that, then you truly understand what joy is. You have to fulfill nothing--nothing except to be!

You know, God is lawless. Lawless! There are no laws in the Kingdom of God. Man, he is a law-abiding creature, but not God! The infinite spirit of your destiny is the flow of this Now and living it. And if your loins have a tremendous calling to do something, do something with them! But do it in a virtuous way, what is called "natural." Do it to complete yourself. Loving another is most natural.

Does not God love us enough to be all that we are, great and ugly, evil and divine? And hath He ever judged any of them to be either? No, He never has, entity, for you are still here as a living testament for that truth. All of the things that you have ever desired in the purposeful darkness of your heart has **not** changed Life. So, you are still loved, regardless of what is in your Soul.

Self is Self: glorious, divine, beautiful. Man is divine. Woman is divine. That is very natural. How does one live to be a very divine creature and to be "God-loving?" Well, "God-loving" is Self-loving. When you truly love Self, then you do not live in darkness; you live within the light of your own laughter and wherever that laughter and joy take you. It may be different than any one else here, but that is their truth, and everyone is right.

To live is to love yourself **now.** Your destiny is to exploit the Now in understanding **you.** Don't divide yourself up; you will never find yourself if you do that and confusion will always reign supreme in your life. Be you, simply you.

One grand thing that you should do for yourself every morning in the quietude of your being before you rise out of your slumber--speak from the Lord God of your Totality and give thanks for the God that you are and the Father that lives within you. That is all [you need do]. And you don't even have to do that, entity. But in loving Self, what you would say to another, say it to yourself. [I realize that it has been difficult for you to say it to yourself], certainly, entity, for you have never known which self to say it to!

"Those who put the limitations upon Man by saying that there is one road and there is one road only, and you must get on this road, for if you don't you will fail, they are the ones that put the thought of failure in the divine Soul of Man. And they are the ones that have invented the narrow road for the purpose of enslavement. It is quick to see that not all can fit on their road, for they have made it much too narrow!"

ALL PATHS LEAD TO FULFILLMENT, WISDOM, AND FOREVER

Wherever you are **is** the "right path." There is not a set path, as it were. [The path] is where you are. You are the maker of the path; thus, you are always on the right path. **The** path is **your** path, which may not be the same as anyone else's. But all paths, no matter how far apart they are or how high they are above others, have one great common occurrence: they are all ongoing in the same direction. Whether your path is here or here or in between them both, it is still going this-away, a proper term, for the Father is advancing. As long as you have the ability to think, the thought **is** the River of Advancement.

All are advancing, entity; thus, all are on their own path. You will always be doing the very right thing for your being. Thus, with that explicit freedom, you will never fail--you **can** never fail! Failure is a no thing, for how can you fail when you continue to advance? Failure means to stop, and nothing stops. All things, all molecular structures move very rapidly. All things are in a movement of ongoingness, continuums, never regression. Thus how can you fail?

Those who put the limitations upon Man by saying that there is one road and there is one road only, and you must get on this road, for if you don't you will fail, they are the ones that put the thought of failure in the divine Soul of Man. And they are the ones that have invented the narrow road for the purpose of enslavement. It is quick to see that not all can fit on their road, for they have made it much too narrow!

You are on your right path. You have always **been** on your right path! You have chosen what you are doing. You are never haphazardly anywhere; you are always very intentionally everywhere.

*

The greatest lesson learned is from the path most desired to seek.

I have three roads. One road is unpaved, rough and simple. Any who tread upon the road are not guaranteed the good and even passage upon it, and even the asses they ride upon the road from time to time will throw fits of displeasure over the unevenness of the road. This path will take you to a kingdom, but it is difficult and simple.

There is another path that is lined with the sweetest marble that is uncut and has no abrasions but is solid in its mass and

"Everything has taught you well. Failure is one of the grandest teachers of all if acknowledged within your being. It teaches you that you are at the hands of your own thoughts and of your own doings. In what is called a longer run, it also teaches you that you have lived in spite of your utter failure and that what has provided you the opportunity to experience failure has been Life.

Failure is a learning experience. And what the ultimate learning is, entity, is that there is no such thing as failure, for you have lived in spite of it all!"

presents a cool, brightly lit path that goes to the same kingdom. And [there is] a road that is by a river, and the river becomes the road, and the river, through its currents and eddies, will stop to pause and to contemplate itself and [then] move itself on. All [paths] go unto the same kingdom.

Now, if you are a lover of fishes and water and the freshness of it, and you choose the river as your road, master, then your desires will certainly be fulfilled, for that which you love is the river, and it is the wisest of choices. Yet if you choose for yourself marble as the road to your kingdom, for you are the lover of perfect and smooth and cool things and the light and the beauty of their translucent qualities--if your life you see as this, to become as the marble is, then certainly you will choose the marble path to succeed in for it is liken unto your being. Yet if you feel you are an unvalued entity, that you certainly do not deserve marble for your road or the coolness and the change in the river, and choose, of your humble beginnings, the road that is uncertain, master, then that will be liken unto your character, and you will fulfill yourself and your desires, and you will reach your kingdom.

You see, you best ascertain the path to choose, master, by the one that seems to you the most pleasing. It will always fulfill your expectations.

*

Failure is a reality to those who **believe** it is a reality! [But] no one ever fails at life. Ever! You have never failed in your life; you have always learned. Everything has taught you well. Failure is one of the grandest teachers of all if acknowledged within your being. It teaches you that you are at the hands of your own thoughts and of your own doings. In what is called a longer run, it also teaches you that you have lived in spite of your utter failure and that what has provided you the opportunity to experience failure has been Life.

Failure is a learning experience. And what the ultimate learning is, entity, is that there is no such thing as failure, for you have lived in spite of it all!

You have never failed; you have always learned! How do you know what perfection is until you have been imperfect? How do you know what your goal is until you have approached it and found it to be differently colored than what you had seen it in the first place? Is that failure? No. If you wish to call yourself a failure and feel that you are deservant, then all the gain you would have gained from that "error" would be lost to you, for it would be smothered in guilt and it will never be put forth practically for you or for anyone else to learn by. Thus, entity, you are at your own folly.

The Father hath never judged anything wrong. Never! Of all of the atrocities that Man hath created upon the plane that we think are atrocious, the Father hath never thought that, for He simply is—without judgement. So if the Father does not judge you, why feel you it necessary to judge you when it is because [of] and through Him that you have life?

I will tell you of a successful entity. It is one who has reflected upon his life and loved all that he hath done, been and said. And where he hath found a pain or bruise, he will bless it and love it, for what an experience, what a wonderment, what a jewel that is in his treasure! And he will see readily that that which he has experienced has brought forth a collective experience wisdom.

Never see anything that you do as a failure, but see it as an accomplishment; then you have never failed, entity; you have always learned. And by that action, a greater vista of opportunity will always be made available to you.

When your beauty is gone and your days are withered, entity, and no one comes a-calling with sweet meats and Syrian whiskey to make your hours better, and you are alone, you will think of how you wasted your life because, in considering you had failed, [you] kept yourself from experiencing the ultimate of happiness and joy, which was everywhere. And what is a grander misfortune than that is that old men like me, through their wisdom, can tell a young entity like you this and yet it means no thing for it is so far away. If you are wise you will listen. There is nothing that be in fashion or society or the modes of vogueness that is worth you thinking you have failed—for anyone's opinion!

Whatever you choose, it makes no difference; choose it for the fact that it makes you happy. You will be a success whatever you choose. And it matters not what it be, be it a king on a throne or a worker in the field. If the king is not happy being a king, then he will never make a good one. And if the worker in the field is happy, never place him on the throne for his heart will be in the field. Do you understand?

Never look at any one thing as a possibility of failure before you have embarked upon it. Rather, look at it as a possibility of happiness. I wonder, entity, if I set you in a wilderness with a cheesesack and a bit of wine, in the middle of the wilderness, surrounded by the Plain of Sharon whose distant mountains hold up heaven, would you know how to survive without being confused as to which direction to go? One day we will see! So be it.

*

When does a person realize that in doing any one thing, whatever it is, that he has made a mistake? When does this realization come to him? When you were doing all of the things that you have guilt about, did you feel during those [acts that] you were making a mistake or that you would suffer guilt from them? Then how could they be determined a mistake? That is called innocence, entity; and it is also called education. Do you understand?

Now, what determines one to assert that these things that they [have done] are "mistakes" is when they have learned [one] lesson and then [afterwards learned] another lesson that counteracts it or is better or sweeter. The guilt means you only wished you knew **then** what you know **now.** [But] how can that be an error? [Life] is advancing Spirit every moment; it is progressive.

Master, you have never made a mistake. Ever! What is there to be guilty of? That you did not "know" when you were doing these things? Master, you knew everything there was to know when you were a participant [in them] or else you would not have participated. Your "mistakes" have been what is called, appropriately, "Steps to the Kingdom," entity, step by step. And knowing full well what you know now could have only been achieved by making the steps. So mistakes, as they are termed, are valuable lessons that equate wisdom, the grand treasures of this and any life.

Feel not guilty for learning. Ever! Feel not guilty, entity, for education; that is called enlightenment. What you must understand is that you have done what you **needed** to do; it was all necessary. And you made all of the right choices, all of them.

Now, to be anxious about a future? Master, you are going to live tomorrow, and, **indeed,** the blessed day to come thereafter, and on and on and on. And what you shall find about those days, entity, is that you are going to learn more and more than you know **this** day. And yet this day is not a mistake, entity. It will lead you into tomorrow.

*

CHAPTER TWELVE

BE THE BEAUTY THAT YOU ARE

"Beauty is imageless. Its by-product is often mistaken as the reality. But what brings the flora to bloom is far greater than the flora itself."

"The important thing that you must learn to do is get rid of the concept that you are the bastard of the universe and learn that you are, indeed, divine—know that you are!

And never strive for perfection for there is no such thing. God is an ever-changing mass of energy every moment; He is better than He was two moments ago. So how can one ever establish perfection? It is the Ongoing Isness that one becomes. You will never have to become perfect though everyone tells you [that] you should be. Well, you already are!"

KNOW YOU ARE ALREADY PERFECT

Who be you? It is beginning to be a suspect in all that be gathered in this wondrous place that they be Worth, indeed. It is beginning to be a suspect upon all that are gathered here that they be God. Ah! a "suspect," of course.

Who be you that I serve, indeed, that I teach, that I love? You be the composite of the Mind of God, the receivers of the blessed Thought; indeed, the Creators of the Mass of the Father. You are beginning, in your wondrous ways, to believe a "possible" of that which is true; that what you be, be splendid in its origin.

This hour in this wondrous day called hope we will teach a bit of learning that all should be aware of in their progress of becoming that which you are beginning to suspect in your being to be a truth--and that is called "perfection."

All wish to be perfect, but what is it that they are to be perfect unto? What is the image that gives unto them the image of "perfection" [so] that their Ideal can become one with the image? Ah, where be it? Well, let's see.

Perfection is a state of co-existence that hath maintained a balance in its totality; that lives and is all that it can be in its framework of realization. Perfection is the expressive, collective attitude of living the totality of what you believe, what you **know** is an absolute in your perfect being.

Expressing "perfectly" is not to express in the image of another but to express in the only image of yourself. If all consciousness and thought-collective varied with each unique, individualized entity--and it does--then how can you express [the] perfection [of] one when yet another will express a totally different perfection? Thus, who shall you copy? Who shall be your ideal? Who shall be your image? If you try to be perfect for one, you will be imperfect to another.

So what is your perfection? What is **your** perfection? Indeed, it is being you! In order to be perfect, you must come back unto you.

What do you determine "perfection" to be? How will you know it when it arrives? Shall it be one great morn that you gleam brightly unto the world and all will look at you in awe and say that you are wonderful and beautiful and all of that? Nay. Perfection is [obtained] in the moment of knowing that what you are is **already** perfect, that you are already the grandest there is.

"You can never determine perfection in the eyes of another. You must determine it for yourself by first knowing that you are already perfect, already sublimely beautiful, already God. To make the perfection grander, to elaborate upon it, to extend it, to take it into creativity, indeed [you can]. But to make it more? How can you make more perfect [what is] already perfect? Hmm.

Being perfect is being you, right here, being all that you are, right now!"

You say unto me, "But I want to be better than what I am!" How do you know there is a "better" than what you are? For you have seen it in someone else? How do you know that your "lesser" is not the betterment to them?

You can never determine perfection in the eyes of another; you must determine it for yourself by first knowing that you are already perfect, already sublimely beautiful, already God. To make the perfection grander, to elaborate upon it, to extend it, to take it into creativity, indeed [you can]. But to make it more? How can you make more perfect [what is] already perfect? Hmm. Being perfect is being you, right here, being all that you are, right now!

What has brought man a bit under other men is that man will always find one to be perfect, and then he will consider all others [to be] less than perfect. If there is only **one** Perfect Man, what is that to say for the rest of the mass, aye? That they are imperfect? What an atrocity! **All** men are perfect! Thus, you do not look for one to give you the stated image or the Perfect ideal; only you know what is acceptable within the totality of your being, indeed.

[Once] you know that you are perfect, can you ever be imperfect? No! There is no such thing as imperfection in an already perfect Ideal. Thus, how can you fail if you are perfect? You never can! How can you be wrong when you are perfect? You never are. And how can you be less than God when you are perfect? You never will be. The simplest and quickest way of becoming [perfect] is to **know** you already are!

Being perfect is exercising the sovereignty of attitude, the sovereignty of a unique personality-self, the sovereignty of a unique beauty which all of you possess, and bringing it forth gladly and loving it gladly. Perfection has already been eminent within your being, for you express perfectly in whatever attitude you bring forth.

When the consciousness reckoning of the totality of this mass of Mankind upon this plane comes to a wonderment that truly there is All Truth and truly there is All Perfection--that all peoples are perfect in their sphere, are perfect in their totality, are perfect in their attitude, are perfect in their beauty--then the security of Man and his established worth will be profound. For no longer shall anyone feel less than the other, and all will culminate within their being the right use of their creativity to express perfectly in a harmonious joy. When all realize that they are perfect, no one will ever fail and none will ever make "errors" or "mistakes." All will succeed in the creativity of their Perfect Being.

To acknowledge simply within the being that you are perfect is signalling to the being that it is God. When God is signalled within the being, joy is eminent, happiness is eminent. When joy

"Only you are the giver of the Ideal of Perfection and what its standard and substance be. Only you know your own calibre of an Ideal. And if it is known within your being what the calibre is, then it is already reached, for if it is known in the mind of man, then it hath already been experienced. And that is a truth.

Be at peace with that which you be. Know what the Ideal is [within you] and then become the Ideal to yourself. Then you have become the totality of what you presume and know within your infinite being to be perfection of the highest point of achievement—and fortunately the point never ends."

and happiness become eminent within the being of man, it is reflected in his magnetic light fields; [and] when reflected there, it draws unto him the sameness in attitudes. Thus, a happy entity who is bountiful in his energy, protective of his wonderful status of perfection, will draw perfection to him; will draw to him happiness, joy, mirth, jolly beings that also express the same as he expresses.

"To become perfect," "looking for perfection"--I hear these words often. I see what is an earnest man, an earnest woman, desiring to be the God of their being "perfectly." But as long as Perfection is never understood, they will never recognize that they have become the God of their being, for the "perfectly" is the hook in the statement. Words that are often used yet never understood are words that inhibit the perfect flow, that inhibit the recognized consciousness, inhibit the totality of becoming what is desired.

Wanting to be God "perfectly," [to] express yourself "perfectly," is an ultimate illusion that can never be grasped or understood until you find out that you already are perfect. Expressing God now **is** perfection. Breathing this moment **is** perfection. And **being** is the Perfection of Life.

I am here to tell you who wish to learn that only you are the giver of the Ideal of Perfection and what its standard and substance be. Only you know your own calibre of an Ideal; and if it is known within your being what the calibre is, then it is **already** reached, for if it is known in the mind of man, then it hath already been experienced. And that is a truth.

Whatever the pursuit be of what you term your perfection, let it not be in the eyes of another, for only another can know his perfection; he will never know yours. Be at peace with that which you be. Know what the Ideal is [within you] and then become the Ideal to yourself. Then you have become the totality of what you presume and know within your infinite being to be perfection of the highest point of achievement--and fortunately the point never ends.

To be Perfect is to be You, all of You. To **know** that perfection in the God of your being is to know that you already are [perfect].

You were never created imperfect and you have never had an imperfect thought, for thoughts are the purest forms of all forms. And you have never been imperfect within your being; you have always been perfect. However you have expressed, into the grossness or vileness of your being or to the height of divinity recognized in your being, you have done it perfectly. Thus, you have maintained perfection.

How difficult is it to become perfect? Only know that it already is there, for it will always be there. You already are.

To make yourself grander is only to open up your perfection to greater awareness, to greater knowingness, that the perfection of the knowingness can become more so within your being [from] experience, [from] learning.

For so long on this plane, people have been taught [that] there is no such thing as Perfect Man. Of course! It was an "imperfect" man who wrote that! He would make the world be as he is; then he is not so lonely. That is an untruth amongst truth. All things are perfect, all men are perfect.

If a man is told that he is imperfect and he believes that, then the sorrow is deep within him, for he feels forsaken, he feels alone and unloved and finds his use a no use. Thus, he becomes a part of the murk and the mire and the stench of this plane, for he has nothing to lose. He is an accident of the universe, a bastard of the stars, forsaken by the only God that he ever saw hope in, and there is no hope for him. How terrible hath been the Soul of Man unto his beloved brother to put him [as] a subservient below all things, to take from him his divinity, his right to be, his beauty, and alas, his conception of perfection.

If Man realizes now that he is already perfect, then he is not lost and doomed, he is not forsaken, he is not an accident or spawn of a mistake. Then he has a reason for being, and his reason for being will remove the "evil" within his Soul and replace it with Joy. Thus, Man the humble will become Man the God, the great, the giver and lover of all Life, for it is his nature to be so.

Know that you are grand, that you are perfect. Love that which you are [and] extenuate yourself into greater knowingness. Take your perfection with you wherever you are and know that the perfection of your being has assured the Light of Fire of your being called the God of your Being. And [know] that whatever you do, you will never be lost again; that you are part of the continuum of all that be [and] that you are the creator of all that be in this continuum.

And alas, one day in your reckoning, that perfection will take you unto the stars, and there you may make your nests and your palaces and your abodes forever. For you who know you are perfect, there is no thing within the mass of perfection that will inhibit your growth to whatever direction you desire to have it take you. So be it.

*

There is no such thing as perfection. Perfection is an unattainable aspect that doesn't even exist. You know, the one thing that destroys greater than war are ideals. An ideal that a society imposes upon itself to be is the greatest destroyer, entity. Do not affix an ideal of how you **think** you should be, because how you **think** you should be shall always be something very remote from what you really **are.** Rather than that, allow yourself to simply be, and whatever feel you and fantasize you in your being is how you are.

When you leave yourself alone and allow yourself to bloom and cease criticizing yourself and cease struggling for a very futile ideal, you will have sublime peace, for every moment you **are** the Ideal of how you are, and every moment you are gaining from that.

Simply be the beautiful master that you are and allow laughter to come forth. And do away with the things that bring harshness upon your being. If there is any one thing that is around you that brings you a reminder of an assault of [an] ideal you are supposed to be and [you] are having difficulty being it, do away with it. It is not worth your life!

The Father has expected you only to be you, [for] your unique beauty adds to the classic whole of what He is. Do not criticize others any longer and do not criticize yourself. Let others live however they choose to live; that is their right to do so. And love yourself enough to allow yourself to live however you chose to. That is what is important. Then, master, you will allow the whole world to be at peace, and harmony will reign in your life.

There is no such thing as perfection. The only Ideal is the Ideal seen in you this moment.

*

Evolution is "the continuous refinement of." In this principle called Life, this dream, Life is the only reality **in** this dream. All that evolves from this dream are interactions that we desire to occur to ourselves. If we had no interaction but were in the dream, we would still evolve because **Life** evolves us; that is the momentum called "God." He is the next moment that is blooming, birthed out of the womb of the Present. He **is** "the continuation of."

My beloved entity, if all you did is sit upon your rump and contemplated all of these things, you would still evolve because life has evolved within you. You think that you must obtain a "higher" status of being. You are taught this through that which is termed beliefs. But the greater truth will tell you this: You have to achieve **nothing** except to be. And in the being process, you realize that you are here; that you are thick in this dream; that this life is advancing; that you and the whole of this consciousness you are "feeding upon" (for consciousness is the sweet nurturing of God) **are** expanding.

"To know this Father, [to know] you, remove every limitation, every dogmatic law, every religious occurrence and simply look at what is left. And if you remove all those things, you find Unlimited Self. But only when you, master, realize that your life is not a struggle but an allowing. Don't ever strugle to be anything. You be—then you find God!"

Peoples are taught they are low creatures, that they have many selves: "lower" selves, "higher" selves, "medium" selves. That is a duality, the duality to split a "house" to conquer it. There is but **one** Self. If the Self **chooses** to be a lower Self, it does so; if it chooses to be a higher Self, it does so. But that which chooses **is** the greater Self: the Isness.

You don't have to be "greater" or "higher." You only have to allow that which you are to be and to know that that which all is **is** you; that as you sit here this moment into this Advancement of Moment, you are being fed a consciousness that is the result of Life; [and] that you **are** Becoming. Those who struggle to become something other than what they are never become it because they are becoming something outside of their being.

You think you must become something else, become greater than what you are? There is **nothing** greater than what you are; that is how it is. God **is.** You, beautiful entity, you **are.** There is no religion about you; there is no law about you; there only **is** about you. The Kingdom of Heaven, this God, this wondrous Self that you wish to evolve into, will bloom like a great and wondrous flower if you remove all of the tapestries and illusions, thick illusions, that lie upon it.

To know this Father, [to know] you, remove every limitation, every dogmatic law; remove every religious occurrence and simply look at what is left. And if you remove all those things, you find Unlimited Self. But only when you, master, realize that you are not a division but a whole and [that] your life is not a struggle but an **allowing.** Don't ever strugle to be anything. You **be**--then you find God!

YOU ARE THE FLOWER OF A MAGNIFICENT GARDEN

I am Ramtha, The Enlightened One, indeed, servant unto the Christus, **born** of the Source, **created** of the Source, that the Great Creator [could] be the Source flowing through the creation "Christus": God-Man, individualized entity.

Creation, as you term it to be, is really the value of Life that **always** has been. There no beginning of that and, certainly, there is no ending unto that. But the Creator, from the substance called Life, is called Christ.

[The Christ is] God, the assumed value, collectively expelling energy to create forms into that which is termed the junction called Matter--this that you call "reality." Christ, beloved Christ indeed, beloved brothren indeed, be that value. Mankind,

"This teaching, I desire you not to call 'religion,' for it is lawless. Religion is riddled with law; it is dogmatic, restrictive and very judgemental. And if any one thing clouds the goodness, the beauty, the intimacy, the forgiveness and the lovingness of God, religion does that.

What I give unto you, it is called Love: I will love you into experiencing unlimitedness."

womankind, humanity—it is "God playing with Himself." It is God creating from the spectrum called Matter. It is God, indeed, eloquently disguised as limited, wretched entities. Indeed.

What makes you so valuable? Why have you been that which is termed the point of concern, if you will, of entities who have propogated themselves upon this plane to live for you, exemplify for you, intervene for you, teach you, die for you? Have you ever wondered why you be possessed of such a value that would cause this to occur for eons and eons?

Now, there have been many assaults on you. We have ventured to many avenues to get you to listen. But as Gods would have it, your destiny is cloistered in your "point of view," and your point of view is the limitations of your acceptance.

For those of you who have a need to know, have you ever wondered why you are so valuable? Why there have been wars in your outer space on your behalf and wars to come on your behalf? [For] you, indeed, belong to that which is termed a wondrous race. The race is of God in its highest perimeter, its seat of intelligence, its seat of discriminating creation.

You, who have the will to think quietly without any ear listening to it, who can dream any dream, quietly contemplate any contemplative value, what gives you the power to do that? What gives you the credentials to manifest it? You! You are, in this lowly wretched state as most would have it, God in the form called matter, an intelligence that is the King of Kingdoms.

You are very valuable, you are very precious, because the life that flows through you, the thought that is coming to everyone of you, however you entertain it, **is** God. It is the same link that I am and all that have walked and gone before you.

You are very valuable. You are worth universes, you are worth stars, you are worth Eternity, because without you, none of that would exist. How beautiful is the flower if you close your eyes and don't look at it? You have determined its beauty **and** its existence. Your will has determined that it is either beautiful or it isn't there afterall. What sort of power rendered in you is that?

You have options to live this life however you choose to live it. Learning to live it in a more purposeful direction for greater results, as the term is, I can teach you to do that.

Now, I have esteemed your value as great, for what I am, you are also. And I love myself, grandly. Thus you be myself also that I love, for that which flows through us is the same.

This teaching, it is not in accordance with devotees. I do not want you to be devotees. That is an experience, certainly, but that only leads to experiencing being the "devotee" and never the Master.

"For you to become unlimited is only to be you, happily, and to live that every moment. Being you is being a truth; being an 'ideal' is being a duality that never knows itself, loses its powers and walks this plane in madness."

This teaching, I desire you not to call "religion," for it is lawless. Religion is riddled with law; it is dogmatic, restrictive and very judgemental. And if any one thing clouds the goodness, the beauty, the intimacy, the forgiveness and the lovingness of God, religion does that. But what I give unto you, it is called Love: I will **love** you into experiencing unlimitedness.

Being God and living in what is called a moment to moment, day to day existence does not mean that you abstain from that existence in order to be that which is termed God. Do you think you must conform to be a diety that walks on light, has wings on its back, and alas, has melodious tones to its voice? Well, nothing is more beautiful than you are. What's wrong with walking on the earth? Indeed! And being clothed however you are clothed? You have wings on your thoughts; that is better than having them on your backs.

To live every day does not mean that you must be anything other than what you already are! You will be happiest--and the Father understands this--when you are left alone to grow, given "food" to nurture your thoughts, to bring them into existence, and allowed to be. God is best loved, He is **best** loved unrestricted and in lawless freedom. You are to simply be who you are, but **allowed** to be.

[Do you] know why you are neurotics, **indeed,** [why] you are riddled with diseases? Because [in] all of your existences, you are being taught to be that which is other than you! There is nothing wrong with you. If there were, then God surely hath created a great flaw, and I assure you, beloved masters, He hath not done this.

What is wrong with being you? Nothing. Each of you have added to the virtue of creative relativity. If only one God here was so elected to choose the path of what is called relativity [for all to follow], all of you would alas be lost, because you could not possibly have the same path. If that were a truth, what would have been the use in making you so different--looking different, thinking different, feeling different?

You are the flower of a magnificent garden. Your seed pollinates and creates new flowers that are beautiful and more lush in their deepening hues. You, indeed, are valuable--just being you.

For you to become unlimited is only to be you, happily, indeed; and to live that **every** moment. Being you is being a truth; being an "ideal" is being a duality that never knows itself, loses its powers and walks this plane in madness.

You know, being you every moment has created this consciousness for whatever degree of good or bad you determine it to be. But [when you are] left alone and allowed to bloom, **however you are,** the consciousness will become God the

"My beauteous brothers, God would be nothing without you—an outrageous statement, but it is a truth! You have brought about Creation; so the value of your existence is very important. And for you to continue as a race of entities in this form, it is very important for you to learn of your own sovereignty and value, as well as every one else's."

Almighty. That is how it is.

So, I have not come to mislead you, enslave you, captivate you; I have come to free you and to tell you it is all right, as it were, to be the splendid entity that you are. If you want to know how to become a grander "you," how to be the genius that lies only a thought away, that is simple: Don't try to be like anyone else, think like anyone else, look like anyone else. Be You! [Then] all of the "blocks," as you have appropriately termed them in your understanding, can be removed [so] that the flow of Thought can enter freely within the context of consciousness.

My beauteous brothers, God would be **nothing** without you--an outrageous statement, but it is a truth! You have brought about Creation; so the value of your existence is very important. And for you to continue as a race of entities in this form, it is very important for you to learn of your own sovereignty and value, as well as every one else's.

God, the Divine Source, the Wondrous Life, it is all around you. It wants to be you, steadfastly, and to live you, happily--whatever that means to you. To everyone here, it will mean something different, for no one invented happiness. If [someone] did, none of you would obtain it except that which invented it. Happiness is Self-realized.

Be happy in this life, whatever it means to you. Assert the God that you are to give you the power to have dominion over this kingdom that you have created. If you are not happy with yourself, change it! Only you have the invested authority to do that. If you don't, you will end up following others who pretend they **can**, and alas, you shan't ever learn anything!

You have the option to change every single moment. You be a God that has created its will, that has created its life precisely how it wishes. You are not the outcasts of the Kingdom of Heaven. You **created** the Kingdom of Heaven! And you are valuable because what you have created this day will intensify greater in the tomorrow that is to come.

What [must be] understood is that you are where you are because you **want** to be there. Want, entities, equates happiness. You forget who you are and do not give credence [or] value to the Power that is withstanding within you, and that you can change in any moment. Knowing that you are God helps you to understand that you created your situation and only **you**, indeed, can create yourself right out of it. I am here to teach you, explicitly well, the science of doing that.

I, Ramtha The Enlightened One, only got to be [enlightened] by living. I have lived as you have lived, indeed, and sought for knowingness, for I was an ignorant man. The knowingness brought forth answers, expanded the awareness, created compassion, and

"No one can make you God. No one can cause you to be uplifted and holy. Only you can do that. You allow the Source to allow that to occur. I and no one else can help you until you accept your greatness, your worthness, and [know] that you are loved and important.

I will continue to teach [you]. And little by little you will hear and feel, and you will learn a little bit more and a little bit more. And perhaps through this, you will find that you are beginning to be a reality and will stop worrying about mine."

God was born within the entity.

What I have learned and accomplished is not far away from any of you. But no one can make you God. No one can cause you to be uplifted and holy. Only you can do that. You **allow** the Source to allow that to occur. I and no one else can help you until you accept your greatness, your worthness, and [know] that you are loved and important. And only when, alas, you can accept that can this teaching of becoming unlimited--going back to the Source, glorified, immortal--can that be. Indeed.

I will continue to teach [you]. And little by little you will hear and feel, and you will learn, indeed, a little bit more and a little bit more. And perhaps through this, you will find that you are beginning to be a reality and will stop worrying about mine.

WHERE ELSE IS THE GLORY OF GOD BUT IN THE BEAUTY THAT YOU BE

I am Ramtha the Enlightened One, indeed, servant unto that which is termed the Supreme Cause, unto that which is termed the Divine Essence, unto that which is termed the Divine Thought, unto that which is termed the Mother-Father Principle, unto that which is called God, indeed, the Eloquent and the Almighty.

I am Ramtha the Enlightened One, indeed, servant unto that which is termed the Christus: Man exhibiting the beauty of his being into that which is termed the Godhood of Humanity; Man that has come forth as God, the Creator of Creators.

Christus, indeed. And who be that? Not that which is termed some forlorn messiah from afar, but that which is termed the Resurrection of Christ, the Embodiment of God, as it were, into that which is termed You, my beloved brothren.

What be that which is termed your responsibility in being God, Christus? Unto that, what attitude [must] possess you that you may become that which you so long to be? Your responsibility, as it were, is to be nothing other than the superb entity called "you."

I have watched many of you at your dreams and your imaginations and that which is termed your working existence, and the lot of you are playing games of great mischief in that you are imitating everything else save you. What is wrong with **you**? Think you must be a messiah that you don't even know? Indeed, think you are to create that which is termed God and

"Being Christus is being you. It is liking whatever liken you. It is grasping whatever wish you to grasp and holding on to it. It is you formulating the brilliance of ideas and seeing them through. It is your opinion, alas, also [being] important. It is your voice that is heard, indeed heeded.

Create. Liken your creation. Speak your truth and love it for the way it sounds. Look into your mirrors, longingly, and find beauty in every place that you look, for where else is the glory of God but in the beauty that be you. Do not be like other peoples; indeed be like you. You are God [and] your decisions have worth and value, [for] they are indeed what all of creation comes forth from."

make Him so great that He is beyond the reach and realm of your inhabiting, indeed of your being?

I tell you, entities, there are many of you that have sat in this audience for that which is termed a space of time in your time, and **still** this perplexes you. God, the Infinite, is the jewel that you be. You--learn to be yourself! That is your responsibility. [And] to love yourself with all your might and with all your force and with all your being, that the love of Self be greater than any one thing outside of the perimeters of your being. How else do you love God with all of your being, with all of your breath, and with all of your life? It is transmitted to **you.**

You want to be great masters? Learn to be happy. Know how to be happy? By being yourself--you! You never were wrong, indeed ever. Ever! You were always right, indeed. Even further than that, you always "were," and that is the prize of all of the decisions you have ever made.

Being you means being happy: being happy with the decisions of who and what you are and loving yourself into a state of accepting the truth that Self offers. You think that God has one truth, a set regulation of laws that you must abide within? If [that] were [true] it would color all of you; and I fear for your beings that you would be colored all the same. That is boring and mundane!

You are loved for you and your **unique** vigor, your unique beauty, your unique creative Self. What else is better than being **that**, indeed? Know you I had nothing to pattern my life after save a few stars, a lot of trees, an unfurling wind that was wicked in its freedom, morning, night, sun, moon, dust. The only Ideal that I had [was] what I perceived those values to be: my self-perception.

Being Christus is being you. It is liking whatever liken you. It is grasping whatever wish you to grasp and holding on to it. It is you formulating the brilliance of ideas and seeing them through. It is your opinion, alas, also [being] important. It is your voice that is heard, indeed heeded. It is you. Who be God? Well, my beloved, He is you. Not that you are to be Him, for what are you to be? You are to be yourself.

Create. Liken your creation. Speak your truth and love it for the way it sounds. Look into your mirrors, longingly, and find beauty in every place that you look, for where else is the glory of God but in the beauty that be you. Do not be like other peoples; indeed be like you. You are God [and] your decisions have worth and value, [for] they are indeed what all of creation comes forth from.

Contemplate this, I charge you. Contemplate and weigh the brillance of yourself and start looking inward and start facing the beauty that you find there. I assure you, not one of you will find wickedness or evil, but a true kingdom and true virtue. You only have to look.

*

Everyone that is here has picked perhaps the most arduous experiences for them to experience. There are seven heavens, indeed. There are seven perceptions of consciousness. This is the First. It is called the Plane of Demonstration. Here, a free-wheeling Spirit is confined within the confines of a heavy body and thus are not free-flying as they once were. And here they [must] contend with a thick consciousness that is so condemning and so judgemental, for it is based on the **appearance** of an entity rather than the **essence** of an entity.

You have chosen to come into a lifetime, entity, where it is called "fashion" to look certain ways; and if you are not, you are despised or you are not loved because you are not what is called "beautiful." [Such "beauty" is] an enigma, for true beauty cannot even be seen; it must be felt.

You have chosen to come here, beautiful entity, and you are caught up in a consciousness that is very condemning of everything save its own ideal. And to that ideal, it enslaves the whole of humanity to struggle to become it--only for it to change when it has run its course. This is very arduous for anyone to live in, that I understand, particularly this time in Time as the perfection of the human body is coming closer and closer to the decree as it once was.

You are a splendid example of being the outcast in this society. You are a splendid example of being the "unloved" in this society because of how you appear. But I assure you, entity, you have a beauty within your being that when you leave this plane, Glory shall you be. And so awesome is your light and the colors that immerse and twinkle and emerge there, that you have not the thought of beauty to even contrive the conception of how you shall appear.

Love that which is termed the inner-Self and strive not to please **anyone**, for you will please no one, ever, except yourself. And in that, take heart and jubilance, and be free with it. **Be** who you are. The Lord God that is the Lord God of all things shall never forsake you, for you are the Face of God. Take heart in that.

I will teach you to love yourself because of **you** and no one else.

LIVE THE TRUTH OF WHAT YOU ARE

Divinity was not put in a prophecy of holy, divine words as a road to becoming enlightened. Rules and regulations inhibit the flow of free thought. Enlightenment and divinity is procured when a balance, an understanding, a love is seen perfectly within the individual [such] that he lives according to his word and his truth.

How you become "amaruge," divine, is by being you. If everyone had one truth to live by, and that truth had specified laws, regulations and amendments according to who was in power, then you would look like everyone else and they would look like you; you would think like everyone else and they would think as you. That is how absurd **one** truth is. And evidence that it is an absurdity is that no one thinks alike and no one looks alike.

The unique, individualized "you" adds to the sum total of the All. The only truth there is, is that everyone has it! As they have it is as they are. They refine it, perfect it, balance it, become it--only through realization of it.

To become the totality of your truth is to become an enlightened entity. To become the totality of your truth means you live [as] a total unit; that you do not suffer the pains of duality; that you are together in a perfect alignment and express perfectly. That is what is needed in Mastership. That [is] indeed Christship.

God is not **one** formulated thought. He is the truth of **all** thought. Anyone [who] expresses his truth perfectly in his own eye, in his own point of view, in his own understanding, becomes closer to the I AM, the Truth, the God, than that which expresses the duality.

Live what you are. Once you have turned your attention to living what you are, you will indeed perfect you, because for the first time in your life you are listening to you and not to others. And once you begin to listen to you, you will only accept the perfect Isness of your being. And when you see for the first time your truth, and listen for the first time for your own words, [that] is when you, in your being, will correct them to the point of being. Then you come closer to God, the Perfect Thought, the Perfect Realization. For when that is mastered, all else will follow. But it is first living it. Living it!

Love what you are. And if you find any one thing not beautiful on your being, change it. Now, this does not mean that you walk around being restrictive. It does not mean you walk around having your own truth in spite of everyone else's, for perfected truth sees beauty in everything. Perfected truth sees its truth in all other things, for truth **is** all things. When you realize that you are the giver of it, entity, it will put you in All Thing's kingdom.

*

You do not live what you know, for what you know is greater than what you live. And if you lived what you know, you [feel you] would be scrutinized by everyone around you, for then you would lose the "image" that you have purportedly lived for so long that gives you identity into the conscious social world.

The wondrous thing about "pitifully growing old," as you would term it (I term it "becoming"), is that you are able to lose the images you have fought to obtain to be accepted by the society which views "beauty" as the supreme object and "gold" the supreme supportive system. Once you let go of all of those things, then you come unto a knowingness or a utopia that allows you to see who and what you are, because it is "time" to. No one here cares about you if you do not look the image or the part; that is how it is.

So when you no longer have to be and [to] struggle to do those things that will cause "acceptance," then you come into a time, a ripening, where you will be blooming, born free. Then you can experience your knowingness without ridicule or criticism, for they won't care, for you are not what they conceded you to be, nor are you fashionable, nor are you young, nor are you physically beautiful. My master, that is a wretched kingdom, and it does not adhere to the true beauty of all that is, which is unseen. But that is a "fortunate" aspect of life that does exist.

You do not live what you know, for you have chosen to have two knowingnesses: one for those who "count" and one for you when you choose to listen [to yourself]. Do you understand? If you did what you know you are and lived it supremely, you would have a fear of being rejected by most that are around you. If you did what you know, you would be afraid you would lose, and all you would obtain is the "unknown" that is uncertain. You live [this] duality for "survival," as most do.

Master, I will tell you straightaway: The kingdom we are preparing here has nothing to do with fashion, nor does it have to do with social ideals of acceptance. It has to do with the "inner qualities" within an entity: that is the rare and beautiful kingdom.

Entities are not happy, master, that live "dualities." They live facades; they live in fear; they are "hunted creatures." They have to live in such scrutiny, into such misery, into such neurosis to be certain ways for the critical eye of society that they have little worth that they have gained in this experience except how to be unfit to express it.

I tell you: You are loved by an unseen Source that loves what you are, through and through, and that warrants and witnesses your being every moment that you are. And that if all of the world denied who you are and did not love you, master, this Essence, that is the All That Is The All, would be your kingdom.

Live for who and what you are, whatever you concede that to be, and love it. And speak "even" when the evenness is there. And feel when the feeling is there. And when weeping comes, let it come, for that is the Voice of the Soul. And when the laughter is there, laugh--regardless of who laughs around you. Do not look to see if they are in agreement. Who cares! Be who you are, and cherish it and love it and live it.

And one last thing to you: When you have lived all that you are spent on living for society, [and] when night falls and there is slumber in the air and all is still and quiet, and the stars twinkle benevolently in their heaven, and the moon in her journey waxes and wanes all the way until dawn, and there is nothing that you have to live for or be for or do for--in the quiet of those moments, entity, you will question your own honor and your own nobility, your own truth, and the quality of your existence. And if your nights are not filled with slumber and peaceful dreams, then perhaps you need to re-assess how you are living in the moments of day when you have to live for all the perplexities of everyone else.

Live through the honor and noble character that is acceptable to you--regardless of what is acceptable to anyone else.

*

Feeling that you are not equal to everyone else, that you are not as good as anyone else, is [because] you don't know who you are. And the only entities that you do know are the images that walk before you and project an idealistic attitude that seemingly is perfection or beauty or goodness or whatever you wish to term it in your proper terms. But they are only being responsive, entity, to a "collective consciousness" that tells them to be that way. They, in turn, are asking, "Who be I that compares to the rest of the world?"

Insecurity [comes] from not knowing [Self]. When you learn who you are, moment by moment, and you turn your proper attention to **yourself,** little by little the pieces of your beautiful life will formulate before your own eyes; an exquisite creature will emerge--feeling, sensitive, compassionate, understanding, loving. But all of those wonderful traits are a no thing unless they are put into practice by the individualized Self. Only then do they become a magnificent reality.

Compare you not to anyone, for there is no one that you can compare yourself to--no one. In doing that, you will be left utterly alone with finding out who you are. And that will be a splendid adventure! Know you what happens when you find out who you are? You become a wizard. You become a God. And your self-assurance and self-esteem allows the world forgiveness--and that is a great gift.

*

Everyone determines the whole of their future; no one else does. They determine the exactness to which they do or do not do things; no one else does. They, entity, determine the unlimitedness or the limitedness to which they know and understand things; no one else does. To have the freedom to be explicit, to be multifaceted, is to remove that which is termed the negative "cannot," and be a doer and Be. That is all; you have to do nothing else.

Lord, you are the greatest lover of yourself. There is no one on this plane that ever has [been] or ever will be that can love you to the manner which you need to be loved [other] than **you.** You to you have survived **eons**--ten and one-half million years of that which is termed human experience. There is not another entity in this wondrous structure that has endured all of these things with you except you. You have never failed you! You are always you--to be more exact, **God**, the principle that I speak of. If you depend on any one here, they will let you down because they are giving unto themselves, not unto you!

"To you, for you," master, is the ultimate mastery, the greatest of all, because you are your greatest friend, your greatest benefactor, your greatest lover, your greatest God; and that has been proven by the mere instance that you are here this moment, ten and one-half million years later.

To be all that you are is unlimited freedom. That is what the Masters are, and they became it because they **wanted** to, more than anything else. And that energy had to be found **within** their beings, not outside of it. Don't be afraid to be you; you have never let yourself down. You have only to find that which is termed the richness of what you are--by being you.

Here in your society, everyone dresses like everyone else. Here, everyone prepares their tresses in accordance with fashion and style, an atrocity of limitation. There are very few here that are originals, indeed. Those that are the originals, they are the Lord Gods of Totality. They are the ones living for themselves and no one else, and they will advance further in this knowingness than those that are succoring unto society for its demands.

*

This world, of itself, is a grand place. The goodness of nature is abundant; it has never judged any man or any action, ever. What is direful about this place is it permits a child such as yourself to be intimidated, to be stripped of innocence and virtue, to be in a hurry to become an adult so that you can be "noticed," that you can be loved, that you can be "somebody" on this plane.

This plane has worked very hard at destroying love, freedom and the divineness within the Soul of Humanity. And how have they done that? [By] laws to govern and to distinguish peoples from one another. [By] laws to self-elect one to be powerful over others. Or [through] self-governed idols of your own choosing that represent a perfection that you [feel you] grossly lack, for if you had it you would be the idol. And here, beauty is recognized only for the skin and never seen for the Self. That is an atrocity! Outside of this consciousness, the abundance of life here is the emerald of this universe.

The Winds of Change are heavy upon this plane, dear entity, for there are many things that have been set into motion of a becoming of this Age to come. And one of them is the ability for entities such as yourself to become little children for as long as they wish and not be in a hurry to grow up to escape their youth into death and to wonder where all of the joyous days of their wonderful, gleeful Self went when nothing but solemnness and despair surrounds them.

You are a child of your society and a product of it. The only way that you can rise above it is to know you are worth rising above it. It is time [to] give to yourself all the exalting you gave to the opinions of everyone else. Whether you speak not ever another word, if all thoughts are turned for your delight, for your God-self, for your being, you will have expressed the Totality of Isness and the joy of the Father.

Don't live for anyone else any more. And do not go around looking into other people's lives and find lacking in yours. Be happy. Be a child again. Know what it is to find joy in the simplest of things. To be a child means that you are in possession of an Ego that emits truth from yourself; that has the inablility to judge, for it has never been taught fear, it has never been taught imperfection, it has never been taught violence or ugliness. It simply is.

Ponder that in the days to come in your time. We will bring out the child again, entity, and start over. So be it.

*

Simply be. Be! What things are more important than the status of Being? They are only conjecture. Be. Then you will be all of the things that you need to be in the moment you are

"Be Happy! Love the God that you are and bless it. And find fruitfully within your being Joy. Never deny your being your love or your happiness. And do not, above all things, criticize it; that is like taking a mighty sword and running you through each time. Eventually you will die of your wounds of insecurity."

expressing them.

Wonderful lady, listen to me. We take to ourselves what we conceive [to be a] perfect situation in life that seemingly works for someone else and we think it must work for us too. And we bring it here to ourselves and try to put it in ourselves, and ourselves say, "It just does not fit, for that is not my way. I have my way, and in my way I am uniquely different. Let me be how I need to be. In my ultimate expression, I am God. And ultimately realized, little by little, subtleness by subtleness, I will be perfect if you leave me be."

I wish to tell you this: I teach on what I know, what I have been and what I am. And I know of a truth, not a philosophy, that works for all peoples, however manner they wish to apply it to themselves. They do not wish to be like I am, for to be like I am they would lose themselves. They wish to be like they are. Man's undoing of himself is trying to be the truth of other men and how they live rather than how he lives.

Be Happy! Love the God that you are and bless it. And find fruitfully within your being Joy. Never deny your being your love or your happiness. And do not, above all things, criticise it; that is like taking a mighty sword and running you through each time. Eventually you will die of your wounds of insecurity.

*

CHAPTER THIRTEEN

BE SELF-ISH:
LIVE FOR THE LOVE AND JOY OF SELF

> **"All of this is an illusion. The particulars of society is an illusion. The particulars of judgement are illusion. The particulars of living for the causes of others is an illusion. All of this is an illusion. Living for Self is the only reality there is. That is guaranteed."**

"It has been taught prudently here [to] forget Self and serve others. A tyrant wrote those words!

You can never serve anyone else, entity, until you have first served yourself. And you cannot love another entity until you have established that sovereignty in your own being, because how do you know what it is [that] you are to do until Self has experienced that?

Be Self-ish, as it were—Love your Self. Do what brings you happiness and live in freedom. Then, you will have the capacity, as a Master does, to love everyone else, regardless of whether it is returned or not.

Imagine God being selfish! Well, He is, for if He wasn't, you wouldn't be here!"

PUT YOUR DESTINY BACK IN YOUR OWN HANDS

[Others] don't care how you live; they only care how they live. They don't care what you have to say, only what they need to hear or need to say to express. So who here do you live for other than Self? If you don't have to live for anyone else here, you would never have self-doubt, ever. Cease living for everyone else and all of the ridiculous ideals, no matter how "Godly" they are. Just be you. That is divine, purposeful, intentional; that is God.

When you cease to [live for others], you can, alas, love every entity, for no longer are you feeling a spectacle to their critical eye. [You can] let them stare or talk or be anyway they choose to be because you love them enough to let them do that, for it doesn't matter any more to you how they think of you, only [how] you [think of you]. That is rising above the murk and the mire and seeing this plane for how it certainly is.

Live for you and no one else--no one else. Then you won't doubt yourself any longer.

*

If you want to live according to others, then prepare yourself for complete confusion, misunderstanding, lostness, sickness, unhappiness, miserableness, and into death! And they will come and weep when you die. That is a blatant truth!

Love them, but their opinion is good for them. Let your opinion come forth and be defined, for that is what is going to separate you from the mass; that is what is going to make you different; that is what is going to help you become God--supreme, singular, active entity. What is the will in having a will if others think that your will should be their will?

I worry not what others think of me, entity, and if I change one iota, as you term it, to what they think I should be, then none would come listen to me e'er again, for I have fallen from grace into disgrace by becoming their attitude.

*

Limitations occur when you live upon the opinions of other entities. And where they get their opinion is from the limited source of consciousness that they are aligned with. When you live according to what other people think you should live like, then you are limited in the spheres of understanding and you never know yourself; you only know the illusions you portray in order to satisfy the mass--and that is a truth! Herd animals do that for protection; they give self-esteem to one another, protection in their ego.

When you stop asking the opinions of others of how you do anything, of what they think of you, and begin to ask yourself, you will experience a life of unlimitedness, for who could ever know what is good for you but you. Begin to ask what think you, and then follow your own great advice; it will never let you down.

*

Parents have wonderful ways of thinking that their children's happiness depends somehow upon their enslaving them to their concepts of wisdom and happiness, when they have really only lived a very small priority of life in order to have earned what they have.

Parents are wonderful entities, for in spite of all else, they are doing what they think is best. They all are right, and they are expressing a truth. On the other hand, there is nothing wrong with how you live, nothing, and you must choose, out of love, whether you wish to be how they wish you to be or how you wish to be.

What you must define is this: If their love for you is based on what they want you to, and the love is lost if you do anything outside of that perimeter, then you would have to value for yourself [whether] perhaps in your life's journey you would [find] yourself a greater, [more] profound love, and find those to which you could express it with that are more steadfast in their freedom. Too oftentimes love is given on "terms." It is terms that restrict [love's] movement and its beauty.

It is a truth [that parents] are self-fixed in their own reality; that's where they should be. [But] you must determine what you want to do, and then once you know what you want to do, do it and proclaim it to them. But then you must also be prepared for the consequences. If you wish to continue living how they wish you to live so that you can be possessed by them, then you should not complain, for it is by your own choice in doing.

*

What is the greatest obstacle [to achievement] is trying to fulfill a goal that is seen through the eyes of a different person, trying to become it through their vision and not your own. You can never become what another person wants you to become. You can only become what you are. That is simple; that is the way it is!

When you set goals that are based around the wills of other entities, then you are putting your achievement in their hands, and, verily, if it is ever accepted, it will not stay long there, for you will never stay long within their accepted view. And if others hold the prize of your achievement, when you get it, you will not keep it for long, for there will always be someone behind you that will be more willing to compromise to whatever degree they can to achieve what you have struggled for for so long. That is also a truth.

If you are in your sovereign Self and your goal is set for **Self** to determine when you have achieved, then rarely do you not ever achieve. Self is the greatest critic and yet the greatest friend, the greatest lover, the greatest being you will ever know and possess. And that opinion should be sought after more than anyone else's.

Re-look at your goals and who holds the treasure of them. Who will say you have "arrived" (a most notable term here on your plane) when you have. Evaluate when **you** have, what you determine your achievement. Relook at them clearly and evenly, without the opinion of anyone else. And never ask anyone else if you have achieved; they will never know that; only you know that within your own being. Set the goal for yourself and achieve it for you.

Learn to put your destiny back into your own hands. Learn not to ask others' opinions of yourself—ask yourself! Your Self can make you magnificent if you only let it. Your Self can give you peace if you only let it. And your Self, entity, will be with you all through this life, where others won't.

Achieve for you. If your achievement goes unrecognized by those around you, so be it! It never needed to be recognized to be called achievement.

HAPPINESS IS A SELF-CREATED REALITY

You must do what makes you happy on this plane. There was not a great applause here when you were born, indeed. The whole of humanity did not turn out to witness your birth; only you and your mother. So why be you so busy, entity, living for the expectations and the reprisals of things that you "should" do that you don't when you could be living a happy life for the fulfillment of yourself and, much to your surprise, to the happiness of everyone else!

"Live for you. Do what you want to do! As long as [you] live for the expectations of [others], you will never be happy and you will never lead and you will never accomplish, nor will you ever be remembered."

The happiest entities on this plane are those who do precisely what they want to do, and the miserable ones here are the ones that are busy trying to make everyone else happy and doing what they "should" do to appease for the sake of that which is termed notice, love, compassion and kindness.

Live for you. Do what you **want** to do. As long as [you] live for the expectations of [others], you will never be happy and you will never lead and you will never accomplish, nor will you ever be remembered.

God is lawless. He has not said, "Do this and do that, and don't do this and don't do that." Man does that. God only wishes you to be happy, however that is: that is the kingdom called "heaven," and in that consciousness, everything is achieved in a sublime state of happiness.

*

When you reach beyond to find that which is termed true happiness, joy, it shan't **be** because someone tells you [that] you should be happy. It shall be, entity, because you yourself have incurred it through your individualism.

'Tis not a fearful thing to be yourself; it is only a **new** thing to be yourself, something you have not been for a nigh a long time in your passing and counting. And being what you want to be does not mean that you turn war against the whole society; that is rather fruitless. It only means that you look within and find the beauty that you possess, inwardly and outwardly, and compare it to no one, because there is **no** comparison. And since there is no comparison, you are rather original, unique, and the beauty of what you are adds to the overall beauty of that which is termed the conclusive whole.

Do what you want to do. When you start doing what you want to do—a new adventure, mind you—it will be different, but, nonetheless, it has made you happy. And if others do not approve of it, assess your Self and see if you still want to [do it]; and if you do, flow through it and become it.

Because others are not going to approve of what you are doing, does that mean that they are wrong? No, entity. 'Tis their truth expressing. Allow them their individual opinion. Give them the grace to have their own truth. If you do, you become noble and very God-like in your original character that can still allow love for everyone else, even if they don't agree.

*

You are taught to **be** something? Hmm. You already **are** something! [Entities] think that being something [and] being admired and loved by many purportedly equates happiness. Well,

"Don't strive for anyone to understand you. That means you are taking away your own premise and living for someone else. Don't do that! Do, instead, live for yourself, and if they wish to understand you, they will.

You know, [others] can only see what they possess. When entities cannot see you for the good you are, it is because they cannot see it within themselves.

Be an understanding God and love them. And if they cannot see the beauty of your perfection, it is because they cannot see it in their own Self; and life, however long they permit it, will alot them that experience for them to learn by."

it doesn't! To base one's thoughts of happiness upon the premise of other entities is futile. Self may **never** accomplish being **anything**, or building anything, or becoming anything, except its own, intimate, innate Self. That is called happiness.

Happiness is not giving into the social structures that are placed on you for expectancy, but rather doing what fancy pleases your heart, your Soul, your body. To be happy is to be yourself. Who could ever be happy be being the duplicacy [duplicate] of someone else? There is no happiness in that, only mocked pleasure.

*

The world doesn't care if you fail, and neither does anyone else! They only care if **they** fail. Your priorities are a bit misplaced, for your priorities of happiness is what everyone thinks about you, [that] hopefully it is in a good turn and that anyone can see blatantly that you are successful and esteemed and noble. [But] those qualities, entity, are going to change by those around you.

You have placed your whole happiness in the opinion of someone else and in their judgement. And you have placed it in things rather than individuals. Perhaps you should learn what happiness is.

[Happiness] has nothing to do with anyone else's opinion or a tally of gold or properties earned and owned. It has nothing to do with society, for it is a rebuker of happiness. It has to do, entity, if one is gratified within their own Self.

Happiness lies within yourself: **you** are the richness. When you lose that, entity, you have lost it all!

*

Master, you know, there are many entities that are coerced into doing things because their families have thought them to be a good idea. But what do they know of you? And they think because they had a spasm and created you that perhaps they have control over your entire destiny! And heaven forbid if you should go against it!

Now, what determines that which is termed success and adventure is if the entity **wants** it. Want, entity, is the clearest, most brilliant note of acceptance from you to you that what you are doing is correct. Entities prodded into doing things against their will are miserable, unhappy entities all of their lives, for their will to do as they will has been taken from them, [for] they do not wish to disappoint family or anyone.

The key here is that you must do what makes you happy, what brings you adventure, excitement. The ability to create from **your** perspective, entity, rather than someone else's [is what] gains to you a loftier perspective and attitude about your divine Self. And if you want to be a bum in bumdom, entity, and if that pleased you, you should seek it out heartily and do it—regardless of what anyone says.

Now, want is the key. There is no divine premise or source that can tell you what you should do that you do not already know, for who are they to tell you of something for you to do unless you, the creator, have thought of it first?

The important thing here to remember is never to do anything, no matter how far you are into it, if you lose the joy of it and it becomes monotonous and mundane. Do away with it and do something else that brings you happiness, for perhaps what you needed to learn from it you have already achieved. Go wherever you want to go, do whatever you want to do for as long as you want to.

*

Master, which is greater, as it were: to keep [others] happy and bear the pain yourself or to be happy and let them have the pain until something else comes along to make them happy again?

Master, I desire for you to know this: There shan't ever be another entity like you. Not in the whole of this plane is there another [entity] that is unique like you are. You are the only "you." It is a certainty [you are] one of a kind. But that does not mean that you are not replaceable in the hearts of those that adore you, because you are. And though [you may be] hard-pressed to believe and understand and accept [this], that is the course of humanity.

They must get on with living, entity, in spite of that which [you do]. In the void of their being, they will replace you quickly, that they do not suffer, as it were. You will be the one that will suffer for engaging in that which is called self-guilt for finding your own happiness.

I beseech you, master, do not live for others. Everyone can tell you how they want you to be, and that would make **them** happy. But all in all, that is to no avail unless it makes **you** happy. This plane is used to being told what to do simply by being made to fear [or] to feel guilty.

In order to become steadfast, to understand the one thing of all the Father desires of you called joy, you must serve that which is termed Self; that is where you find the Father. And if what you must do, you must do to acquire happiness, [or] what you must do [is] to let alone those things around you that cause you unhappiness, then that is your destiny, certainly. If you do not partake of it, you shall have lived this life, your youth vanished from your being, [have] become that which is termed an elder, and you will dream long dreams and read scripts [about] others and wonder where your days went.

Happiness is a Self-created reality. It is not group-created; it is Self-created. And if [others] become hurt [by] your choice, master, then that is by their own decision to refuse to understand; nor do they have enough love in their being to allow you to be what is fulfilling to you.

I tell you blatantly: You are replaceable, as those that are around you **you** will replace; that is even speaking. But in order to gain happiness, [the] joy of [your] own Self fulfilled, that is what you must do. Do you understand?

Most entities fall into that which is termed the chasm of guilt, unhappiness and insecurity because they have for so long done what everyone else wanted them to do. For them to think on their own and to become active on their own is a great and large thing to ask.

Give yourself patience. Be. Love yourself. Encourage yourself for happiness. It will come when you are ready. When Self can be gratified and earnestly adored first and loved first, there is a great humbling that occurs in an entity, [for in] that, it can reach out and have compassion for other entities **without** sacrificing its own happiness. That compassion is called mercy and grace, and a saint knows how to deliver it. In that, you must love the entities, regardless of how they act towards you. Love them enough to allow them to express however they choose to express, entity, because **you** are doing the same. That grace and that love and that compassion is what the whole of humanity needs to allow it to be what it is they need to be. You see?

Love them. Give them the freedom, entity, to have hurt if they choose it. Do not try to change their minds. Just love them.

*

Now, in regards to that which is termed the sibling accepting that which is termed the lover, aye? That is very difficult for siblings to do unless they themselves are lovers.

My beloved woman, listen unto me evenly. Love your sibling because unto you have been born from that which is termed the fruit of your womb another entity, a God, an eminent entity that can express and create its own kingdom. But this entity did not come here in this lifetime for you; it came here, entity, to have its own life. It is very arduous for parents to understand that,

"To you, for you," master, is the ultimate mastery, the greatest of all, because you are your greatest friend, your greatest benefactor, your greatest lover, your greatest God."

for they want to believe on the contrary. That is why they go through so much preparation in raising the sibling—so that it will be their own ideal, rather than the sibling's ideal. Knowing this full well to be a truth, you must ascertain within your life what brings you happiness. Your sibling shan't bring you your happiness; it is not its responsibility to do so; it is yours.

Desire that which brings you happiness. [And] if the **whole** of the world, entity, say unto you [that] they are finding great displeasure in the lover of your countenance, it does not matter. Love for you and the blessings and the virtue of what brings you happiness, for the whole of the world shan't make you happy—they don't want to! Understand that.

Take to your bed, by choosing, by choice, and by happiness, who wish you to have there. And when, alas, the happiness is no longer there, it does not mean you have lost anything; it means you have gained everything that it was supposed to give you [and] 'tis time for another adventure. But **you** must live for **you** and to make your own happiness. I tell you staightaway: if you don't, no one shall give it to you; it is not their responsibility to do that. You see? [And] if the sibling finds displeasure, love your sibling and be happy for its opinion.

*

YOU ARE YOUR GREATEST LOVER

Love that which you are first. And what be love? Do unto yourself all that you would do unto any one entity that you loved and caressed and found amusement in. Then all that results from love will be joy. And the result of joy will be peace. And in peace can you hear the voice of God. In peace can you find the experience of your being. In peace are your eyes taken away from the illusion of colored lights into the deep purple and indigo of a sky that reveals Heaven.

*

[You are troubled by] excessives? Indeed! What be an "excess" and what be a "moderation?" What are their limits? Is excess unlimited? Well, if it is an excess, that means it doesn't have an end, for if it had an end, it would only be "moderate." True? True.

"There is no one here, though they say they are your brother, that will die for you. There is no lover that will die for you. There is no friend that will die for you. There is no one, entity! That you must do yourself. Thus who, ultimately, should you love and caress and care for?"

What is the wrong in being excessive, for excessive is only a state of being that means you are an "unlimited" entity. Why **ever** be moderate about **any** one thing, entity! I do not **want** to teach you moderation. **Anyone** can teach you that! That is the plague of this plane!

I wish to teach you to become **un**limited! **Un**limited is having excessiveness in thought, excessiveness in taking the contemplative part of your being to the heights of your being; to understand, entity, that you are not a simple man; that you are a divine God living in the guise of something struggling to be moderate. No, I will not teach you how to be moderate. What I will teach you is how to be wise.

All of the things that are "good" should be taken into an unlimited sphere. To determine what is the good of your being is up to you! And how you determine that is to recognize that you, of yourself, are the only one that will **ever** love yourself completely. Only you can be the ultimate lover of your being. Only you, entity, are the ultimate friend of your being. Only you are the ultimate teacher and advisor of your being. Anyone else's opinions will always be less, for how could they possibly know you, for they are not you.

Understand that you, to yourself, should be prized above any and all others; that your opinion of you is divinely a truth; that how you look at yourself in your reflector is how you truly see yourself. And if you find all that you are in the wonderful adventure of "you" a mystery, then what a profound beauty that is.

There is no one here, though they say they are your brother, that will die for you. There is no lover that will die for you. There is no friend that will die for you. There is no one, entity! That you must do yourself. Thus who, ultimately, should you love and caress and care for?

How does a regal lord care for a good woman? Hmmm. It is an adventure to touch her skin. It is like silk. It is the color of cream. It exudes the scent, the aroma of lilies. And the body is firm, yet soft. The skin is resilient. The eyes, entity, there never was a sea that held the depth, the vastness, the color, hue, liquidness of the eyes of a good woman or how she uses them. And the flush is natural upon the cheek and the forehead. And the hair is brushed to a fine sheen and smells of all lemonwood scents and wonderful flowers; that when you put your fingers in it, it flows from your hand and makes a hand that is calloused feel like a cushion. And [the] mouth is so beautiful, its breath sweet and tender.

And when you stand off and look at the refined hands and the beautiful feet and the perfect carriage, you swear by your soul, man, you've never seen anything so exquisite; that there have never been an art ever formed to captivate such a living beauty that exudes life, that is **all** that can be seen in the totality of a perfect being.

And when a man sees that in a woman, he is seeing the greatest beauty in **himself** in that woman. He will never speak a harmful word to her. He will never abuse or tear the tender skin. He will never mess the beautiful hair lest it lose its shine. And he will never be harmful lest those wondrous eyes become reddened and shed their water over rosy cheeks. He will treat her, entity, as a virtual Goddess, for she certainly is!

That is how **you** should teach, that is how **you** should respond, that is how **you** should become to **you**! To love yourself. To look upon the grandeur of your being. To hold yourself divine. To clothe yourself in what you consider to be the finest against your skin. To anoint yourself. To perfume yourself. To feed yourself that which is good and lies lightly upon the tongue and in the gullet. To drink that which brings warmth to the being. And to never take anything upon the Self or the personage of your being that would harm, break, destroy, maim, or cripple it. For how grand is you! For you will learn to live with you, you will learn to live **for** you, into eternity, when no one else can.

Love is born within one's Self that it is thus given to others outside of ourself. When you learn to see yourself as a man sees a good woman, entity, then excessives, in your infinite wisdom, are all God. And you will not harm or hurt or damage or defile or dishonor yourself ever again. And that will bring what is called the noble virtue of acceptance to you. Then we will have well-rounded our God!

Excessive, entity, sometimes is only misplaced, for the recipient of it is often misunderstood. I will help you understand the beauty that you are and have you become worthy of your unlimitedness--in a very wise way! Take care of yourself. You are worth it. You for **you,** dear master.

I will send a runner with flora. Enjoy them. They are the signs of new life and color and hope. And when they bloom, they are you.

*

LOVE OTHERS BY BEING AN EXAMPLE OF SELF-LOVE

No one needs you to interfere in their life. But be glad of that, because they are living their life precisely how they want to live it. You should do the same.

To be more loving and giving is to first begin with Self. When you do that, master, then you will learn that you can give to no one, because everything they want from you will be what they term their fulfillment, and, much to your dismay, entity, it will be the ending of your happiness.

You do not give to people to make them happy, master. You simply are, and you are to live for what brings **you** happiness. And by that very act, by living it, that becomes an example to others to do the same with themselves. No one needs giving to.

*

To do in this life what we do not want to do, to be entrapped and to live a constricted, enslaved life for the sake of others, is **not** virtuous! It does not hold any reward at the end of this life, for as it is done, [so] have you become a servant to other peoples' wants and you have allowed yourself to be possessed, regardless of your will. And one day, entity, they will see that **same** attitude, and they will become their own victims [by] doing what is called the "right" thing and forefeiting a prize that they have found that brings them the height of glory and the deepest point of intimacy, ecstasy, pleasure, hope, beauty and life! And [they] will give that all up, for that is the "noble" thing to do for others that depend upon **them**.

I will tell you to do what you **desire** to do, that the ideal that you do will set a precedence for those that you love and care for. What I am saying has not been said very openly here; though it is the desireable thing, it is not "acceptable," as it were. If you wish to be acceptable [and] follow the rules of your society in the enslavement of others, then you will learn to die a hungry, indeed a lonely, miserable, impotent old man. And that is a truth!

Do what is in your heart to do. Then you are living a truth--perfectly!

*

Master, you cannot be answerable unto others. You can only be answerable unto yourself. When you do what brings you happiness, it is a teaching to those that observe. [And] if they would do the things that bring them happiness, it would not mean the enslavement of you to achieve it [for them]. That is a truth.

What must be learned here, indeed, is to love those enough around you, because you **do** love yourself, to let them be [and] allow them to express however they **wish** to express, whether they are disappointed in you or alas depart from you or alas [are] saddened by you--whatever. If that is demonstrated openly,

"It is a noble thing when you have nothing else to do to want to serve the world. But as history would have it, everyone that has tried has been burned, hacked, hanged, poisoned, assassinated and done away with! Be who you are—for you. In the being, you lift everyone.

Love what you are and live for the radiance within you—awesome power—and love it and clarify it and exalt it. Then you have done the world 'a good turn,' as it were."

master, you will find that the disappointment of the others around you will become less and less and a great strength will grow inside of them, for how else is an ideal achieved but by **living** the ideal. Words, they are empty; they mean nothing except to the creator of them. You must practice this within your own life.

Continue to do what brings you happiness. Then you will not have cancerous diseases, indeed, diseases of the mind, diseases of that which is termed the embodiment; you will be a happy entity and you will have been a wonderment to those around you. That is how it is.

*

Why think you that you must serve? Who says that serving others will bring them happiness, thus bringing yourself happiness? Do you know you can never make anyone happy, and that if you go out to serve this very fickle world, they will hang you, because oftentimes their happiness is certainly not yours. 'Tis a truth! And what your idea of what the world should be like in a utopia state will not be the world's. The collective consciousness forbids it. That is not how you help humanity.

The way humanity is enhanced is when **one** entity blooms and becomes the vessel of Love of Self: [a] noble creature of esteem, knowledge, virtue, compassion [and] wisdom that lives unaffected by society, fashion and trends—a virtual hero. Anyone that can sustain beyond such a consciousness **deserves** recognition. One who blooms and loves himself completely, understands himself completely, is volatile to himself, becomes a "light" to others.

If you look at a great city, you will see the consciousness like this: it is bowed. The deepest, highest point is in the vortex of the city, the center part. The consciousness become weakened, thin and pale, to the outer perimeters of it.

The consciousness is created by the collective consciousness of all that inhabit the city. Thus, an outsider, who thought nothing of the ways and the wills and the murk and the mire of the city, issues into the city and begins to feed upon the collective consciousness [there] and becomes a virtual changed entity. This is an enslavement, and those who live in such a structure are never known for who they are; they are only duplicates of someone else's creation.

When a God enters into such a situation, he lifts the "bowl" of collective consciousness, expands it, and adds to [it] love, knowingness, isness. And all who are feeding upon such consciousness will begin to look around them and wonder where the feeling is coming from. And the entity passes in the marketplace and utters not one word, [but] simply at his passing, everyone stops and looks. Their Spirit **knows** that there is

"None can [give] unconditional love; they must become it. Live it in your own life. Be unconditionally loving to you. Let that be a light to others to spur them to go "within," to be kind, to find the beauty that they possess so readily.

Unconditional love does not go out to all peoples, but come from within all peoples. That is the way it is."

greatness amongst them. And lo, he will have entities following him out of the city [who will] want to know, "Who are you? What are you doing? What do you know?" And the entity speaks and says, "It is the Father within me that you have seen through the Father within you." And he does not preach to them; he simply goes about and lives for **himself**, and by doing that, becomes an explicit ideal--not an idol--for others that observe.

It is a noble thing when you have nothing else to do to want to serve the world, but as history would have it, everyone that has tried has been burned, hacked, hanged, poisoned, assassinated and done away with! Be who you are--for you. In the being, you lift everyone.

You are man, Christus, God! If man is exalted into his Christhood, he can change the entire universe with a thought; that is how powerful he is. When the Christ transcends into complete God, then he is no longer limited by the boundaries of flesh and lays out and becomes a platform to which all life continues to emerge from and in to. And it is done with you!

Love what you are. **Love** what you are, and live for the radiance within you--awesome power--and love it and clarify it and exalt it. Then you have done the world "a good turn," as it were.

*

Unconditional love can come forth from you and be practiced and lived that it becomes a sustaining principle in your life force. To **commit** yourself to unconditionally love others, master, is not the way it is done. It is first committing yourself to you and then to others.

None can [give] unconditional love; they must become it. Live it in your own life. Be unconditionally loving to you. Let that be a light to others to spur them to go "within," to be kind [to themselves], to find the beauty that they possess so readily. Once they have experienced the love and the taste of honey, they will want more of themselves and will ask more of themselves, and they themselves shall deliver more.

Unconditional love does not go out to all peoples but comes from within all peoples. That is the way it is.

*

Do not serve Mankind; they will never appreciate you for it. Love Mankind. Be. The light that you are will attract in the darkness that which seeks the light, and they will come, as you see [in these audience], from all places. And that which seeks the light seeks to become as the light is. That is called Love, not serving. You are not here to serve anyone.

"How can you be all things to all peoples, master, when you have not been all things to you?

Find peace and happiness and joy and the tranquility of life, that your shining light and example of perfecting you may be a light to others. Then you are giving them the permission of your own sweet countenance to express a calling to their ideals independent of yours. Then always love them and permit them to express freely according to their will."

You know, master, if only you possessed within your wondrous being the ability to love every entity here, to love them and to hold of great importance their value, you should have a most arduous time making your way to your bed, for you would continuously have a hoard in front of you who needed what you and you alone can give. Such a treasure is the ability to love, that such would your name be, that your service to Mankind will simply be the light that you are without [your] doing anything.

Cultivate that wondrous ideal within your being. That which needs the love will find their way to you, from the darkness to the light. And love them, love them. See into their beings and love them, for in that, your life will be greatly lifted and gratified.

*

Since peace and happiness and health are all different to the views and to the lives of different peoples, what may be your peace and happiness and health, master, may not be your neighbor's view of what peace and health and life is. You see? How can you be all things to all peoples when you have not been all things to you?

Find peace and happiness and joy and the tranquility of life, that your shining light and example of perfecting you may be a light to others. Then you are giving them the permission of your own sweet countenance to express a calling to their ideals independent of yours. Then always love them and permit them to express freely according to their will.

Complete your life and find peace and happiness therein. And if you look for it, master, you will find it. When it is established there, it is a certainty that you will be a light to others to find their own way, I assure you.

*

Being of service to others? Most say to be that which is termed a philosopher or a teacher or a rabbi or whatever, that that is the way to help all humanity. The truth is, humanity will get helped when it wants to get help, and most of the time, entity, it will turn a deaf ear to anyone who is struggling to do it--and rightfully it should, for who is to say [that] anyone needs help? Only when they ask--that is when they need it. The other times they are doing precisely what they want to do, and **that** is their state of happiness.

In servicing others, I will tell you a great truth: You will never make them happy--no matter what you do, no matter how you live--because their happiness is not in you; it is in themselves, and they are going to live and do whatever they want

"Consider yourself above everyone else and anything else always first. The most pious creatures on this plane will say, "Behold, entity, that is called selfishness." Indeed it is! And be glad that it is, for when one is selfish enough to ask Self first and to love Self first, then one has the capacity to help and to love everyone else, for then he knows what [love] is.

Loving God first is loving Self first. Be kind enough to yourself, always. That is an example everyone needs to learn from."

to do that brings them that happiness, and that is what they should do.

To be in service to others is to live your life and love who you are, adamantly; and living it so that that which you be is a light unto the world if it wishes to look; and leaving them alone to allow them to look. That is how you can be of service--by **not** being it, but being who you are.

Teachers have come and gone on this plane, some wonderfully famous and some forgettable and some unforgettable. But it really hasn't caused much of a difference because everyone has lived how they wanted to in the first place. Infinite wisdom, entity, knows that.

So what [do] you do? You love them immensely for the freedom that they express. No matter if they hate you, love them for expressing that will to do that, [for] they are Gods that are doing that. As long as you can love them in every phase of their being, that allows you the strength to love yourself in every phase of your being. And how grand of an entity be you that does that? Simply being who you are is enough.

Consider yourself above everyone else and anything else always first. The most pious creatures on this plane will say, "Behold, entity, that is called selfishness." Indeed it is! And be glad that it is, for when one is selfish enough to ask Self first and to love Self first, **then** one has the capacity to help and to love everyone else, for then he knows what [love] is.

Loving God first is loving Self first. Be kind enough to yourself, always: that is an example everyone needs to learn from.

*

Everyone wishes to make the world happy when the world would be quite happy when you leave it alone. The greatest contribution that you can make is to be this wondrous entity that loves that which you be. What greater gift is there [than] to see one singular entity in this wondrous place called humanity expressing how they are? They become a light and an example to others, but only to those who wish to see.

Loving, master--and I use this exalted term to which the basis is called Love or God--is loving one's Self enough to allow one's Self the privilege to do what brings it happiness, what nurtures Self; then, with the same great wondrous enlightenment and wisdom, to allow the world to do whatever it wishes to do. Even if they were all to despise you, [it is] to love it enough to give it the freedom to do that. That is called Love; that is called God.

Love yourself to where you are an example. [And] who cares if anyone watches? 'Tis your life, entity; 'tis your virtue. There is not one here that would give up their life for you, so why should you make them happy? You make yourself happy, and in that process, your light, indeed, will be a light to the rest of the world.

Everyone wishes to save this place, but the saving grace of this place is for everyone to leave it alone.

*

Master, the world doesn't need any help; it doesn't **want** it! That is free will that equates active God. They are getting everything they want precisely by not wanting any more than they want. Never help anyone, master. Don't! Because they will never appreciate it; they really do not care. You will teach them now and they will forget it tomorrow, and you shall be the one that is hurt by it. That is Gods! That is the way they are.

Now, for you to learn would be the greatest; then teach by doing [what you have learned] in your own life. The whole of humanity learns by observation and its free will. By watching you demonstrate this remarkable feat (though it really isn't) helps the world in an unenslaving manner. Teachers, entity, who wish to go after Mankind to help it are the greatest enslavers of all!

*

You never teach anyone anything unless they ask. Asking permits the will the encouragement to know. If you teach without them asking, you are not teaching; you are enslaving, and that is not for you to do. People do what they **want** to do, whatever that is. People **believe in** whatever they want to believe in. That is alright; there is nothing wrong with that, for who is to determine that theirs is not the truth. **The** truth is [that] everything is the truth!

How do you help anyone? When they ask! When they ask, then you speak it forth from the Lord God of your Being. But you tell them this is only what you believe and have found to be a truth within your own being. And when you are finished, tell them to do with it as they please, that they are not regulated by your likes and dislikes to adhere to what you have just told them. Then you are loving them and allowing them to choose.

*

To expand yourself, kind master, that you may love and understand and be a helping aid to others is to first be that to yourself, that you understand what it means to love and to serve others. Love and understand yourself, master, without price, without, as it were, bargaining. When you do that with yourself, then you have expanded the realization of that effort and of that thought into a greater concept that becomes a permanent reality within your being. And when it is done there, master, then it is understood more perfectly and can be thus applied unto others.

[Others] are drawn to us according to our light. None come unto us haphazardly, as it is so termed; all come unto us for reasons. And when you have expanded **yourself**, master, through kindness and understanding—not through complexities of intellect, but through the simplicity of our own beauty—and give unto yourselves endlessly, master, you will draw unto you those that can be taught simply.

*

CHAPTER FOURTEEN

LISTEN TO THE WISDOM OF YOURSELF

"There has never been anyone that has lived or that ever will live that is a greater teacher unto your being than you. You have all of the answers there. And if, alas, you do not find them there, you are well equipped, I assure you, to secure for you the proper knowingness to implement the answers."

"Listen unto the Lord God of your Being.

And when you are in doubt of any one thing, speak from the Lord God of your Being and ask of its mysteries, and behold, they will be revealed unto you.

If you are in darkness and the knowing is the unknowing, speak from the Lord God of your Being that light be given unto the unknown, and behold, it will be.

And when your heart is in limbo and you know not the purpose [of others] into your life, speak from the Lord God of your Being that it be revealed to you, and so it will.

You see, this is different from chants or prayers or moanings or agonies or whatever they do in ritualistic practices.

I have given unto you a 'key' of sorts; it is called 'the Lord God of your Being.' It fits the 'doors.' Use it; it works well, to be sure."

YOU ARE YOUR GREATEST TEACHER

How you learn is [by] listening to you. And take from your language the thoughts of failure, guilt, fear, hurt; the thoughts of can't, will not, impossible and negative. When you remove all that, which is the mundaneness of Mankind, you will find your splendid Self. Then, when you listen to yourself in the mode of clarity, you will know the God within you.

Everyone follows everyone else's ideal, which is collective consciousness that presides and looms over your plane like stagnated air. No one has reached into the depths of their being to find a new way and, through understanding, a new truth, a new isness. That is why they are a mystery.

You are given your thoughts daily to eat. You are given your thoughts to slumber on at night. And you are given your thoughts to clothe yourself, that the clothing of your thoughts will be an acceptance to everyone else's. And that lacks creativity of the individual Self--which is God! Reach far down within you and ask **you,** and stop and listen to **you.** That is how you learn of the Father and His sublime Isness.

*

You know, entity, you cannot see anything that you do not first contemplate has a reality. Then once you contemplate the reality of it, and if it exists, from that moment on it does exist. Then you have gone on to another understanding, yet another adventure.

How could you go into your Spirit before when you had not reasoned that there was any place to go? Now that you know your Spirit is there, commune with it as you commune with me, and then listen. You have to listen clearly, for your ears are tuned to awkward sounds that represent subtle thoughts; it is the subtle thoughts that you must listen to. And once you have refined your ear so cleverly as to do that, then you are your Spirit. And the more you listen, the more you become. This is how it is done.

The atrocity of limited thought, [of being] closed-minded, [is that it] is the one thing that keeps you from your perfect kingdom, keeps you from the glory of God Almighty and from yourself, because as long as you have limited thoughts and a cloistered mind, you never venture into the unknown, or speculate or contemplate [the] existence [of greater realities] for fear [that] it [will] mean change. And certainly it does, because there is more now to contemplate, to view, to understand, to be

"Learn to listen to the feeling within you. It will never forsake you. Never! Go by the feeling that is in your uttermost being, entity, and let that be a lamp unto your night. It will always find your path right where you are."

a part of, than there was before in a tidy world that lives and dies.

Simply contemplate your Spirit and listen to it. When you do, you contemplate God. He is subtle. Listen to the word that is not a word. See the reality that is not a reality. Become.

Be your Spirit. There are no "doors" there and there are no forbidden walls there. There is not a conglomerate babble of direction of how to become it. It simply is! Live in a state of "is." That is all.

*

Of that which gives direction to the Soul, one be that which is termed the altered Ego or the collective ego-understanding of man living in a limited sphere. Altered Ego is altered God, judgemental God. [The other is] that which is termed the divine Spirit, and that is the **feeling,** entity. The Divine Spirit is in reality the God of our purposeful being. It never misdirects you. It has [its] greatest interest in your own interest; thus it has no reason to diffuse, deface, defraud or placate itself in a folly upon your being. It **is** there, entity, to guide you, for you are the result of its being.

Learn to listen to the feeling within you. It will never forsake you. Never! Go by the feeling that is in your uttermost being, entity, and let that be a lamp unto your night. It will always find your path, entity, right where you are.

*

The Spirit of your being, the God of your being, entity, if you listen to it, knows infinitely what you need and desire. If you go by the quiet "voice" within you and start listening to that, it will never lead you astray for it has only your better interest at heart since it **is** your interest.

The intellect, suffering from the altered Ego, created by the altered Ego, always must find a complexity to the heights of simplicity. It allows the mind to feel the virtual ebbs of ecstasy in intellectual fantasy. And it has made simplicity such a puzzle, entity, that it will take nigh many lifetimes to solve the mystery, hence giving credence to our own being and showing how powerful we are and our state of absolute pompousness!

There is no mystery to Life. If you look around, you will see all the answers. If you listen to your Self and do what your Self tells you to do, then you will soon find the manifestation of that doing.

The Father is the simplicity of the line. He is the totality of Life. All you have to do is look at Him. And if you wish to

"The way that you find out who you are and live is to never go against the feelings within your Soul that feel to you as acceptance. Always follow them. That will take you to the Eye of God. That is how you get there."

make light of His being, then do so; that is what the intellect is all about! So be it.

*

Do not go by things intellectually. 'Tis a fool who does. Go by the feelings; that is the thought that is born of the Spirit that is causing a certain feeling within the body without words. That is what always you should listen to.

The Spirit of your being often rocks before you. It is always communicating with you, and what obviously intellectually should be the answer, not always is! Go with your feelings. There are many things intellectually everyone knows, and there are even those scoundrels who are very proud of their intellectual foolery. But they don't know how to feel. Don't align with them. You allow the feeling to become both the feeling and the intellect. You create, in essence, your own theory, your own truth, your own Isness.

*

You already know all there is to know. You already know that because that which is termed the knowingness is closer than the hair on your head and sweeter than the beat of your heart. It is closer to you than all of those things. And yet you allow yourself only to know but so little of it. Through this understanding and this enlightenment, you will be able to know all of the answers. Indeed.

I am your beloved brothren and love you greatly, and do not mind imparting that which is termed my wisdom upon you, and be desirous that you apply it. But master, there has never been anyone that has lived or that ever will live that is a greater teacher, lover, friend, confidant, as it were, king, indeed, unto your being than you. You have all of the answers there. And if, alas, you do not find them there, you are well equipped, I assure you, to secure for you the proper knowingness to implement the answers.

You are a great God. Do not look to others for answers, entity; look to You. Only you know the answer to what you need. You understand? And know that that which you have chosen is the truth. It is! And as you do that, your God within shall flourish, and your union with yourself will become eminent. And entities shall seek after **you** for knowingness. When they do, you impart to them that which I have just imparted to you and ask that they use it. Then, entity, your life will be happy and, of course, it will belong to you and no one else. So be it.

*

"The atrocity of meditation is that one can never still the mind, for one can never still God! The Thought Principle is ongoing in every moment; it is expanding in every moment. And in the moment of its expansion, it collects from all conscious entities its knowingness.

You never still the Mind of God; it cannot be done, for if it could, this moment would be the last of all moments, and they would never be again, and neither would life or light or breath or wind or waters or stars or moons or heavens or all understanding!"

In this dream, in this understanding, there is no such thing as "no such thing". There is only truth. Ego means God; altered Ego means limited God. Always [the voice] which you hear is truth, always. Always. Truth performs its visions for a specific emotion for the entity to feel to learn by. How the visions are performed and the words that are spoken, entity, are incidental; it is what is gathered by what has been experienced [that is important].

The "voice within," as it were, is not a voice: it is a feeling, it is an urgency, it is emotion. Thought does not become the reality until it is accepted into that which is termed the auric field through that which is termed the immortal body [and] expressed through the central nervous system as a feeling; then it becomes reality.

What you are hearing is the God of your being. And because your neighboren's God of its being is speaking a different truth than your God, does not mean you are wrong. There is no comparison to your voice anywhere. Listen to what is spoken within your Self.

The greatest atrocity that was ever committed on this plane was when God was taken out of the masses and put as a singular entity, and everyone put under rules and regulations called "dogma." Then that meant that everyone was the same and not different or unique.

Master, though you are one God, you are different and unique, and your beauteous truth, indeed, needs to be listened to. Where you are going is not where he is going or this entity is going; it is only where **you** are going. And when you stop comparing your voice to others is when you will truly Become.

Listen to what it says by feeling it. And pray do not go against its wisdom; it is uniquely for you. When the voice is contested, that is when alteredness or limitedness or "man" begins to interfere with it; that is called confusion, a divine state of emotion.

Prayer, Meditation And Contemplation

You are trying to be still to pray and to meditate, but what do you think they are? What is the use of trying to think of a prayer or still yourself for meditation, entity? If you are trying to be still in order to be aware of "the presence within and without and everywhere," you will miss it completely, for it is not still!

"Start listening to your thoughts, entity, and when you start listening to them, you will believe that there is nothing greater than you. Then you will start making sense to you and your life, and for the first time in your existence, you will have answers that mean something, for they are coming from a sincere entity to a sincere entity: you to you."

What are you trying to be aware of, entity? When you are trying to be still and listen, what are you listening for? A trumpeter? Soft music? Running water? Brilliant lights? What are they going to do? They are only going top make you think about **them**! What is the use of prayer and meditation if you ignore the answers that come? Your answers, entity, are thoughts.

What do you think the "Voice of God" is? An alien? What do you think you are listening for? A completed sentence? The Voice of God, entity is the River of Thought--purely that! The "presence" you are trying to listen to, entity, is your own thought processes without [your] judgement standing in the way.

The Voice of God is the thoughts that are coming to you. Where do you think they are coming from? What you are trying to listen to are answers, but the answers you are seeking are not going to be from an entity appearing outside of you and divinely telling you them; it will be you in your everyday thought processes, which is the most important value of life, meaning it is **every day** speaking to you in [your] language.

The Voice of God is not harps or the music of clouds passing by; He is the Thought that made those occur! The Voice of God is the River of Thought. The altered Ego is the dispenser, the alteredness, the judger of pure thoughts. All of your thoughts that you have termed "mundane" and "distorted" is where all of your answers have [been].

Start listening to your thoughts, entity, and when you start listening to them, you will believe that there is nothing greater than you. Then you will start making sense to you and your life, and for the first time in your existence, you will have answers that mean something, for they are coming from a sincere entity **to** a sincere entity: you to you.

There is no "outside presence," entity, none, that hath greater concern for you than you--the Spirit of your being that hath allowed these thought processes to come forth. And [each time] they can squeeze in beyond your judgemental attitude, they add a little bit more happiness to your life.

If you will sit and let all of these "distortions" come, for however long they want to come, you will have answers to every single problem you have ever had. You will have insight into your tomorrows to come, and you will have a reason for being.

Enough of this! I tire of my own words, for how much simpler and bolder can it be? Where do you think I get hold of **my** information, entity? I am the River of Thought in the guise of a personality. So be it.

*

When [men] first believed that God no longer existed within their being, they were put in a most vulnerable, dangerous position because, in that, someone else who did [profess to] have the "Word of God" could dictate to them how they were to live, what they were to do, how they were to do it, when they were to do it—everything.

Many rituals has man gone through for eons to find a way to reach God or the Knowingness, the Isness--from sacrifices [of] human, animal and plant life to the giving up of estates, lands [and] hovels, to that which is termed commitments of life forever [in] convents, to halls of study, to prayer, to meditation. [But] as long as you know you **must** do something to connect with your Self, you will always know [that] you never will.

Meditation is the receiving of thought processes and listening to how you react to them. It is really listening to Self like you listen to your melody. Unfortunately, entity--and fortunately--most entities are very distrubed because they do not do it enough and feel very guilty; so they are enslaved to guilt because they [feel they] are not connecting with God enough. And then they begin to feel very unworthy. And it goes on and on and on, and we are back in the beginning--Man without God.

You being wherever you are, beautiful entity, you are receiving Thought, which is God, and you are responding to it according to feelings. That is daily prayer; that is daily meditation; that is daily existence; that is steadfast knowingness. To be quiet, indeed, allows the stillness of the being and allows Self to be at one with Self--but not to "reach out," only to be.

If you never meditated another existence of your life, master, you will still have done everything right. What one needs to know is that they already **are** God, and they have not to reach any further or burn themselves or sacrifice in any way to reach that infinite thing. Just be who you are. Imitate no one but yourself.

*

If you shall devote more time to sitting and being quiet and contemplating your beautiful Self, entity, that will open up to you yet more areas of adventure--it is a certainty--for you not to serve **anyone** but your own cleverness. If you do that, you will be a happier entity, for that means you are giving yourself an opportunity to experience you--which everyone here needs a little bit more of.

If you had moments to pull away from the murk and the mire and the clutching hands of the marketplace long enough to contemplate your own inner peace, you would find an inner value, an inner truth, an inner guidance, entity, that behold, you never knew existed there. That will allow you to rejuvenate, will allow you to collect, to become expansive, clever, brilliant, that when you arise from it, entity, you go about your task in a different point of view, a different aim, a different objective that allows you to be more certainly you rather than only a number or a laborer or a slave in the marketplace for someone else's value and point of view.

What brings esteem to a man is when he has his own idea, true? If you are needing self-confidence, stop doing what you are doing and think about what **you** would like to do in a state of being. That is where ideas are born, inventions are created, philosophy understood—magic created. Contemplate you! Obtain your own self-worth by giving yourself the opportunity for the God within you to listen to the Source. It adds increasing knowledge, increasing awareness, knowingness and value that you can implement right where you are.

*

Master, the atrocity of meditation is that one can never still the mind, for one can never still God! The Thought Principle is ongoing in every moment; it is expanding in every moment. And in the moment of its expansion, it collects from all conscious entities its knowingness. Thus, being a part of knowingness, entity, is being a part of all that is. Meditation is the hour to let all of that flow through you for assessment.

You never still the Mind of God; it cannot be done, for if it could, master, this moment would be the last of all moments and they would never be again, and neither would life or light or breath or wind or waters or stars or moons or heavens or all understanding!

The Mind of God is the River of Thought. You don't **control** your thoughts; you **assess** them. In a state of pondering, or meditation as you would term it, one contemplates the thought values that are flowing through his wondrous receiver. He ponders upon them and assesses them. The thoughts never become a reality unto his own being unless he **feels** them through emotion. It is through the feeling of emotion that brings them into that which is called "manifested reality."

In meditation, it is rather like sitting in an audience and listening to everyone else's point of view, including all life. So when you are still and listening, you are listening to God in all that He is, everything that He is! So what is the purpose of that? It takes you beyond restrictiveness. It has you contemplate things you would never contemplate before, and perhaps in the contemplation of those, answers [will] abound in the Soul that is searching for them. And the answers manifest in a three-dimensional world, after they are felt, for that which is called experience.

[In meditation], you are listening to God. And who be He? Entity, He be you. **You!** So you never control your thought; you only assess them. And the vilest and most beautiful of all thoughts shall you hear, for who determines vileness and beauty save the viewer of them--[and] that is you!

*

How do you [communicate with your Spirit]? Seek you a place and love the place you seek. Find you a quietude, as it were. Put forth the head of your being unto the north and your feet unto the south; thus, you are "polarized," as it is seen. Once the magnetic fields are at peace with one another, then speak forth what you desire [to know] from the Lord God of your Being. And be quiet and expectant, always expectant.

And if you hear not even a voice or a whisper that plays upon the ear, be not disappointed, for perhaps the greatest realization shall be in the materialization of [your answer] in attitude, or perhaps emotion, or in being in the three-dimensional aspect of its reality.

It will always come. When you are looking for he answer, master, that means you are expecting it; thus, it is expected, and it will be.

CHAPTER FIFTEEN

ALLOW YOURSELF TO BE

"If that which is God is the embodiment of Self, and it is Self that you are not pleased with, how can you ever love God or say that you love God?

In order to understand that which is termed Rolling Thunder, to understand that which is termed the love of the Omnipresent Isness, you have to understand and love you."

"There are no rituals, there are no chants, there are no dogmas, there are no sorcerers, indeed priests, indeed oracles, indeed wizards that can allow you to be who you are. All of that is a no thing. The only thing that allows you to be is to remove judgement against yourself. It is that, simply."

REMOVE JUDGEMENT FROM YOURSELF

Contemplate this for a moment. In your most direful moments, as it were, have you ever wondered why God hasn't asked you why you are doing this? Why you are being this way? Why aren't you another way? Well, He has never done that because all of the ways that you are are beautiful unto Him, because life does not end in this moment, in this fretting, in this depression. It is going to go on and be sublimely more beautiful than its yesterday.

If the Father allows you to have the freedom to express your colorfulness, entity, then do not be so harsh upon the countenance of your being because you do not fit the boring modes that society says you must in order to be pious, holy, and divine.

Everyone wants everyone to behave [in] a certain pattern; except those wanting them to be that way never practice it themselves! That is a bit of hypocrisy that is also colorful. But one day, when the whole of this plane no longer has to feel that living this life is fundamental survival, as their instincts in their genes have taught them to be, they will stop living in this madness, as it were, and start finding out the true joys of this sublime existence.

Your whole commerce, entity, the whole of your education, 'tis not built on happiness; 'tis built on survival. And with that, you purge everything frivolous from your life in order to be meaningful and dutiful to that which is termed the marketplace. That is a boring life.

One day there shall come a time when you shall overcome all of these emotional difficulties that cause you to be that way, and you'll understand what it is to live in freedom and be happy in that understanding. So be it.

*

Everyone possesses Ego. And everyone should possess Ego and always will possess Ego, for Ego means "God"; that is what the term equates. Altered Ego simply means that: "altered God." What equates "God" is unlimitedness. What equates "altered" is limitedness.

If you remove from your being judgement for **you,** entity, you will allow an unlimited virtue to come forth, and your Ego shall be the God that it is! There are no rituals, there are no chants, there are no dogmas, there are no sorcerers, indeed priests, indeed oracles, indeed wizards that can allow you to be who you

"It is very simple to love yourself. It means that there is nothing to consider but love. That is how love is. God is in a state of Isness, ongoing 'being,' totality. Being equates itself to Isness, which equates itself to God. When you do not have to stop and judge your attitude, then you are God!"

are. All of that is a no thing. The only thing that allows you to be is to remove judgement against yourself. It is that, simply.

How do you do that? When you arise in your morning, master, lay there and contemplate yourself, quietly. Think about you. Think about you! Think about how beautiful you are and the thoughts within the deep secret wells of your being. And think, entity, how beauteous that image is. And then see that image in everyone else. When you do that, you will have removed judgements, and altered Ego will become Ego--unlimited! And that, entity, equates a master. If you do that, you shall grow and know, and you shall become, and you shall ascend in this lifetime.

*

The greatest alignment occurs when you remove from your being "good" and "bad"; when you [no longer] say, "Alas, this feeling is greater than this one." When you remove good and bad and say, "I am what I am, and that which I am is the expressive God living in the moment," you will find that joy will occupy your being at all times. That is how one stays aligned.

The Soul does not judge thought; it only aligns it. If a thought comes through that saddens you, your being will be engulfed in sadness. But that is not "bad." Who is to say that is "bad?" Who is to say that there is a reality termed "bad?" And who is to say that if joy comes into the Soul that [it] is better than sadness, for many's joy is **found** in sadness. You see?

Be. Do not condemn yourself and, above all, do not be crucial to yourself (a very good term here is "negative" towards yourself). And if you are blue, turn blue. And if you wish to be purple, be purple! But above all, **be.** You see?

If you will allow yourself the emotion to experience without determining it to be a good feeling or a bad feeling, you will keep the alignment within you at all times and you will always feel wonderment. Do not weigh the principles of perfection and imperfection. Weigh them as **Isness**--"I am what I am." And the less you judge yourself in any way, the greater benefit you will receive, for you will grow and manifest greater in your "Am-ness" and in your "Is-ness."

Allow yourself to be in whatever measure that being occurs. That is all. You understand?

*

"Know you [that] everytime you condemn the body the 'death hormone' is flung within it and the body begins to degrade itself, only to the dismay of that which inhabits it.

The body is a wondrous, beauteous chariot. But if it is not loved, it must obey that which is given it, and it will decease itself!"

You do not want to have a "good" attitude, for that equates that the balance of "good" is going to be a "bad" attitude. Attitude is your point of reference for your unique creativity. The grandest thing to possess is to simply become the attitude of "Isness," which means you ponder not if your attitude be "good" or "bad" but that it "is." And the way you do that, lord, is to love yourself, to take your attention into Self. Then, when love of Self begins its road of ecstasy, it will not be a matter that your attitude be sufficient; it will be a matter that you love yourself grand enough that your attitude is the isness representation of the Self which you love.

Be. Love what you be. Honor what you be, earnestly. Then you will be exceedingly glad that you have an attitude to appreciate that which you are and always will be.

It is very simple to love yourself. It means that there is nothing to consider but love. That is how love is. God is in a state of Isness, ongoing "being," totality. Being equates itself to Isness, which equates itself to God. When you do not have to stop and judge your attitude, then you are God!

*

The definition of peace is not contentment; it is **allowance of Self.** In other words, [it is] accepting who you are and loving who you are and being peaceful with that. Most aren't on this plane. They are struggling to be an ideal of what society says they must look like. So they are starving themselves to become wretched twigs, and they are doing things with all of their countenances to look like a certain ideal. It is very hard to find happiness in a starving entity or one that is continuously making their countenance to look like someone else's.

Loving who you are--that is being peaceful. And that is a blessedly good thing, master.

*

Have you ever compared your wondrous body to someone else's and found it lacking? That is not loving the body. Have you mimicked others, thinking they are more beautiful or grander than you? That is not loving the body. Do you despise that which you are, have hated the way you look and anytime been insecure or regretful of Self?

Know you [that] everytime you condemn the body the "death hormone" is flung within it and the body begins to degrade itself, only to the dismay of that which inhabits it. The body is a wondrous, beauteous chariot. But if it is not loved, it **must** obey that which is given it **and it will decease itself**!

"It is all right to be unhappy. You know, master, in my life I was unhappy a great deal of the time, as you would ascertain time to be in moments to moments. But in that unhappiness, there birthed from ignorance, and pestilence, and a barbarian, a great and immaculate truth, a frontier for adventure for the whole of Mankind. I only had to be unhappy with myself to realize that truth."

Fashion is very limited. It is an atrocity, for it construes everyone to look like one individual or group of individuals. And everyone struggles arduously to look that way, and they fall into great neurosis because they are unhappy with themselves. Yet beauty, it is an unseen essence. It is an invisible essence [that] no one here possesses in outer portions.

There is no one else like you. There are entities everywhere, but there is not another like you. You are unique: that which you offer in your splendid Self no one else has. When you consider that value and treat yourself as [the] unique and wonderful entity you are and cease to modify [or] change [yourself] to look like anyone else, your body will never die of disease nor will you age; the body will be in a state of joyfulness and will continue to live and support that mechanism that gives it life. And when [others] are struggling in their neurosis, enraged with madness, trying to starve themselves to be acceptable [and] to be "intellectual" and [are] dying of it, you will continue to live and see generations come and go.

To keep the body flawless is to keep harm from it of thoughts of rejection, hate, bitterness, copying, unhappiness, dissatisfaction, but rather loving it for what it is. You will never have anything wrong with it as long as you do that.

Love yourself. Be pleased with who you are and the way that you look, and know that you are an "original." And that is a wondrous word!

LOVE THE EMOTIONS YOU FEEL

The state of Isness has no declaration of separateness. In other words, Isness is not "good," for it it is "good," it equates a balance called "bad" or "evil." It is not "perfect," for then it would equate "imperfection." So it is neither perfection nor is it good nor is it evil nor imperfection; it simply is an expressive value.

Isness is being what and who you are; and whatever you are feeling, to feel it and to live the emotion. [Living] that emotion is the God of your being allowing you to participate in an adventure that perhaps is unheard of in this society; but when you do [participate], your Self is excelled and elaborated for it.

Isness is without judgement. Isness is loving yourself without judgement—doing the things that you feel without judgement; not that they are good or that they are bad, but simply because they are.

Living in Isness is living in the moment. It is living the adventure. It is living the feeling and loving who it is that is living it. That is a state of Isness, for that is what God is: an Isness who judges not you or anything, for all that you be is Him in **His** Isness.

To live in a state of Isness is to be what you are and not be despairing on what you are. Nor [is it] to judge what you are nor to lessen what you are but to love it, for there is a reason you are the way that you are, and that is for the beautiful experience of the value which you are learning.

The Soul hungers for that which it has never experienced before. The reason that you have a Soul is to occupy thought [so] that thought can have a basis of reality through feelings or emotion. When the Soul hungers for an experience, it means [that] it lacks the data from that experience. So, it draws a feeling [that] captivates the whole entity to be emerged upon the adventure to gain the wisdom for itself.

And then, when the experience of Isness is finished and the emotional storm has subsided, the adventure and all that it was worth gained something that surpasses gold and time and beauty. It advanced itself into wisdom, which is indicative of the Soul saying to you, "You never have to do this again, for you have already experienced it." Then the Soul will take on [another] hunger, and the entity will be drawn to do other things because it **needs** to.

Isness is being what you are and loving what you are--even if no one loves you for that. Worry not if they do or don't; only concern yourself with you. Then you are living in the totality that God meant you to live in. What you are goes beyond beauty. And it goes beyond perfection. And it goes beyond that which is termed "right and wrong." It goes into Destiny, into the Fulfillment of Self--that is the only thing that is important.

You are loved from an unseen Source that loves you greatly; that is even greater than the seen Source. And all your secrets **are** known; and all the things you have done **are** known. But are they weighed against you? No. And for what you feel you must do, that is understood. You are not judged any less. You are not judged; you are loved, for you add to this eminent whole. Remember that.

*

You cannot understand the great stars beyond the solar system, [you cannot] see the things that the eye cannot see until you have loved yourself enough to have given sight to Self without criticism. To reach out in thought [and] grasp ahold of knowledge that this world has not yet possessed, you have to love yourself. And, in all essences, that is the greatest reward there is.

If Self is "bizarre" and "weird" or "enchanting," that is all right: Self needs to be that way. And if there are critical eyes on that and you fall vulnerable to other's criticism, then you will always deny what is the truest nature of Self because it is not acceptable by others. Then you [will] pass this plane and come back over and over and over again, only to get lost in future ideals because you never established the premise of Self-love.

Whatever you are, love yourself for being that way. And do not become vulnerable to the criticism of others. Let no one separate you from your God, and that is what that means. And soon, this wonderful thing of Self-love will bloom into a wonderful flower. And entities will come from all over to smell the perfume and fragrance; and they will test you, for you will be unique and different, and true happiness will abide within your being, naturally.

I am happy when I am oppressed, for that is simply how I am expressing. I am happy when I am depressed; I am simply expressing that. And I am happy when I am pouting; I must be or I wouldn't be doing it! And I am happy when I am laughing; it rolls my whole being into fervorous excitement that allows a little weight to fall off. That is being joyous with Self.

When you have come to the point to love your beautiful being, you will pass this plane in a sliver of light, for there will be nothing heavy about you any longer, and there will be nothing that will cling you here any longer. And you will birth all the stars and all the heavens to come; you will be a part of their activity.

It is simple to reach God. Reach yourself! That is where you find Him.

*

Finding out who you be will never happen, because who you be be the continuum of Thought. You be singularly the continuum of what I refer to as God. And how do you know God? Only when you have become everything in the moment that is expressing itself--and that is into Eternity!

To know yourself is to have the quest for existence that goes on and on and on, for it will take that long to know who you are. You will never have a point of understanding that you can

"The Love of Self on a daily basis is accepting the emotions that Self is experiencing, learning not to judge them, [but] allowing them to be. If you are feeling a certain way, feel it until you are tired of feeling it; then simply change your expression [and] it will change in a moment."

say, "Alas, this is who I am!" for in the next moment of consciousness, of being God, everything will have changed in will into the next moment of Future. So, [in trying to] identify Self according to the frivolous wills [of others] and an advancing time, one never knows who he is.

To assimilate that you are God is to assimilate that you are all things. And because you are all things, you are open to the nature within your being to change. And how wonderful that is! Why would anyone want to be stagnated, caught in a moment of time, when all eternity passes him by? That would not be good for any one thing, and, fortunately, that doesn't exist.

To know who you are is to understand your feelings at the present. But greater, it is to accept the flow of change within yourself. When you accept that you are vulnerable to future tense and that you are vulnerable to wills, then you are God!

So, I would not wish for you to categorize yourself. I am desirous of you to become a master, lord of your being: to have dominion over the weaker aspects of life that would have dominion over you, that you can put them into proper priority to give you a greater sight to see yourself, that you can advance this wonderful enigma called time, that you grasp all that the Father has to give without anything holding you back.

What this means in simplistic terms: Who are you? You are an entity energy that has consummated itself into mass, matter. What you feel this moment may change the next. Understanding that you are God that has such options is one who can love himself in freedom to exercise those options.

Be who you are--now! And if this now changes in the nows that are yet to be born, so be it, for that makes up the fundamental Self that is called God. And love yourself for everything that you are, above all things.

*

You know, you are composed of the only reality that exists: You! You cannot understand other people, you cannot even give credence to anyone else, because you cannot **feel** for anyone else. They remain an enigma or mirrors that reflect the actions that you already identify within your own divine Self.

When I say unto everyone that life is the only reality there is and [that] all of this **is** an illusion, I am speaking a most profound truth. The only reality is feelings, and that is what one possesses in the innermost parts of his being. **That** is reality!

To know one's Self is to know how one feels. Always know who be you. And never become defeated [if] you utterly fail to understand the masses around you. God doesn't expect you to; only to [understand] what you are, and that is the singular most

"Always, above all things, have Self first and its joy and happiness. For if you ever betray your Self, entity, you have betrayed the justness of God and Eternal Life. The refusal to recognize that, entity, is a fool! Do you understand?"

important reality of all.

If you did not have you, you would not be able to see the color on this plane or [feel] the wind in your hair like a caress. If you did not open up to feelings, the world would be an illusion and a dream, for without you it is nothing. So the value of Self is of the uttermost importance, for without it nothing exists.

In being in this simple form, in allowing the emotions to emerge in this simple form and allowing you to be appreciative of you, however you be, you are loving God in the highest form and appreciating life in the grandest form. I am desirous of you, master, to love yourself, infinitely, and to appreciate yourself, infinitely. And whatever ails you, appreciate yourself for the feeling of that. And give value to life because you are here, entity, to give credence to it.

Always, above all things, have Self first, and its joy and happiness. For if you ever betray your Self, entity, you have betrayed the justness of God and Eternal Life. The refusal to recognize that, entity, is a fool! Do you understand?

*

You can wallow in as much melancholy and self-pity as you wish; there is nothing wrong with that. When it is a permitted principle, you will soon get tired of it and go on to something more thrilling because it can become tedious and boring. Removing it and making you do something else does not render it; knowing it is all right renders it.

Being melancholy in your various moods is really an exploration of Self. You will learn more about yourself when you are in such somber states, and there you truly go to where you would never venture before. You'll go into darkened places and there you will bereave yourself until an answer flows through you to light it up. [That is] the way one heals.

It is all right to be [melancholy]: it is very productive, it serves a purpose. And it makes you happy doing it, for [otherwise] you wouldn't do it.

*

This plane is the most restricted and the utterly most limited because it is the lowest frequency of all other existences. We have called it, very much so, the Plane of Demonstration, for a pure thought and a pure spirit enters into a matter of flesh [and] then becomes vulnerable to the pain, the hunger, the transitionary effects of thought over the body. And then the body becomes scrutinized by other embodiments. And Man sets up very soon a cloistered ideal as to how everyone should be, taking the individuality away from each entity in doing it. And then, you must not only put up with the body, but you must also put up with the ideal and live according to the ideal. And so a pure thought and a pure spirit has become very scrutinized and not so pure any longer.

When you are fighting such odds from a purity of thought and you are swayed by a consciousness that is poisonous with limitation, it is very difficult, entity. [Even] saints have been in their moments [that] their despair is so great they would have laid [down] and died in a moment rather than feel the wretched pain and agony of such diversity upon this plane.

So you are not alone [in your depression]. [Many] feel this severely, indeed, because they are sensitive [to] thoughts around them that are far worse than words are. Most people in my beloved family and yours and those [on this plane] have all felt depression.

The sweetest time in life is when you are a little girl or a very old woman. When you are a little girl, it is play, endless hours of frolicking with little reponsibility save school. And when you are older, you have passed that which is termed the focal point of beauty here, so you no longer have to struggle to impress anyone. You can relax and be who you are and be happy with yourself and watch the world in all of its frantic illusions trying to accomplish a "meaningless" dream. But the interim is a very direful point.

I have had such days, entity. But I tell you this: **allow** yourself the depression. When you have had enough, you will surface out of it and you will become wiser for it. And each time you go into your oppression again, it will not be so devastating as it used to be. To **avoid** depression, that is the worst thing you can do. Allow yourself to frolic in it so that you know what it is, and then come out of it. That makes you strong. That also gives you wisdom to understand. In depression, all of the frivolousness is removed and the blatant realities of feeling are left there to look at. And in that understanding, entity, one begins to know himself a great deal better.

This plane is of the test of fire, I will assure you. If you pass this plane with all things intact and wisdom gained without ever being brutal upon your beautiful being, then you become a God of the seventh level--and **that** is how it is! It is very easy to live only one lifetime here and dare never to come back. And I would say altogether that that is perhaps the wisest move anyone can make!

My sweet lass, the reality is that you exist and that you feel all of these things. Learn the lesson of judgement and do not impart blasphemous things upon your beautiful being, that when you do fall into the enigma of the realities of oppression that you understand precisely that that is what it is. And do not look for others to despise you or make yourself feel less than what you are because you do that.

Conquer love of Self, entity, by loving yourself, no matter what. And if individuals ask you, "Are you happy?" say, "Indeed, I am happy when I am oppressed and depressed." That is a good way to speak.

*

Confusion is an emotion that truly equates the word "options." When you have many options to consider, oftentimes your being will be caught in a state of confusion. This state is an emotional state brought forth by the Soul. It is a divine and proper act to be confused, and it is nothing to be ashamed of or feel wronged of.

When you decide what it is you want to do, it will become very clear within your beauteous Self. But until those moments arrive, be patient and allow yourself to contemplate and be confused. Confusion is a necessary and scientific emotion.

And another thing--Don't ever be rushed into your decision. Allow it to come from straightaway knowingness; that is living God right within yourself.

*

There are no degrees of how one does in this kingdom; there simply aren't. There are, however, that which is termed levels of **feelings** of how one is in this kingdom.

You are always God; even in your unhappiness, in your vulnerable state, in your displeased Self, entity, you are still God. And how does one rate that which is termed "omnipresence," indeed divineness? You cannot. That is why improper, unsuitable words as these were created to describe and communicate something that is beyond words. You always are, even when you are unhappy.

When you are unhappy, it is all right to be that way. Everyone thinks it is wrong to be unhappy. It is not! Unhappiness is the birthpains of a realization of **another** realization which means [realizing] another feeling which comes heavily impregnated with wisdom--another pinnacle of life.

You should have the pleasure to be unhappy. When a person gets that way, they are ready for that which is termed changes; they are ready--the peach is ready to fall from the tree, you see? It is a pleasure to be that way; it is the only way change can ever come or be accepted.

So, in order to remember that which is termed your God-self, you never have to remember it, you simply have to know it. Knowing it is living it and understanding that it is all right to be unhappy.

You know, master, in my life I was unhappy a great deal of the time, as you would ascertain time to be in moments to moments. But in that unhappiness, there birthed from ignorance, and pestilence, and a barbarian, a great and immaculate truth, a frontier for adventure for the whole of Mankind. I only had to be unhappy with myself to realize that truth.

CHAPTER SIXTEEN

LIVE IN THE FOREVERNESS OF NOW

"If you do not know how to fulfill this moment, it will never be fulfilled in the future to come. Now is when live must be experienced—and only in this moment! As the next moment progresses, you are moved into the next moment of progression, and into the next and the next. If you try to live ahead of that, you will never know what life is, for you will have escaped the very moments that have permitted you to experience it."

"There is no past and there is no future. There is only the ongoingness of this Now; there is nothing else. This Now permits Eternity to follow; a future permits nothing! Everything that is lived in the Now that is a worry upon the future never permits [you] to be; that is how entities die."

LIVE IN THE FOREVERNESS OF NOW

Live For The Now

Live for the Now, for the future has yet to be designed. In living in the momentful Now, you never restrict or limit yourself; you allow yourself to simple be. When you are living in [a] "future tense," you take away your ability to be free, for you will labor for something that is [only] conjecture in the future, hoping for that time to bring you fulfillment, when [it is] the Now [that] brings fulfillment.

If you do not know how to fulfill **this** moment, entity, it will never be fulfilled in the future to come. Now is when live must be experienced--and only in this moment! As the next moment progresses, you are moved into the next moment of progression, and into the next and the next. If you try to live ahead of that, you will never know what life is, for you will have escaped the very moments that have permitted you to experience it.

Live for the Now. This purposeful Now will make the Nows to come great and more valuable.

*

The "river of God," or the "river of Thought," is endless in the ideals that can be brought forth and implemented into this, your society, into this, your "vibration." But it only comes to one who lives into the Now and thinks not of the future. What is the "future?" How can it be seen? It is only seen through a film called "Now"!

When you live for the future, you have not lived **this** moment; you have lived an expectation, and that is conjecture. If you live Now and speak forth what you need Now, what you want Now, in the Now the ideal, the door, the runner, will come forth, but only when you learn to live "properly," and that means living this moment.

There is no past and there is no future. There is only the ongoingness of this Now; there is nothing else. This Now permits Eternity to follow; a future permits nothing! Everything that is lived in the Now that is a worry upon the future never permits [you] to be; that is how entities die.

"Time is the destroyer of life. Time is what makes you grow old. Time is what takes your youth away. Times is what takes your bones and makes them dust.

You know, master, time is such a reality here, it is an unreality! Can you reach out and touch an hour? And they question if I am real!"

Time: The Abominable Enslaver

This plane is the only plane with darkness; it is the **only** plane with darkness. Thus, you have a day filled with wondrous light and an evening, when the enchantress is in the mood, with some light. But if you look into your blue sky, my dearest master, you will see there is not a calendar. And if you look into your water, there is no clock. And if you look to the wind to tell you what year it is, it will blow you hat off!

Now, we must presume from that that if "time" is not in the fundamental understandings of what your nature is, [then] life is merely an existence that is ongoing in its cycles of nature; and we must presume [that it is] Man that indicated and evolved time for an understanding. Indeed.

As long as all of my beloved brothren live for the future, [they] have lost the Now. And you know why they live for the future? For they go and labor in order that in a future time they are paid a pence for it, and the pence is counted on labor, measured by time, that determines their worth; thus, they live in the future. You see?

Burn your calendar. Live your moments as they come. When you [project your desires], your projections are meted out **Now**; their fulfillment is in the Now--the Now, the Now, the Now!

Live for the moment. Life is in the moment; it is not "in time." Time is the destroyer of life. Time is what makes you grow old. Time is what takes your youth away. Times is what takes your bones and makes them dust.

I understand the difficulty here when an entirety is based on time. The only way that will ever be obliterated is when the Great Light comes as the end of your century closes, for the enlightened entities will not be enslaved by the illusion, the enigma, time.

You know, master, time is such a reality here it is an unreality! Can you reach out and touch an hour? And they question if I am real!

[Time] must be [reckoned] with individually, [by each] man [determining] his own understanding of what a moment is: individually and in his own way befitting his own attitude and his own kingdom. It is up to you to decide how you wish to live and how your moments will be counted.

If I put you in a wondrous place, master, that had [no] windows in it, and I took away the water mill and the water clock, and I put in there entities that all looked alike, and I put you [there] for two days straight without any light changes, do you know you would not sleep when it was "time" to sleep; that you would find your belly empty way past your time to have sup

"When you start living by feelings, not times, everything you have ever wanted shall come forth and be born within the spectrum of your grasp—if you only allow it."

and way past your time to breakfast, that perhaps your sup would be at midnight and your dinner at noon!

You see, if I did this to you, then you, my beloved master, would live according to your **needs,** not according to a clock that says it is time for you to eat, or it is time for you to sleep, or it is time for you to worry, or it is time for you to hurry, or it is time for you to rush. You see? So how does one make such a "room" possible? In his attitude!

This kingdom enslaves itself for things, and most things are unseen, unfortunately, like "future." [In] this kingdom, [there] will come a day when none have to work for the other. When a master becomes a master, do you know he does not toil in the field? The bread is manifested before him. Do you know that he need not go to the marketplace to purchase, from some pence he has earned, a meager and humble wool for this shoulders? You see, he manifests it for himself! **That** is the privilege of being a master! That is why it is worth **becoming** a master. That is why all [should] put all that they have into making themselves greater. And all [should] put themselves in such a place that that greatness can surely come without the interactions and interruptions of those that would limit it or enslave you.

Ideally, [a] God does not have to work for anyone. And, ideally, [a] God's garments are God. Where [else] would he get them from? You see, you are still stuck on this plane in saying, "How can I deal with time?" when I keep calling you a "master." What you should be dealing with is not "time," but you, the master, becoming greater than it!

Time is an abominable enslaver. It is the greatest enigma you "non-believers" believe in! You can't even **see** a moment or an hour, yet you [only] believe in [things] that can be seen. Well, believing only in what can be seen is an unseen enslaver!

Time is not dealt with in the Ongoing Isness, for there is no such thing. Time only rushes you into your hour of death. It ages your beauteous being. Time oppresses, depresses, and causes neurosis in you. Why worship you this terrible enslaver?

I do not give credence to time. I give credence to seasons. Indeed. Everything has its season and what is called "its change." When I walk with you and move with you, I do not move with you in your time—and never will I! But I will move on you when the Soul is the tenderest, when it is ready for the experience. And if it be a hundred years from this moment, it will still be. Or a day. or another moment, or a year—it will still occur.

You are so impatient! When you start living by **feelings,** not times, everything you have ever wanted shall come forth and be born within the spectrum of your grasp—if you only allow it.

*

"The only reason that anyone grows old is that they are expected to; they think 'old.' They have days that celebrate, in great hosts and with all sorts of frivolities, their birthday. Treacherous entities that celebrate getting older, [for they are] hurrying with great laughter and expediency to dying.

When you do away with [such] things [as birthdays] and 'age' and the concept of 'eternity'—and astrologies—you will do away with aging and dying."

Time is a powerful illusion here. And for time, you have learned to measure distance laterally. Thus time is the ruler of the illusion of moments [that are] measured by distance measured. The Now provides no time and no measurement. Thus, the Now was a million years ago, and as I speak to you this moment, one million years from this moment will you see me speak to you again--in the same moment. Because it is all in the Now and it is not measured by time and lateral movement, thus is my reach into forever. Where I am with you Now, this moment, will I be with you in this same moment ten years from this Now, but Now. I have the capacity to do this, for I do not love and worship and adhere to time; nor, entity, do I adhere to measure. I adhere to Thought, the sublime magic that created all of this illusion.

How do I know you? I become you in the moment I speak to you. And in the moment I become you, do I open the door for that which you will need this year, two years, four hundred years to come. In the same moment, I have already done it. But you, you must live in time in order to accept that. I am the Runner of the Future. I am the Manifesting God of this Now. It is already finished--for everyone here.

*

The Soul cannot help but live in time, for it is encased within an entity that is continuously producing itself life after life after life after life, whose ending and beginning of life is dictated by time, the illusion. The Soul never changes its continuousness--which is called "forever." Time equates an ongoingness that is measured and weighed; but foreverness is the Now; it is the continuum. The Soul is also continuum.

[If] you cease in time and start the beginning of Now as forever [so that] this Now is all that is important, the Soul will continuously record "now" rather than hours that are indicative of what you call "birthdays" that advance you into death.

Live Now, entity, and the Soul will regulate the hormone activity within the body that allows the body to sustain itself in an equallum that is called "Now."

The only reason that anyone grows old is that they are expected to; they think "old." They have days that celebrate, in great hosts and with all sorts of frivolities, their birthday. Treacherous entities that celebrate getting older, [for they are] hurrying with great laughter and expediency to dying. When you do away with [such] things [as birthdays] and "age" and the concept of "eternity"--and astrologies--you will do away with aging and dying.

"To be impatient is to acknowledge time. And to acknowledge time in the pursuit of being impatient means that you are rushing to your death.

Every moment that you do not live in ease and acknowledge the Now as being the Now Forever is called being impatient, [and] the moment will slip by into an eternity, and the ending of your life shall be in moments away. That is what impatience brings the entity. That is the acceptance of time and the acceptance of death."

In the beginning of the onslaught of Man, even unto as close as three thousand years ago in your time, entities were living until their five hundredth year. Only [when] Man became what you call "civilized" and limited, did his life span shorten. When the calendar was created, so was the ending of the life span of Man. That is a truth.

[Time, an] illusion? Indeed, but the most awesome [one] that rules this plane, for you are permitted to act only within the realm of time: that warrants and limits the activity of an entity upon the Plane of Demonstration.

You know, your Soul does not have any wrinkles on it! The Spirit that often walks in front of you, brilliant light, has always been a brilliant light. And the immortalness of the Soul that you have, that you could not occupy thought **unless** you had it, never changes. It only equips itself with the wisdom of experience and the virtue of adventure that allow the reasoning part--the Spirit, Soul, and Ego--to come together and be poignant in its decision and attitudes.

Patience: The Master Of Time And Death

Patience does not mean, entity, that you are sitting there, waiting for the world to turn over on its side and burp! It means you are in a state of "being." Patience is merely being, being. Your state of being will be different than anyone else's state of being, for then you are without pressure, you are without demand, and you are allowed to create. Being is the most magical thing anyone can do for their illustrious Self, for then they remove all the "have to's" and get down to living how they really are. It is an art.

*

To be impatient is to acknowledge time. And to acknowledge time in the pursuit of being impatient means that you are rushing to your death. Every moment that you do not live in ease and acknowledge the Now as being the Now Forever, every moment you do not do that, it is called being impatient, [and] the moment will slip by into an eternity, and the ending of your life shall be in moments away. That is what impatience brings the entity. That is the acceptance of time and the acceptance of death.

Patience is a most admirable virtue, for in it an entity learns to live Now and see that his kingdom has manifested Now, and [that] whatever he is wishing for his future to bring, he only has to feel it in this Now, for in the tomorrow to come, which shall be another Now, that which he has felt shall manifest.

*

Patience is the master of time. Impatience is the victim of it. To be impatient, entity, is to never know love, for love is outside of the providence of time. It is outside of the providence of measure, degree, calculation. When you become patient, you become not only the master of time and illusion, but permit love to occur; and that brings peace and joy and happiness and understanding, and that I will have you find. If it takes an eon, lord, for that to occur, it is worth it; it is worth it. Then you can experience love and you cannot be the victim of your own "untimely" death.

*

If you can go faster than the Father goes, entity, or go unto that which He has aligned Himself to produce, that which is called "infinity," then you have a right to be impatient. If you could, you would not be the molecular structure you are; you would be pure Thought, for only thought contemplates infinity and its end, for only thought is expedient enough to reach infinity that never ends. Thought is the thing that make infinity a space.

Impatience means you are trying to become something, yet you have not affixed the realization of what the something is in your being. That is impatience, entity. How do you get over that? By becoming the knowing of what the ideal is that you are impatient about becoming. Once that is known, you need not be impatient again, for you will have acclaimed yourself to it.

The greatest usherance of death in this experience and in that body is from stress. From stress, entity, the body is geared, and it wears and it tears and will shorten its life span by half. An impatient entity, one who hurries through moments, is rushing towards his death.

Every moment that you watch your clock or count the hour glasses, entity, or watch the sun come up and go down and feel that the whole time has been spent uselessly, that day has been lost to you and life forever [and] you are running toward your death. If you continues to live in this type of anxiety due to impatientness, one day it will all be finished and your desire for impatientness will all be granted, for that is how the Soul works.

The Soul, entity, is the subconscious being that controls the life flow within the body. It also controls the death hormone within the body. When entities live impatiently or they live by that which is termed affixed time, they are living at a much [more] hurried rate than that which is very relaxed and enjoys the moment and lives not for tomorrow but for the Now, as everyone should. They will outlive you, everyone of them, for your Soul is gearing for you to die.

If impatientness is worth an early death to you, then by all means, go and do it. But there is not one person or one thing or one ideal or one experience that is worth your anger or your impatientness, entity, for there is not one of those things that will die for you—not one of them!

There is no illusion, entity, like Now. Now is the greatest place to be in. When one has all of his aura intact, entity, life is the most expressive and the most exquisite treasure there is. In that, one can discover love, adventure, self-esteem and self-gratification.

Never escape Now; there is no place like it. Live this Now like it was forever. Love this Now like it was forever. And to be unkind [and] uncompassionate to anyone, [it] is not worth it, for that only brings inharmony within the being and destroys the Now.

Love everyone. Allow them to be who they are, for the are expressing God, just as you be. And when you love them, your worries become less, master, because you allow them to be; then you allow yourself to be; then this life blooms.

*

Now, a little advice: Give unto that which is termed your Self the acts of humility and do not expect of your Self any more than you can readily comprehend. And what you can comprehend [that] you can be, **be it,** to the grandest of all that you are. And then, when you have filled that space and begin to grow and there's a little void there, expect to be even grander, and you will be! But do be kind unto you and allow [yourself] to express for a little while. Have mercy on your being. It will grow if you do so.

*

Searching: The Illusive Quest For Fulfillment

No, entity, there is no "search." If you think there is a "search," that you must continuously search, do you know that you will never "find," for each moment your priorities as to what the search will bring you will always change.

There is no search; there is only Now, living in this Now and who you are. That is the totality of the only reality there ever was and ever will be. If you go out searching for whatever it is, you will never find it; you never do. If you live in this moment and love the God that you are and the beautiful entity that you are and know that you can create from your mind whatever you wish, that is fulfillment, that is expression; that is not searching. And, after all, isn't fulfillment the end of what everyone conclude a search to be? Fulfillment is already here. Simply be.

My truth has differed from yours, for yours means that you must go outside of your embodiment to find a Christ, to go outside of your embodiment to find a God, to live arduously in search of fulfillment that will always be outside of you, when I will ask [that] if they are all outside of you, then what is ever the use of being who you are? Mine says they already **are** you, that you are **all**, entity, that you ever need and that there is no one, no one, greater than you—no one. If you realize that, then you have all that you have thought to be existent outside of you; it will come forth like a great well from your own being.

Your truth has said, entity, that this harmonious and inharmonious life is meant to search or to equalize or to balance in order to learn, when I say that all those thoughts are certainly true, for as long as one knows them to be a reality through the process called "belief," then they will be. Then one is never fulfilled nor is he ever happy, for he has set in motion a precedence for himself never to obtain. How pitiful to never obtain.

But the same thinking can be reversed and everything [will be] Now, explicitly complete Now. Then you are fulfilled every moment. Then you are all you ever wanted to be every moment. Then you never leave this life feeling like you ever lost anything; you leave this life for a greater adventure.

Change the way you think and speak, and your whole life will change, entity. All of your dreams will come to pass, in spite of you; but I will have you know that no one brought them into being other than you.

*

Master, do you know how oftentimes the flow of genius has tried to get through the receivers who fight it by dismissing it as "imagination," or dismissing it as "unintelligible," or dismissing it because "it is not applicable to theory?" All of the time! In this life that you are trying to accomplish here, what has been the answer for you and the "carrier" that will carry you through it, you have dismissed because it is too simple.

In letting yourself "flow" and "be," you will not fail, you will not lose track of you--or those who are trying to change you. In being, entity, means you cannot come from the central focal point **of** being; you simply are there: there are no degrees to it. Be who you are.

You know, searching has its merits, for truly, when you search, you will find something. Unfortunately, it is not always the something that we need because it puts us back into search again. If you just are, entity, and allow yourself to live completely in a moment, unobscured by contemplative thoughts of an unattainable future that cannot even be imagined, for it is not even conceived, and quit struggling against a harsh wind, the answers and what you are looking for will come, first in thought. Then you will not have to search; then you will not have to go through arduous training, as it were, philosophy, as it were, schooling, as it were. In being, you will lead you to what you need to know, for the Soul recognizes what it is lacking. It, entity, will show you what it needs, but only in a state of being.

Do not struggle; it will get you nowhere. And if you go looking for [answers], entity, you will not find them in what is termed the "obvious" places; I wish you to know that.

Goals: The Forerunner Of Failure

When you set many goals for yourself to achieve in this lifetime--some for your teaching, some for your learning, some for your loving, and some for your being--then you relinquish [in this life]. Don't set so many goals; then you can start to live, and the moment is superb when it happens. You [may] say, "Alas, master, we cannot do this; it is not practical in our society." Well, society is not even practical.

Goals are well and good, but they are also indicative of failure, and that, entity, brings many entities to grow up into this life being very conscious of failure. Learn to live in this Now and **this** moment. Allow yourself the flow.

Routines that you can set are understandable, but never make out that which you attempt to achieve in that routine. Simply allow the days to come, and whatever will be in those days, allow them [to] be. You will find your whole life changed and enriched.

And, after all, you who have been seeking so much enlightenment, so much knowledge--high and low you have been looking for it--you will never get it or understand what you have

"When entities look back into their past for answers, they never find answers for their futures, for they are too busy [with] their heads backwards to see the Now when it comes."

been looking for until you allow yourself the life to find out about it.

Past Lives: Looking And Living In The Past

Every person that you lived to be was different than what you are now. What you are this day is a direct result of all that you have ever been. And what you are now is greater than you have ever been before. You would not even know who you once were nor recognize it because you have refined the element called "Self" to a point beyond the recognition of what once was. That which you once were, if they were to look upon Self this day, they would call you gallant, a genius, a heretic; they would call you "possessed"; they would call you many things, for you are beyond their understanding even in those days.

When entities look back into their past for answers, they never find answers for their futures, for they are too busy [with] their heads backwards to see the Now when it comes.

I have also found that entities fantasize about their past in a most romantic, heroic fashion, for when life here is very plain, dull and boring, they can always conclude that they were very heroic in battle; they left many woman behind weeping for them; and when they did return, the whole town turned out in a celebration that lasted for eons. Or they were more beautiful than any woman in the world at that particular time and had every man as a lover in those days. But I say to you that the present is far greater than anything I have just mentioned in the past, for the knowledge is greater.

*

You have all lived many lives. Your lives have been illustrious, romantic, barbaric, infamous, famous, no things, some things, part things, all things! They have been everything! But I will tell you a truth: All that you were then is not as grand as you are now. You are the greatest you have ever been, entity, for you are the cumulative knowledge and experience of all the lives you have ever lived into this Now. You have never been better than you are now, no matter the disguise or the illusion or the experience.

Those who continuously look back into the past to find out who they were they are never finding a future and never know the Now, for all of their Yesterdays make up their Nows, which causes an entity to be less creative, less prosperous, less loving of himself and insecure.

Learn to live in the Now—the greatest life there is, the greatest being there is, the most beauty there is. Be grand in this life and experience you. Ride the wind, entity; sail a thought to the moon; lay a splendid thought on the Sun that it will know who you are; sit upon a star; speak to the water. That is all you, it is all God, it is all life—the greatest purposeful reality there is when all else is illusion.

*

CHAPTER SEVENTEEN

BECOME: BE CHANGEFUL, BE ONGOING

"When you change, you do not lose yourself. Change occurs not by becoming something else, but by removing the things that inhibit [your] seeing the totality of yourself. This is what is called 'becoming,' an appropriate word."

"Change, 'tis the key that opens the Door to Eternity. Change provides change provides change provides change. And of all those wondrous adventures, there is not one thing within them that is fearsome, that should take your life from you, that indeed would leave you crippled and sad. Not one.

The wonders of that which is termed the Father is that It never ceases. Always accept change. Always."

BECOME: BE CHANGEFUL, BE ONGOING

Change is never a retardation, for if the Father is ongoing, evolving, expanding movement, then what the Father would have to do would [be] to stop going onward and go back the way He came. That is what people fear change is. But the Thought does not do that; It is an ongoingness. Change raises you above the ongoingness to another level, another attitude, another perception, but it never retards you or takes you back.

*

Go and find your adventures. Life is teeming everywhere. Unfortunately, because Man is so insecure and so much like a herd animal, he feels that if he leaves the herd and casts himself for the adventure, something is going to get him. Not [so]: he can only find greater things than what he left behind.

Man is a **continually** creative source, that the next moment holds majesty far beyond the moment that now [has] become the past. You can only better yourselves; you never degrade Self. Self cannot be degraded, and you cannot go backward in life, [for] life is ongoing.

The greatest treasure of life is not what one became in his working capacity or how much gold one earned or how much land he has or how many vineyards that he has or how great his fame is: that is very fleeting. What one does grasp in his life is that he lived his life in such a manner that everything that he did brought forth joy, and, indeed, because of that, his kingdom was fulfilled.

Do you know [that] in happiness, God's manifestation of the Source and the Force that flows through you--if you were to put it forth into that which is termed a mathematical understanding--is that which is termed fourteen billion times greater than when you are in sadness?

In happiness, genius is born! In happiness, indeed, the Glory of Self is created! In joy and happiness, peace becomes the tranquil state. In happiness, one becomes fulfilled; one knows the Kingdom of Heaven. So what is **worth** doing or laboring for that does not bring you happiness?

I urge you to reach out, entity, for you will have something to grasp if you do so.

*

"Those that are secure entities never know the vistas of a different land; they never know the adventures that await for them moment to moment to moment.

To break free is to go beyond, into the unknown that is speculative, conjecture, uncertain. And out there, entity, you have all the freedom to take, for the first time in your existence, your own God-given brilliance that you certainly are and apply it in a way that you deliver yourself from the enslavement of someone else's ideals and create your own. It gives purpose to an entity."

Freedom means having the adventure to create your own security. When you are secure means you are safe, but it also means someone else is taking care of you and **they** are having the adventures; you are reaping the benefits, but without doing or becoming or allowing your own creative brilliance to occur. You are a follower.

Those that are secure entities never know the vistas of a different land; they never know the adventures that await for them moment to moment to moment--and it is all creative. To break free is to go beyond, into the unknown that is speculative, conjecture, uncertain. And out there, entity, you have all the freedom to take for the first time in your existence your own God-given brilliance that you certainly are and apply it in a way that you deliver yourself from the enslavement of someone else's ideals and create your own. It gives **purpose** to an entity.

Secured entities are secured and safe from that which is called "predators," [but] they **live** fearfully. Entities that break out of this create their own boundaries and live in a state of perpetual happiness, for they are continuously creating every moment; they have to depend upon no one!

You cannot become in the shadow of someone else's ideal. You must become your own ideal. You must cast your own shadow to become what only **you** know you desire. And your destiny is to fulfill that in the moment you feel it is necessary. **That** is true security, but also the truest measure of freedom.

True warriors, true Masters, rebel Gods, they abhor being taken care of. A true Master, entity, a God creative, will go on the marshlands or the high plains in a great storm and weather all sorts of things for his freedom, for he is his **own** entity, his own individual--and he can lose nothing! They are the heros; they are the trendsetters.

To break away and Become is to ask Self what it wants, what it needs, where it would like to go, and then do it, little by little by little. Then you are creating a happy entity.

There are many who stay in bondage for contracts--marriages, indeed relationships, businesses--because everyone depends upon them. They never even thought that the greatest dependency of all is themselves, and they are denying [themselves] moment to moment to moment, and finally, alas, never know who they are when it is all said and done, for they have denied themselves for so long.

Become! Ask what you desire; it will manifest. Go the directions you wish to go. Feel! All of the things [you desire] will manifest for the greater glory of the God that is within you. And certainly your "boundaries" will change; adventure always changes them. But who is to know what lies beyond the next vista, what can be conquered there, what can be earned,

"[What] I am speaking of is asserting yourself, not that you be an image to humanity, but that you be the image to yourself that you are searching for simply by being what you are. For all the wondrous things that are, God knows you may be the next brilliant light that alas the world has been waiting for. But you shall never know, entity, until you pursue it and find out."

what can be measured from there. It is not risk at all--it is Life! And you will never starve or go unclothed, and the elements will not take their toll on you, for you are a free Soul; that kind of entity **controls** the elements. That is all you have to do.

The reason why everyone feels so insecure, the reason they don't know who they are, is that they are brought up in regimented spectrums as to how they should live, what they should do, what they should say, how they should act. No wonder they find themselves so utterly undesireable or "bastards" of the universe!

[What] I am speaking of is asserting yourself, not that you be an image to humanity, but that you **be** the image to yourself that you are searching for, simply by being what you are. For all the wondrous things that are, God knows you may be the next brilliant light that, alas, the world has been waiting for. But you shall never know, entity, until you pursue it and find out.

*

There is no such thing as a bad change. If the change, entity, was "bad," you wouldn't be changing in the first place; you'd be staying where you are! That is logical.

Now, all changes are good, for they create a different sphere of existence; they create forth, as it were, new entities, new enterprises, new adventures, and a greater way for us to know ourselves. All change is good. All!

*

Change should always be looked forward to, for it lets the waters run free within your being and does not permit stagnation to occur. Change offers adventure, and with adventure there is excitement, disappointment and all of those wonderful things that help to evolve you to a greater state of appreciation for yourself and perhaps others.

Change, when most make it, [they] are greatly disappointed, for it is nothing that they expected it to be. They wait for open arms and everything to be made ready for their debut into appearance and [for] everyone to notice, when most never do. But when all is settled and the reality of beauty is seen, the value of what has happened to Self is grander than any vision ever expected.

*

The greatest way to acquire that which is termed "growth" is not to measure yourself by anyone else. There is no one that you can say that you are less than or that you are better than or that you are equal with, entity, because you do not understand who you are yet. So, to look at someone else and to measure how far you have come is being most unfair to yourself.

Thus, you must ascertain what it is about your being that you love, like and dislike. And what makes you unhappy or you dislike, master, you can master the change in a moment. Of the realities that you have surrounded around yourself that you look at everyday in your time, and the relation of that object unto the Soul makes you feel unhappy, get rid of it! If it is clothing, jewels, if it is a hovel, if it is entities--whatever it is, whatever you look at [and the] association causes the memory of unhappiness or oppressiveness to occur, do away with it, entity.

It takes great strength and substance for any entity to do away with the things of unhappiness because he is throwing away his identity. You have kept these things and your moods and your tempermants because that is how you can equate that you are; that is what gives reality to yourself. If all in a moment the objects, memories, personages, hovels are thus thrust away from your being, then how can you identify yourself? Then you are left rather bare, entity; but you are **also** left peaceful, for there isn't any more unhappiness and the reminder of it. [And] what occurs in the void, entity, is adventure.

Everything that has created unhappiness started out an adventure. If one has learned to decipher the difference between joy and unhappiness, he shall be very careful into what adventure he is a particpant in and what things he brings unto his countenance.

Decorate your walls with things of joy. Put upon your being those things that make you happy, **regardless** of what the world thinks of how you dress. And be unto yourself all things careful to bring about that which is called joy, master. If you do this, you will elevate yourself into very much a level called peace, and there you can manifest the whole of the Kingdom of Heaven at your doorstep, because you have **room** to enjoy it.

Now, what is that called? Loving one's Self. That, in its first steps, takes great strength to do, but it must be done; it is a necessity. Once you do that, master, you will become fulfilled within your being and you will have happiness in your being. And once you have obtained that, you have a compassionate understanding of other people. You will **allow** them to do whatever they want to do because you realize it is a neccessity for them to learn the things they are learning. And in that, when you pull away the restrictions, you can easily love another. Then, master, you love like God loves. Then you will be complete in this life [and] will have achieved what it takes entities **eons** to achieve.

*

What is a future? Tomorrow? The next moment? One hundred years? What is that to you who hold onto yesterday. You will **never** have a tomorrow, entity, [if] you are buried in yesterday. And if all of your yesterdays are worth the sacrifice of tomorrow, then so be it; that is your truth [and] you shan't **ever** let go. But I tell you this: you [may] hold on, but when you are ready to let go, you shan't recognize anyone around you nor know where you are, for generations will have passed you by and you will be an old man who weeps in his sorrow.

You cannot undo yesterday; that is reality that has been coagulated of Thought, manifested, and belongs to the ages. Tomorrow is like a child: it is ready to birth itself into a ray of brilliance, freshness, vibrancy, and all to learn of a spectacular day that is to meet itself. Tomorrow holds the infinity of virtue in conquest upon conquest and adventure upon adventure.

Entities who hold on are never remembered. But that which lives in tomorrow, entity, and for its adventures, are called heros and seemingly take on the enigmatic ideal of the whole society.

*

Master, you know, everyone here holds out that which is termed their wondrous arms for showers of blessings, as I have heard the term called, and they all get them. What is, indeed, the difficulty in allowing them to come and doing someting with them is that often the showers of blessings mean a change. And Mankind, in his nature, is very much like the animals which the Gods created to be very herdlike. Man is very insecure, and he will always be that way to those that need him.

Problems, nonetheless, are secure, and entities hold on to them because it is something for them to hold on to and reflect upon that gives character, imagery to being. So, alas, when the utopia of happiness comes given to you--the blessings are here--it is up to you who are God, who possess that which is termed Divine Will, to allow the changes to occur [so] that the goodness, indeed the blessings, can manifest to fulfill the existence that you have.

The Father, the Source, continuously presses toward you your joy and your kingdom. But if you grasp to yesterday and to that which is turmoil and trouble and hurt and all the things that give credence to the value called you, you shan't realize the pleasure of the adventures of blessings.

*

Confusion is, of itself, when one reaches that which is termed a point to where he has nearly completed, yet has not accepted the completeness of his journey, and there is a new [adventure]

"The 'birth pains' of Self we call, in our understanding, 'divine fire.' That is the burning away of illusions that really entrap the splendid Light that is within you. It is letting go of the illusions, realizing that they are a no thing [and] that the true identity [of Self] is the spark of divine essence that emerges outward and is gleeful to the world, for it sees the world as a mirror of its own spectacular beauty."

pressing arduously at his door.

Confusion is, indeed, a state where many linger who are afraid to let go of the old, yet the old is boring and finished because it is familiar to them. And they are frightfully anxious to open the door to the new because it is the unknown; they do not have dominion over it and [they] fear they cannot be declarative as to what will come. Because of that, the emotion called confusion dominates the existence of the entity.

Master, there is nothing in the unknown, there in **nothing** in the unknown that can do anything to you except to make you greater. The unknown is the great adventure; it is the conquest, the acceptance of, the being a part of Majestic Life, wherever it is. But because it is not old and certain, it is fearful to your being because your life is governed by fear.

When you realize that there is nothing created that will ever put out your light, ever; when you realize that what is unknown equates unlimitedness, which equates "manifesting God," you will never be [confused] again; you will only want more, entity. That is when the fire becomes unquenchable; that is when Becoming becomes a very rapid movement and many lives take place in one lifetime. That is because the entity is ready for Life and all that it has to offer.

"Divine Fire": The Birthing Of Self-Love

If you want peace and happiness, then the Christ of your being [will] get rid of those things that have caused the unhappiness--the boring, the mundane--and reach out for those things that are guarantees of peace and happiness; and the transition is painful. It is the birthing of change. It is called, in ancient tongue, "arorist," divine fire. But the result will be peace and happiness.

*

The "birth pains" of Self we call, in our understanding, "divine fire." That is the burning away of illusions that really entrap the splendid Light that is within you. It is letting go of the illusions, realizing that they are a no thing [and] that the true identity [of Self] is the spark of divine essence that emerges outward and is gleeful to the world, for it sees the world as a mirror of its own spectacular beauty.

When the pain is getting quicker and deeper, it means you are coming forth like a babe coming forth from the birth canal: it is having to elongate its head and stretch its body and [is] being squeezed [by] great muscle pressure in order that it may grasp life.

When the Self is birthed, the pain will slowly become less and less, and the Love of Self--an entity that represents the spectacular essence called Life--comes forth. Then you are having to live for no images any longer, no ideals any longer, for no one any longer, except your own point of reference in your world.

And one day, you will arise from your wondrous bed, early in the morn when the dew is sweet upon the grass, and you will say, "Alas, it hurts no longer. I am what I am and 'tis beautiful unto my being." That is when God walks the earth, unfurled!

*

Master, when a woman births the fruit of her womb [and] a delicate yet heavy sibling is expelled, it is very arduous and very painful, but it is done in a state of grace and a state of love.

And behold, when the sibling comes forth expelled, and the mother, anxious to see that which she has housed and nurtured for so long, [hears it] cry or let out its first movement, the pain is readily forgotten and the child embraced, and the wonderful interaction of mother and child begins.

When you want more, when you want to become greater, when this becomes necessary, entity, only by simple desire, you are going to bring forth the pains: that is called [the] "fire" of the birthing of change. But when the child is expelled, when the change comes forth, the adventures and new beginnings are jolly good, and the pain is forgotten.

[When] you want to become greater, to understand more, the blocks, the limitations that you still live with within your little shell [will] be broken away, and they [will] tear away from your security. You have been secure on the premise of what you have been able to establish: that denotes Self, a reflector of sorts. But if change is in the making, the reflector will do no longer; it must be pulled away that something grander can take place. That is what is occurring--and you created it.

In the middle of childbirth, it is very difficult to say, "Ah, alas, if this would only go back up into my womb!" You want to get it over with. Now, it will pass, and those secure identities will be put into shambles, and brilliant and new reflectors will come that magnify you a little bit better.

*

CHAPTER EIGHTEEN

FOLLOW YOURSELF TO GOD

"I will tell you blatantly and emphatically: To become God is not [to] become in the image of another entity, including myself, for then you are denying yourself truth that goes beyond the teacher."

"All things that open our eyes to the possibility of other things existing outside of our limited, cloistered lives is always good, for it will lead us on, for where it ceases, master, [the one] who is becoming what he is seeking will surpass it and go on to further planes. It is a roadway of sorts, a stopping point, a well in the desert, that you have learned from it and gained from it.

Be who you are, master, not under the direction of Ramtha The Enlightened One or Buddha or Joseph or Yeshua, but be of the following of who you be, God that you are, unique that you are, supreme that you are, and set your own pace, for none can be a God for you or teach [you] of their Godself. You must be aware of who you are and what you are.

FOLLOW YOURSELF TO GOD

To put another man as an ideal is to limit the structure of your tranquility, your purpose, your dignity, your destiny, and give acclaim only to one who does not deserve it. If you were to put forth your own image, as it were, on your own neck, the knowledge, the becoming, would intensify a hundredfold, entity, because then the Source is properly directed.

Man can only realize that which is termed his Godhood, his enlightenment, his unfoldment, **through himself** and his proclaimed love of himself. Man cannot follow another and become the other, ever; he must follow himself to become that.

You are God. You follow **you**, you love **you**; chant unto you, "I am, I am," because there is nothing else. Then you'll become the wind, indeed, you'll become the Thought, you'll become the Forever. Put all that you've ever wanted anyone else to be into you and just be. Just become you, who are as beautiful as a morning sun, entity, and as mystical and magical as a starry evening in your time. Identify Self with Self: that is what I desire you to do. Then you will become the holy man, the divine one, indeed, because that is the only way to get there.

I will tell you blatantly and emphatically: To become God is not [to] become in the image of another entity, **including** myself, for then you are denying yourself truth that goes **beyond** the teacher.

That which is in the flesh, entity, and is vulnerable to death, has not known that which is termed Unlimited Life. In order for you to become the I AM, you must become the **individual** and not the small, intricate group that lives by the teachings of one man. That one man is not you or anyone else!

Becoming is a solitary process. Becoming is the self-acknowledgment of you, a divine principle that can gather itself up and be fertile and bloom in your own space. In order to be That Which Is, to go on to greater understandings, master, you must become solitary in your own truth.

I tell you, I am emphatic indeed on this, because if you ask, you are going to be told the truth and how it is seen and understood here because your life is important enough to be **worth** that! Master, I am emphatic about everything. That **is** who be I, but I am an even teacher, entity, and I teach what is even and how it is understood and how it is seen. And if one asks, I will give them the answer. If you don't want to know, do not ask. But I will be even in this and in all things. That is how it is!

"Do not live under the ideal or auspices of any one else. Follow no man to God. If you do, you shan't ever become that which you are following. You must live for the fire that is you. Hold and love your Self above all other things, for then you love God."

Whatever you think of me and what speak I, I do not care, for what feel I unto you shall never change, entity. Never. And that only became possible in searching for that which is termed God without dogma and limitations and expectancy of anyone except myself. So, [when] you come into this audience, I will tell you to let go and be unto **you** that which can sustain life, and to learn and to blossom, [and will] encourage you to be who you are. That is how it is.

I tell you, I don't have to make you into what I am or to clothe you all the same or [have you] put my picture around your neck or in your castle to love you. It is you and your beauty and your select individuality that I love.

The days of such followings and self-ordained teachers are coming to an end because the consciousness is beginning to change here by things that reach much further out that are unexplainable, that have a true science and a true relationship [with] life that is tangible. That is coming. The Mind of Man is coming to a greater understanding [in] which this shan't be necessary, and that is how it is.

I love you greatly. Stretch yourself to understand what I have just told you.

*

Entity, if you studied under ten teachers, you would be in even greater confusion, for [each one's] conception of "what is" will differ. But I will give you a clue to what settles good in your being: If it rings true in your Soul, it is. And the greater truth is: Anyone that teaches a limitation upon anything, entity, is not as advanced as some are.

There are great teachers on this plane that are "magicians," and they do wondrous things, but they still believe in death, and they will die. Even though they are great in what they have learned, they have not excelled beyond that, entity, to take it further and to take what they believe into a continuum rather than to death and dying and birth and life.

Is God limited? If He were, entity, Life would not be ongoing and you would not even have the ability or the option to be confused! Look at the simplicity of Life, its principles: it is ongoing and unlimited. That, entity, will give you a clue as to whether what you are reading is good for you or not. If you are reading of intellectual ecstasy that doesn't mean anything and leaves you only befuddled and baffled, it is an imbecile that is writing it. That is a truth! Who would ever write anything that a poor simpleton couldn't read? Listen to what is said and how they say it, entity. If it limits, separates, divides, then they need to take **their** life a bit further.

"If what you believe in your being is limited form, then that is your truth, and that is correct and precise. If you believe in an unlimited form, that is your truth, correct and precise. And if you are searching for something to believe in, don't believe in either—believe in you! At least there is some validity to you. Do you understand?"

I will tell you this: You may be confused all you would like, for my wisdom will only confuse you even more, for you will go to another and compare it. And I will give you [the] choice to do that. I am an Unlimited God who believes and is an unlimited God, and I see the progression of Man not in hierarchies, but in equalness of ongoingness; at least I give him a chance.

The equality of Man is the equality of God. To limit Man is to limit God. To limit God, [then] there is no thing. To separate Man from his divinity is to separate divinity from God. If what you believe limits the thought processes, it limits, indeed, the thought process of the Father.

All things are God, even the papyrus to which they put [their teaching] on is God! But to philosophize and to conjecture a proper teaching--I will tell you this: **You** are the proper teaching and learning. If what you believe in your being is limited form, then that is your truth, and that is correct and precise. If you believe in an unlimited form, that is your truth, correct and precise. And if you are searching for something to believe in, don't believe in either--believe in you! At least there is some validity to you. Do you understand?

Don't ever struggle with it, entity. Do not ever be arduous with the simplicity; then you complex it like everyone does. Believe in you. Write your own book and then be confused about that!

Love what you are. There is no thing, no entity, no thing greater than you are! That is a truth. You are the giver of your own truth, the dispenser of your own law; you are a sovereign. Do you know, entity, that whatever you want to believe in will be? Thus, all things are truth. So now you choose what be proper for you, what you wish to believe. No one of my being will say you are wrong.

There are those who firmly believe that the world is going to open up and descend upon Mankind in such a flurry and burn them off the face of their existence, and all kinds of abominable things. If that is their truth, let them believe in it. If we have the option to believe in a "positive" or a "negative," why not believe in the "good," why not believe in the positive mode? And then once you know that that exists, why don't you take it a step further and believe that all is and will always be? Then that rather frees you from confusion, for you have established your **own** belief--which everything is! That is all. So be it.

*

What you hear from a teacher, you are hearing **perceived** truth and how they see it, how they have learned it. And someone else will teach you yet a different understanding. What you are not grasping is that though they are right, so are **you.**

"The God within you speaks a very subtle tone; it is called feelings. The feelings manifest the path of enlightenment if you follow them."

What you learn from all of these teachers, inevitably, is that you are the greatest teacher, for only you and no one else knows what is best of all things for you. How **can** they know? They are busy living there own lives and assessing from **their** point of view. Only you know what is good for you. The God within you speaks a very subtle tone; it is called feelings. The feelings manifest the path of enlightenment if you follow them. Then, master, you will have assessed, lived and understood from **your** point of view--and it will all be right.

Live for what you feel inside; there is truth. And live it and manifest it to where it is the glory of you. Be your own teacher, your own savior, your own master, your own lord, your own God. That is how a true master lives.

*

In regards to a "guide," I will tell you a great truth: Those that hear what is termed "different thought waves" occurring to them, or hear the presence of another entity around them, think that the presence belongs to someone else, when the presence is their own divine Self called the Spirit of their being, which is the light field that surrounds the embodiment. When you pass from this plane, entity, it is that divine essence that guides you through the passing.

You do not have a guide, entity. What you have is yourself. [What] they call "teachers," "guides," and "gurus" and the like, in essence, entity, it is their own Self teaching Self! Purposeful explanations should never be given to an outside source; the credit should be given where it lies.

Your grand teacher is the "light" of your being called your Spirit. It, entity, is the keeper of the Soul. It, as well as the altered Ego, teaches the Soul. It is direct God, meaning it is pure knowingness, pure understanding, pure being. It may not be nearly so glamorous, as it were, as [having] another entity as a guide, but I assure you that there is no other entity that can comfort you and help you better than the Spirit of your being once it is enacted.

So what should you call the "voice" you hear, in proper form? "God!" And that is you. And if you speak to it, you will hear answers very clearly within your being. You **do** possess all knowledge. Know that, and allow it to occur to you.

*

What is sorely in error in this audience [is] that everyone thinks that it is prestigious to have a great many guides. But for them to be so arrogant to think that entities who pass into another existence have nothing better to do [other] than to stand

"You are your greatest lover. You are your greatest friend. You are Life personified in the beauty that you are! You are your greatest voice. You are your wisest man. None, none who pretend to be wiser than you or far greater than you can give you the truth of your own perfect being for they have found it not in theirs! And it matters not "the vibration!"

around and watch you all day--if that is what is awaiting for you, perhaps you should reconsider passing!

I have met entities that have **thirty** "guides," a whole host that is around and watching every move the entity makes! How boring!

*

Guides? I wish to tell you this: When you leave this plane, what do you think that life is after here? Do you think it is one continuous service of all of the outlaws on this plane? Nay, entity. Who wants to pass from this plane only to be a guide to you for the rest of your life? Do you not think there are better things to do?

There are not guides, entity; there is only Life, and this is one level of seven levels of **many** dimensions. And whosoever leaves here goes unto those dimensions that are best suited for them.

For any one to nurture this plane and to be a guide, as it were, unto [others] would be sort of like a penal colony, and there is none. You have no guide except that which is termed the God within you and the Spirit that walks before you, which is your **own** Spirit; that is the Eternal Self that has always been with you from the moment of conception of the Thought into Light. The Spirit of yourself walks before you and is often mistaken for another entity; but in truth, it is you, your great and wondrous, beauteous Self.

You, entity, are your caretaker--and the greatest of all of them.

*

What is called our "higher brothers" or "spiritual guides" or "teachers," they are of no good, master, until you have become **you.** There are no spiritual guides or teachers **greater** than the Spirit of your being, the God of your being. If you are so inclined to believe that others have greater wisdom, greater sources of amusement, greater guidance than you, then you know not of this "maiden" in life.

You are the totality of your being. It is better to align yourself to **you,** the Spirit of your being, [for] it has greater power and understanding than any of those that you give credit to. Thus, in this credence, find you, master. You!

Who be you? You are your greatest lover. You are your greatest friend. You are Life personified in the beauty that you are! You are your greatest voice. You are your wisest man. None, none who pretend to be wiser than you or far greater than

"You are an all-powerful entity, for you are a God. And God set you not free from His being unprotected, unguided. What was the guide? Free will, master. What is the protection? The Spirit of your being."

you can give you the truth of your own perfect being, for they have found it not in theirs! And it matters not "the vibration!"

You are an all-powerful entity, for you are a God. And God set you not free from His being unprotected, unguided. What was the guide? Free **will**, master. What is the protection? The Spirit of your being.

Speak from the Spirit of your being; it is beautiful, for it is the Source. And from it, all that is needing for you and your beautiful expression, so shall it be.

When you let others guide your life, you have no life to be guided to but only **their** hopes and aspirations. Be your own guide, your own teacher. And then those that are termed "spiritual friends" will be that: friends. And they will gain and love you for that which you are, for you are a source of enlightenment for the "seen" and "unseen". Do you understand?

I am a magician of sorts. Thus I give you the "magic words." They are: "From the Lord God of my Being, I call forth the God of my being into action, into now! Come forth! Give unto me life. And whatsoever its purpose or its direction, let it come." It is magic, for it works!

*

The sovereignty of man means complete freedom to express, not as "radical" movement, as it were, but as man to express man's individualized Godself will in accordance with man's sovereign kingdom--which is his life.

There are great masters in the land, and they are magicians of sorts, and they do wondrous things, save [they have] one great flaw: they believe in death, as it were, and they die! And another great flaw is [that] they believe in humanity as the rabble of the universe and of themselves [as] the deliverer. Though they are well and good in what they do, the explicit purpose of Man is to become God in his silent awakening and to live as himself: God unrestricted, in a co-creativeness with his own design.

Others can give unto us advice, and always we listen. But we also must learn to assess it in our own kingdom. If anyone takes you and replaces you according to **their** schemes and designs, and tells you [that] you must be this and must do that, and [you] must follow this law and this regulation and this writing and this and that, then you are not a sovereign God and a sovereign man: you are man the rabble, man the slaughtered sheep; you are not the shepherd.

Learn to be you, at your own will, and govern your life according to you. In what is termed "the final analysis," [each is soley] responsible for all his actions; and [in that], you [are]

parted from guilt, responsibility and enslavement through the entrapment of emotional feelings by those who care [about] you. So be it, man the sovereign!

*

CHAPTER NINETEEN

LABOR FOR THE JOY OF EXPERIENCE

"Whoever asks you, 'What will you be when you grow up?' tell them, 'I will be everything I have ever wanted to be as long as it brings me joy.' That is a wise man's answer. That is a grander way to experience unlimitedness."

"A very limited thing that that which is termed your family structure teaches here [is that] you teach and rear up your siblings to go into that which is termed the school processes, which supposedly is to teach; actually, it restricts the thinking process.

Then you impart upon them a very heavy responsibility: that they are to "become something"—a labor. And the more long-lasting it is, the more arrogant and self-respecting that is is supposed to be.

What a pitiful folly! To do one thing would be a life enslaved to boringness and misery, ending in cardiac arrest."

LABOR FOR THE JOY OF EXPERIENCE

When everyone seeks that which is termed a "labor," you know they seek it for a lifetime. What a bore! [When] you have manifested yourself to learn for yourself only one labor, that is not only limiting and boring, entity, that will also cause unhappiness, erracticness, and madness within your being in later times to come, for then you will have gotten yourself into that which is termed a "pickle" in order to survive.

When your labor no longer brings adventure, it is time to become something else. The greatest destiny that you have is the ability to learn **many** things.

What I have found unto those who have gone long and arduous into schools of scholarly limited understanding (which is always based on theory [from] someone else's point of view) and have spent so much time to procure a document that can be burnt in a moment [and] to learn what is called "an acclaimed profession," and if that is all they do, they are very limited; they are no more "intelligent" than the entity that experienced fifty labors in his life, for he has acquired knowledge from all of them, whereas the one solitary has only acquired frustration from his.

Whoever asks you, "What will you be when you grow up?" tell them, "I will be everything I have ever wanted to be as long as it brings me joy." That is a wise man's answer. That is a grander way to experience unlimitedness.

*

Lawgivers are well and good, indeed. So are weavers; they are well and good. The lawgiver be not distinctive from the weaver. The weaver works with his hands, and if he is to put forth mist linen in its finest, sweetest move, he weaves the woven substance in water, and his hands are raw, but his product is beautiful.

A lawgiver, indeed, he represents the justice or injustice [of] whosoever comes unto him. If he is pleased with that which he does, then that of his status is no different than the weaver, for the weaver is pleased with his mist linen and the lawgiver is pleased in his representation of justice or injustice.

Master, it is an illusion; it matters not [what you choose]. What matters is the attitude in which it is pursued and learned and gained. If you wish to be a lawgiver, you will do exceedingly well, as you would [if you wished to be] a weaver. It is how you think you will be: that determines your genuis or ingenius. Indeed. You see, it is not the labor that is supporting of you, but rather you that is supporting of the labor; it is your attitude. You could be a beggar and be one beautifully. You see, it matters not; it is how you do it.

There are unhappy weavers. They will not put forth the mist linen, for they desire not the rawness or the redness or the callousness upon their hands. Thus, they put forth the rough wools, poorly dyed. And there are lawgivers that do not represent those peoples that come unto them and barter for their freedom; it is what is called "selling them off." A good one never does this; those that are unhappy with what they do do this. You see?

Whatsoever you pursue, pursue it from the Lord God of your Being, indeed [from] the direction of your being. In doing so, beggar, weaver, lawgiver--whatever you choose--you will master it.

*

There is no gold worth the spending of one's life laboring in the fields, bent under the sun, if you do not want to be there. Labor at what you want to do. Find that which you choose to do, that you enjoy doing, that love you to do.

Man is a compulsive creator. If he cannot create, but only work under the assumption of another man and his ideal, he will never succeed, he will never be happy. Man must be his self-imposed creator.

Do not work because it is for gold. Labor because that which you are doing is creating, you are learning from it. Gold is only the "side effect," the "aftermath." Then you are living for you and creating for you. Don't do what you "have to do" any longer; put it away. Allow thought to enter and become compulsively creative. The gold will be drawn to you simply because you are living in perfect alignment. That is how it works.

*

Of all professions, know you who is the wisest on this plane, who has, indeed, the most esteemed profession of all, who learns more from his profession than anyone else? A bum! Why? For they live in the moment and do only what they need to do to live [and] to get to the next place; and so they have done a little of all things. In other words, they have an understanding of all labor; of law, for they are constantly avoiding it; of life, [for] they are always trying to understand it; and the pursuit of happiness, doing away with all things that eliminate it from their beings. They are the wisest teachers on this plane and have a lot to teach you who are striving for the stars and building it with a golden stair.

To be one professional entity is boring, it is stagnating, it is an atrocity to creative Self. You think you must do one thing, that that is the ideal here. Nay, it is not the ideal.

You will be the happiest in this life when you do what you want to do. If you will pursue life in the vein of it making you happy rather than in the vein of making gold to live through it, you will be the happiest man there is, for you will only work a little while, and then, when you are bored, you will find that there is another "door" that will open to you. And you shall go through that [and] do something else, and you will be jolly happy with that. And then, when you become a little bored, have gained everything [from it], another door will open to you. And on and on and on.

*

You will be successful in what you desire to do, for you love what you do. How can you fail at one thing that pleases you so greatly? How can you not help to experience and to become knowledgeable and expand your truth on that which you love?

You only accomplish readily where your heart is. It is when people succor after things that they do not love and labor at things that they do not love [that] they fail, for they expect failure and unaccomplishment. Thus, you will learn and you will grow and you will become better in what you desire [to do].

*

All labor helps you to know yourself, all labor, for how do you know that you can do all labor until you do it and then surprise yourself in the process? That is learning of one's ability and, certainly, of one's creativeness. Everything will teach you, master. If you be a worker in the field or a king who sits on the throne, they both teach you of yourself!

In regards to "purposeful design" and which [labor] hath the greatest importance on your being, gold never determined that, entity! It is how one feels about what he does: what makes him happy. You know, the worker in the field with his hands in the earth can be happy at what he does and [not] the king who sits on the throne. Thus, he will gain from his experience, for he has learned of happiness and joy; the king may have learned of misery.

Whatever you do, you will always know you; you cannot help from knowing you, for you are the possessor of the contemplative thought that contemplates the moment you are in.

*

"What you "need to do" is stop thinking you need to do anything! And if you are in a state of confusion about what you want to be, it means you are trying to make a decision to be something other than what you are."

What you "need to do" is stop thinking you need to do anything! And if you are in a state of confusion about what you want to be, it means you are trying to make a decision to be something other than what you are.

You are not here to be anything other than you, splendid entity. You! You have the wonderful endowed imagination, which is really the creative center of your being, and from that you will take fancy from time to time to do any one thing that brings happiness to your being. But it is a very arduous thing to tell a sovereign self that it is going to be this or that labor for the rest of its life, for that is restricting, enslaving and boring.

What you do, you do from the sovereign Self as to what makes you happy. And you know, entity, often the humblest of things--the humblest of things--brings the greatest joy, mainly because everyone else is seeking the glory and fame somewhere else, leaving behind all the little treasures for entities who are seeking only happiness.

*

The things that make you happy, pursue them, whatever the pence, for when you are happy, you will magnetize your wealth around you. That is a truth. But first find happiness. [Even though it] is only a pence that you are paid for a hard day's labor and the pence can only buy you a goblet of sour wine [for] your meal at the end of the day, [if] it has been gratifying to you, then it has been worth it.

Soon you will be successful in what you do to the point that you will become valuable, for few people are happy with their success, few people are happy with their labors. Those that are [happy] are valuable, and for their time and effort, they are paid much pence that buys not only a sweeter wine, but a wonderful sweetmeat, a wonderful royal fish in garlic and oil, vegetables that are simmered in the sweet cream, and the whitest bread, and a good cheese and fruit afterwards. And that makes you happy also. You see?

Why so many of the mass are unhappy [is that] they are not complete with what they labor [at]. Once we take a man and strip down all of his illusions, all of the things that have enslaved him over and over and over, and we take them all away from him and have him [with] no thing but contemplative thought, then we say to him, "What would make you the happiest that you could do?" And he would contemplate on that, and right away he would give me an answer. [But] I would do no thing with the answer, for I would let him think about the answer. Then he would ask me, and I would have him think more about his question.

And then soon there would come a time that [he would realize], all by himself, [that] all that he first said would make him happy, no longer will make him happy; that he has envisioned within himself yet something richer, more profound, more wonderful, for he has had to be with himself and not be disillusioned, or not have his attention towards dancing women and frightful men, or jewels or silks or linens or pearl or lemonwood or marble; [and thus] he would have started thinking about the prize that he himself is. Then, through the collectiveness of that emotion, his desire comes expediently, for it is perfectly aligned. It was not my desire for him, or what I thought he to do, but what **he** desired from himself to do; and it happens in the moment.

Now then, he says, "Oh, master I have found what I would like to do most." And I would look upon him and say, "Do not tell me what it is, for you do not wish my opinion upon it; you wish only to do it, to be happy, for that is the most important thing here."

And he would scurry away, and he would find the light of the day robust and wonderful. And he would take his sandle off and put his toes in the saffron dust. And he would find a sweet and wonderful fountain that mulling and busy men have all ignored and not even seen the beauty of. And he would run to [the fountain] and kneel before it and put his head in it and his hands in it, and he would open his eyes and look around in it and drink it and put it on his face and his body, while more proper men would look in disgust. And then, indeed, he would savor it and he would take his small skin and put a bit in it, for it is better than the wine.

And [then] he would go to his labor, and there he would participate in his labor with a light in his eye and a virileness about his body and a vigor and enthusiasm. And all that are there are saying to him, "How can you be so happy with something that stinks, that is so lowly?" They hate it, you see. "No, I love it. It makes me happy." And they'll look at him and they'll say, "You don't get paid anything for this!" And he will say, "But I don't have anything that needs the pay. I am happy!"

And the governor [for] whom he is working sees this zest and this vitality and this energy, that [he] can do the work of six lazy men and three good ones, [and] dispenses of those who have complained. And now where are they at? They are complaining they have been dispensed with!

And when [the governor] gives him his purse of gold for [his work], he takes the purse in his hands, holds it tightly and then opens it up and looks within it. And he sees the gold as being dark and bronze, depending on where the light is hitting it, and how it jingles. And it smells musty in the pouch. He closes it back up and puts it in his loin cloth, and puts his cloak and his mantle upon [him], and he leaves his labor at what is termed dusk.

And he runs down his road that goes down the hill to the courtyard to where the wonderful fountain is, [where] there are a few simple women with their urns [who] have gathered the water to take to their hovels, some joyfully, some arduously.

And you will see your fountain. And you will take your mantle off and put yourself upon your knees and put your head in again. And [you] open your eyes to see that the sunlight is gone, [that] now the water is shadowy and gilt, and it is wonderful. And you refresh yourself and fill your skin up a bit, stand up and put your mantle on, secure your purse, look around, and go to your solitary [abode] where nothing abides except the joy of you.

That is happiness, man. And it takes a lot to come down to the point to where that can be seen, for when others are on such loftier craft and surrounded by such miseries and enslavement [in which] they must toil, they will never know that [happiness], for they do not give up their illusions for freedom. It is a truth of how the vastness of humanity is . . . and, unfortunately, have always been.

*

Insight can be in song and dance. It can be with zephyrs, flute, lyre, harp. It can be in speech, in script with a wondrous scribe. It can be the comedy of laughter, jesters in court. It can be war, battle. It can be politicians, democracies, republics and the like. They are all talents, for they are all creative forms of someone's collective genuis, and the sum total of what they are have made their contribution to mankind and his ebb and flow into time.

Those are all talents. The basic, underlying beauty of all of those, entity, is that they are only different ways of expressing one's truth. And once one knows one's truth, then **he** is the grandest audience of his own talents--not the world!

Your contribution is you, entity. Whatever you do with it after that only heightens your beauty and your being--for you! It will matter not if the world would scorn you if you loved what you were. That is a truth. So be for you, make your contribution for you. Then the world can see it.

*

The greatest margin of success is achieved by anyone doing what they want to do more than all other things. Unfortunately, that element is least considered because they never think of doing what makes them happy; they only think of doing what brings the most gold.

If you would do what brings you the greatest happiness—whatever it is—you will be more successful, not only monetarily speaking (a new word I have learned), but also happy speaking, for when you are joyful, that creates the aura of abundance from the Divine Source. When you are happy, God the Father gives you everything you want.

Consider what you want to do the most, whatever it is; that will bring the greatest success. Gold, entity, should be considered least of all considerations; that is where most think they fail. They only make a certain amount of gold, and unfortunately, even if they were given a little more, that would never be enough because they would only want more, for their happiness is wound up in want rather than [in] that which is called self-esteem and self-gratification and happiness with accomplishment. You see?

*

CHAPTER TWENTY

CALL FORTH THIS KINGDOM TO SERVE YOU

"When you know you are God, infinite happiness occurs within your being for He is Infinite Happiness. Then the Kingdom of Heaven that is prophesied is yours, for the Kingdom of Heaven is Unlimited Fulfillment: that is what it is. And anyone can have that if they only knew they could."

"The entities that wrote of poverty being a virtue were the ones that despised the rich. There is no sin in having all that there is in material values so long as they do not take precedence over your own value, [that] they are here to serve and nothing else. Your kingdom can be vast, as a reflection of your beauty, but if the kingdom is taken away, you will not suffer for it, for you know, innately within your being, you can build yet another. That is absolute freedom!"

CALL FORTH THIS KINGDOM TO SERVE YOU

This plane has set up a cloistered view of what is acceptable. Material values weigh far greater than personal values. On this plane, entity, my beloved brothren are slaughtered all the time for a small purse. They are harrangued, they are judged, they are enslaved for a purse--which is also God, but the priority of that matter hath not a priority of the God that is holding it.

You are the creator of all of this [material kingdom]. There is no thing on this plane greater than you. The values will begin to change, and are beginning to change, for Man is tired of sufferance, of being put hard to the millstone for his daily bread, for that is **not** how Gods were intended to live here!

All that is in this kingdom, as far as you can see, all of the substance that there is, can be yours, entity, and **is** yours, if you desire that it is yours. But it will only come when first you have become the Sovereign that you are, the God of your being, a free-thinker; not a radical, a free-thinker in loving yourself, in finding your own happiness and not forcing it on others, [but] believing upon you and knowing that God, the Father, indeed the Eminent of All Eminent, be you in all the totality of your being! And then, entity, all that is in this kingdom will come to serve you rather than you serving it.

The entities that wrote of poverty being a virtue were the ones that despised the rich. There is no sin, there is no lacking in having all that there is in material values so long as they do not take precedence over your own value. They are here to serve and nothing else. Your kingdom can be vast, as a reflection of your beauty, but if the kingdom is taken away, entity, you will not suffer for it, for you know, innately within your being, you can build yet another. That is absolute freedom!

All that are [on] this plane can have anything they want if first they realize the secret of getting it, receiving it, having it, **being it**, thus being the supremacy; and then holding it steadfast and saying it comes forth to serve--and then it will! Then, they do not have to labor for another's creativity; they can labor for their own creativity for the sake of expression and not wallow and grovel.

Know that God, that is the totality of all things, that is the essence of all things, holds greater than all other things; that whatever He is, you are! Thus the vastness of eternity, entity, you are! Simply know that, become that. When you know you are God, infinite happiness occurs within your being, for He **is**

"Most don't understand what prosperity is. They always hold it above themselves. Lack of self-esteem, lack of self-love equates poverty, equates no prosperity.

Prosperity is only the side effect of a happy entity who allows a creative mind to be born. One sweet morn, when you arise and realize that, entity, [then] you may have anything you wish, for it all belongs to you."

infinite happiness. Then the Kingdom of Heaven that is prophesied is yours, for the Kingdom of Heaven is Unlimited Fulfillment: that is what it is. And anyone can have that if they only **knew** they could. So be it!

*

Everyone thinks that in order to become wealthy, you must work hard. That only makes you a slave; it doesn't make you wealthy.

Gold is born of the thought. If you allow your mind to create and allow the thoughts to come through, wealth will be born in a thought. And there will be those who will come to you, and you may implement your thought to a creativeness that will help all peoples. Then, the greatest joy is not the gold that is derived from it, but the realization of your own creative thoughts seen straight before you.

Most don't understand what prosperity is. They always hold it above themselves. Lack of self-esteem, lack of self-love equates poverty, equates no prosperity. Prosperity is only the side effect of a happy entity who allows a creative mind to be born. One sweet morn, when you arise and realize that, entity, [then] you may have anything you wish, for it all belongs to you.

I will teach you how to think like a king and, in thinking like one, create like one. And from that, entity, you will rise above your impoverished condition and [lack of] self-esteem and become the Lord you truly are.

*

It be not wrong to have all things in this splendid plane, for all things are God. God be the gold that all hunger for. God be the bread that all are nourished by. God be the structure that protects his Son. And God be the pallet His Son lies upon.

In this kingdom, all things belong unto you. You are here to have dominion over all things if you are so desiring. Desires fufill the need, and each desire, as it is granted, lifts our understanding of ourselves to yet a greater sphere, that perhaps our importance and our worth and our value are worth being.

It is well and good to have all your desires fulfilled. I would have them all fulfilled for you. I would not have you do without any one thing, for you are Glory and you are Divine, and all things are deservant unto you, my beloved brothren.

*

"There is no thing wrong with material value, and anyone [who] says that there is, he is an enslaver and judgementor and usually jealous because he doesn't have it.

A great freedom on this plane is to be free of all things that inhibit, that the mind can be at peace. When you become the Lord God of your Being and become a Master, you can formulate whatever you want.

Everyone here needs to be without the worry or concern of gold. And everyone here may have that as long as gold is not the priority but happiness is."

"A rich man cannot get into the gates of Heaven?" The one that wrote that, entity, was poor! That is a truth. A rich man **made** heaven, entity! Do they not have peace of mind enough that they have bought their freedom in order for them to become, that they are not nagged by collectors in the marketplace, that their family does not go hungry and that they provide gold for many others to work for them?

If a man sees that his enlightenment could only come from abstaining from material value, for he would fear he would be enslaved by it, then he should abstain. [But] it is a Godly sense to have all there is. What is the sense of being a God and to suffer the very elements you create. You know, that is only a fool.

Is not "material" [also] spiritual? It cannot be "material" lest it is begat by Spirit! All things are God, all things. Gold is God, entity: God is in all things. There is no thing wrong with material value, and anyone [who] says that there is, he is an enslaver and judgementor and usually jealous because he doesn't have it. A great freedom on this plane is to be free of all things that inhibit, that the mind can be at peace.

Oftentimes the atrocity comes when those who are wanting gold and treasure and material value do many despicable things not only to others but greatly to themselves in order to have it. All should have all they want. When they become the Lord God of their Being and become a Master, they can formulate whatever they want.

Master first the being, that the being has become a Sovereign, that the being is loved totally, that there is no thing greater than you, nothing. When you believe and know for a truth that there be no thing greater than you, then all that be of this kingdom that can serve you is yours.

*

Master, there is not one thing, be it an automobile or a house or fine linen that is not spiritual, for it all comes from the same kingdom; it is a lower manifestation of a great thought. Everything is Spirit. Everything is!

For one to desire things "of the mind" may be gratification to that entity which you must go to a lower form [in order] to reach a higher gratification--which you do when you desire things "of matter." The auto, the house, and even the gold means nothing unless the one who has desired it has desired that that shall make him happy, and thus, in the process, it does. They are only "catalysts" to emotions. One who is desiring fulfillment within himself is by-passing matter and going directly into emotion. Thus, he will achieve and have what you must seek through other means to get to.

"If every undertaking was perceived in its creation that it must have financial backing, most of Creation would never have gotten here. God would had to have to think a little bit longer about doing all of this!"

If it means a great deal to you to have gold, then you may have gold and will acquire it. But what good is it if it is not a bartering system to get other things that make you happy? You cannot eat gold: the body does not digest it well. And the clothing is very heavy upon the being, and though bright, can become very boring. And for houses, entity, you would not live in it for very long, for you would be vandalized, as it were.

Gold is only a catalyst to get other things to make you happy, and they are only catalysts to make you happy. It is all spiritual. If you must find happiness through the vestige of other things, then so be it; there is nothing wrong with that. You may have [whatever] you desire, but you must desire them and manifest them through your own emotion, entity, for only you can achieve that happiness through creation.

*

In this kingdom, everything that is **is**--has fundamental basis in being. Everything has the spark of life in it or it would not be. Thus, in this kingdom, the spark of life that gives credence to the value of whatever is, is God, is it not? For if it wasn't, you would say, "Alas, I wish to meet that which is not God, for it must be the greater." It **would** [be] if that were so; but the Father is the Thought, indeed, the great Thought, the highest pinnacle of Truth. Thus, that which is termed gold is also God, is it not? And that which is termed the trees that forge the pulp that makes the papyrus into what you term dollars is God, is it not? Then applying pure reason, why would it be bad to have God--and **a lot** of Him?

Now, this is a very arduous thing because, you see, this has kept many people suppressed throughout centuries and eons. I will tell you a truth: The Church, in its religious dogma, is a form of great tyranny because they have suppressed and kept people ignorant. They have taken the God outside of them and put Him somewhere beyond the fathoms of space, and made man a bastard, that no matter what he does, he can never do it good enough or perfect enough. They also made it a decree that in order to find God, you cannot be the rich man, so all of the power would be given to the Church, for when man has no gold, he cannot buy his power or that which is termed votes or opinions or the like, or even build another Church in contradiciton to the one established. You must know that all of these things have been taken into very clever account.

You know, if you keep a man supressed by removing God and removing his treasure and giving him a little ground to work, and then forcing him to give the best of his yield to the Church, you will **always** have dominion over him; then man will become the enslaved. That is a great and wondrous plan that has worked, but also it is an atrocity, a great atrocity, for it is bred into generations.

Now, to have gold, there is nothing wrong with that: that is God. You cannot separate money from God; there is no separation. To have it only means that it is a means of exchange, of acquiring those things which you never had and wish to. And are not those things that you wish to have [part of] God's kingdom?

When you are free of the fear of not having enough bread, when you are free of the fear of not having shelter, when you are relieved that you no longer have to have no transports, that is called living in freedom, entity, for then the mind is not occupied with instincts of surviving; it is occupied because it is happy and fears nothing and is in a state of receivership to where genius, brilliance is born. And so what give you unto the great Source that has given you all these things? To **become** the Great Source--happy.

And when you are in a state of freedom, you can create for this plane a greater means of pleasure and freedom for all of those who wish to participate. [And you] lift their consciousness [when you can] say, "Alas, this I am, a rich man, but I can go through the eye of a needle." Then that demonstrates that God does not only love the pauper, He also loves the rich man, for the rich man adorns himself and the Father.

There is no degree of God's love. And there are no degrees of being spiritual, because by being here you are being spiritual, by breathing you are spiritual, for spirit is the unseen, which is the Father.

I will tell you another great truth: the reason that that has become the way of religion is because the poor people despised the rich people [and] decided to take God away from them: it was a curse, that is all.

What you want you will have, and the doors will open to you to build your kingdom on a great and wondrous foundation. And then one day, when all your majestic dreams have come true, you will turn into becoming more infinite, for you've accomplished everything else. It does no good for that which be I or anyone else to tell you to "become" and to become that which is termed the Sovereign if you deny those things you want, for until you are fed, entity, you will never become, and that is the way it is.

Draw your plans and create, and when the doors open, go through them. They will be little doors in the beginning, but they will lead to greater ones and greater ones. And when you have accomplished all of these things, rich man, give thanks unto the Father within you and bless all that you abundantly have, and never you feel guilty for having the abundance. So be it.

*

What think you financial security is? You know, master, when you give entities money, they only purchase more things to have to have more. That is a great truth. Financial security, entity? One should ask for, rather than financial security, to have everything one needs to allow freedom to occur. Finances do not always get it; they only incur more.

If you will do what makes you happy, entity, you will never have problems with financial security, ever. Everyone here needs to be without the worry or concern of gold. And everyone here may have that as long as gold is not the priority but happiness is. Then we have masters that are joyfully free, for they labor not for the pence or the ruby or the drachma but for that which is called happiness; they're doing what makes them happy. Then they **are** secure. You understand?

I have great kings who come into this audience, whose wealth you cannot even imagine, who are looking for happiness. They are wanting what the bum in bumdom has--and we've turned a few of them into them! And they're happy--very much so.

*

Fortune is not given to you, entity. The Source gives to you that which you expect you are worth--and only that much! When you realize, entity, that you are a Sovereign and all belongs to you, you may have all that you want and never deplete the supply: there will always be plenty left for everyone else.

True fortune will never be made at the hands of someone else's ideal on this plane. It is made by your own ideal and inventive attitude, for who will give you a fortune from **their** pocket? None. None! You will have to earn it according to what they term "labor."

True fortune is made from Self, through Self, by Self; that is how fortune is made. It will never be made under anyone else. Thus, what that means is that you must become more unlimited and simpler in your unlimitedness to see the obvious that everyone else has overlooked to make a fortune at it. You have the ability to be a fortune-maker many times over, for not everything has ever been invented on this plane, though the thought has been here for nigh a long time. The true inventors, entity, are the adventurers: that you must become in contemplative thought.

*

PART THREE

LOVE YOURSELF SEEN THROUGH LIFE IN ALL OF ITS VOICES

CHAPTER TWENTY-ONE

LIVE! EXPERIENCE THE WISDOM OF LIFE

> **"To have lived your life fully and experienced all things and gained knowledge of them is noble virtue: that is how you become God."**

"If truth is only to be understood through the application of theory and philosophy through learned philosophers—if that is where all truth is, entity, then life will be forgotten; it will never be.

Truth emanates from all places—all. Learn to listen to it wherever it comes from. And whatsoever speaks, it will all speak truth. Do not close your mind for only books of speculative theory and history seen through the ego-understanding of one man, but [see truth] through experience and life in all of its voices."

LIVE! EXPERIENCE THE WISDOM OF LIFE

You become wise through experience. Gods were like little children when they developed all of this because they had not developed the attitude that collectively of itself would form an alteredness of their pure vision. They never knew what hate was, they never knew what jealousy was, so, consequently, they never knew what war was. They never knew and understood death, so all they knew was life. They never understood joy, for they didn't know what despair was.

It has taken you this long to learn all of those things. It has taken you this long to realize that you have lost what happiness is, Perfection, Isness. Experience teaches you, entity, what to look for; [then] the Soul will no longer have to hunger for the knowledge of the experience.

*

What is a great virtue is to take this life and make it the grandest that you can, to experience it to [its] heights: to its mountains, its valleys, to its caves, to its flatlands--to every part of this life; to be a part of it and to love it. Then you are filled with this life, and when you leave this plane, there is no longer anything else here that you feel you need to experience. Then you will not need to come back here.

Those who come into this life, and they have one little direction because it is acceptable here on this plane, suffer a death of agony that they "should have" done this and they "should have" done that, and they "should have" loved this one and married that one and all of those things. All the "should haves" will bring them back to experience all of the "now can haves" until they are filled with all of that; then they return here no more.

Wisdom is accumulated emotion: that is what makes us different from all others that come unto this plane. You will not experience the things you have already experienced, for you will not have a desire to. The things that are longing unto your being, that are adventurous and that are pleasing to your being, you will always be drawn to for the sake of experiencing them.

*

It takes, in some lives, for man to slay man and to become the slain to appreciate the value and the vulnerableness of flesh. And the great entities that walk this plane, that are triumphant in their greatness and yet humble in the way they pursue it, have been the accursed tyrant and that which is termed the weak victim. They have learned, through the experiences of living, the appreciation of humanity. And that is called noble virtue; that is what it takes to become a saint.

*

A virtuous person [is] one who has lived life to the fullest measure, who has encountered the heights of his purposeful good to the depths of his purposeful good in all of his thoughts. [He] has experienced the atrocities of a creative mind, the vileness of a creative mind, [and] the greatness and propriety of a great mind. He has experienced life to conclude that he has gained wisdom from it. He has learned that he has been a participant in it, and, being a participant in it, he is knowledgeable about that which he speaks.

The wise man, as it were, in giving forth direction in accordance with his experience, gives forth virtue. He has experienced all things [and] has accelerated his being into the heights of knowingness. He knows and has become the splendor that has always awaited him, and has done so through embroiling himself in life and all that it is.

The virtuous [entity] is not lacking in any one thing. He is not driven to pursue any one thing, for he has conquered them all. He has lived life and learned from it. And though he has left one experience for yet another and another, he has gained unto his being, has added unto his being, regardless of those who damn him for it. He has gain in his life and has no regrets.

*

Noble virtue is, indeed, the highest acclaim of mastership. And what do you think noble virtue is? It is not the abstinence of life, to run and hide yourself upon a tall mountain and become holy and burn incense and contemplate God knows what! Noble virtue is the practice of living life, experiencing it in every form that the Soul calls you to do so.

You are driven to do the things you do for the purpose of gaining wisdom, that when you have done what everyone else has done, then you can never judge another, for lo, you have judged yourself. Then true compassion and love shall exist within the Soul; and, alas, that is how God is.

To have lived your life fully and experienced all things and gained knowledge of them is noble virtue: that is how you become God.

*

Spiritualness **is** Life. You cannot separate the learning, the love of God, of Self, from [the] living [of] it.

To learn to be you, to learn to have the knowledge that is only a thought away and to learn to implement it into a happy kingdom, you only have to desire "you" to come forth completely. There is no teacher that has ever lived or ever shall live that is grander and more prudent and more fulfilled within its knowledge than the Spirit or God of your being is. That is the only teacher: you, the God that you are. Then you will learn to live life fully; you will learn how to appreciate fully the existence of all peoples, regardless of their situations, because this **is** spiritual—all of it! Pulling yourself away and becoming ritualistic and practicing that which is termed ancient, boring, monotonous, limiting doctrines, entity, does nothing but frustrate the being. [Life] must be lived through and through.

Spiritualness is called Life. There is no separation; there is none. To teach you, I should make you more aware of you, **you,** [for] that is the most intimate relationship with a teacher you can have.

*

What anyone can teach you, you can find in the sweet waters of a gentle brook or the glorious blaze at sunset or the wondrous colors at midnight [or] in the mute beauty of the heavens. Teaching is allowed when one experiences the laughter of a child that is sweet and innocent, the flush upon the cheeks of some beautiful woman, a maiden who realizes her coming womanhood and does not meet your eyes, the breast of some great steed that is stroked kindly. [Teaching] is wondrous things: it is smells, however they be; it is taste and however you taste. It is being.

This life, **your** life, is your teacher. To run away from it, master, is only to run into more life. Life is the thing that will give unto you the greatest learning that you are seeking for! You must be a participant in it by living it.

There are those that go into caves, that go into temples and partake of learning and discipline themselves to be greater than life, to elude life, to hide from life, to calm their beautiful bodies, to restrict their loveliness and vision. To be what? Pious, deliverers, saviors, lords? They will never know life lest they have been a participant in it. The greatest teachers, master, never ran into temples and hid themselves away, or to mountaintops where they were above humanity. It is for and by humanity that life is procured!

Live! Know what it is to sup a hearty red wine. Know what it is to taste sweetmeats. Know what it is to lie your head upon a silken cushion. Know what it is to listen unto music and the mystery of how the fingers move to bring forth sounds that rest

"Live! Reach up unto your mountaintop and breathe the air and look into foreverness. Find a star that is elusive to you [and] ponder it. Become life. Be life. It is what all must eventually achieve and understand and where your wisdom and your teachings will be secured from. Do not robe yourself and become pious; you will lose if you do so."

your very soul.

Live! Reach up unto your mountaintop and breathe the air and look into foreverness. Find a star that is elusive to you [and] ponder it. Become life. Be life. It is what all must eventually achieve and understand and where your wisdom and your teachings will be secured from. Do not robe yourself and become pious; you will lose if you do so.

Look at yourself and bless and love yourself, and present yourself kindly upon this plane, as a procurer of this plane, as a giver to this plane. Then that which you desire, master, will fulfill itself in wisdom: wisdom is assured, for what is learned, master, is secured. That is how you will know and that is how you will be. It is the greatest teaching there is.

And when a small child comes unto you and asks you the mystery of the stars or the wind, then you, who have been a part of these things, can give unto her, in the simplest tones of your being, the mysteries of the wind and the stars, and through your all-wise experience, broaden her wondrous mind to experience life for the beauty of it.

*

Go and ponder by a brook. Go and sit on top of a mountain. Go and sit in a field during a raging storm. Open your mouth and drink the rain. Get up before the sun and watch the splendor of the birthing sky. Watch the sky become rose and hues of gold, and watch the last relentless star lose favor to a greater light.

I want you to live! Do the rose remain the seed, hushed deep in the ground, and refuse to see the sun? No. Does the bee turn its face to the tempting flower and seek a weed? No. Does a man turn his eyes from a beautiful woman? No. Does the sun refuse to come up because the moon is still in the sky? And does the greatest star outshine the least of them? No. Why should you come out and see the things that exist in a simply coexistence? For [then] you understand the Source, Infinite God, Infinite Life!

What is the fourth color of the rainbow? What is the color of poppy? What is the color of the great lights that come from within the earth and shine brilliantly into the sky? And what does soil smell like? And what does a leaf that has just fallen feel like? Where does the secret world of an insect lie? And what of an elf and a dwarf or a fairy? Where, pray tell, have they gone? Are they real? What are the colors of their wings, their noses, their skin, their ears?

And what is it like to embrace a tree that hath never felt the touch of man, to climb a mountain, to breath a cloud and let it

"To be 'spiritual' is not to sit and ponder whatever or to still your mind or conditon it. Never! Better to get up and go out and laugh in the sun and live! That is how you become God; that is how you become "spiritual."

There is no sacred rite that connects you to the Infinite. You already are! All you have to do is to go and live it to allow it to be seen."

lie lazily upon your being until it is ready to move on; or to live in a cave, to light a fire to warm yourself from cold to heat to light to darkness? What does it sound like to hear a wild cat scream in the night or a butterfly when it speaks to a flower?

Do you have the answers to all of those things? Then it is time you did! Is that **not** enlightenment? Is that not Life? Is that not God? Is it not you who have missed all these things?

*

To be "spiritual" is not to sit and ponder whatever or to still your mind or conditon it. Never! Better to get up and go out and laugh in the sun and live! That is how you become God; that is how you become "spiritual." If you are pleased [to meditate], well and good. But if you don't want to, master, you do not have to. There is no sacred rite that connects you to the Infinite; you already are! All you have to do is to go and live it to allow it to be seen.

Infinite wisdom, entity? What is the good of **knowing** everything? What is the good of a thought if it cannot be reasoned in thought and feeling? You know, entity, a thought is colorless, odorless, imageless; it is only an inspiration of electrum. Only when it becomes a **feeling** does it become a reality. You may have all the knowledge there is, but it is really nothing until you have felt it, lived it, experienced it. So, my beloved master, you may sit and be "in tune" with the hot throb of infiniteness in its ongoing creative form, but you will have missed the deep blue of the sky when it becomes morning.

Your infinite knowledge is imminent. Go and feel it. Feel it! Love it. Plant yourself a wondrous garden. Put a little seed in the ground; let it be nourished and watch it become a bloom of magnificent hue, deep in its color, [with] an aroma that pierces the nostrils and sends you into a rush of enlightenment.

Many think that meditation is what they should do. Well, it is [if] they believe it to be so! But to go into Infinite nature, you get there by feeling the thought into reality.

*

I never appointed myself to become a teacher, entity. I lived all of [life] well enough to learn enough, [and] honored myself by loving myself who had learned all of these things, and, alas, found out who the Unknown God was.

[If] you wish to teach, you will never teach, for teaching will be the principle of why you are doing it. Live! Live and experience. Engulf yourself into life. Love it, embrace it. By the mere fact of your living, entity, it will enlighten and bring joy to the world. Teachers never do; they never do. They are

" 'Tis not discipline of any ritualistic act that brings God into one's being. And it is not the abstinence of life either. It is living life to the fullest measure and finding the Father in every bloom, in every feather, in every laughter, in every embrace. Then you are called happy. Remember that."

never remembered for by what they said; they were always rememebered by what they did.

Do something worth having wisdom over, and that will bring joy to the hearts of others. By the mere fact of what you will become, [that] will lessen their burden of experience and allow hope to be born within them.

Your plane has so many teachers, so many that are noted to be teachers and nothing else—and they won't ever be remembered. You will if rather than teaching, **living** becomes your priority. Wherever you go, you will naturally draw to you that which will seek you out to learn by what you have already gained. And what is [more] important: to have the whole world come and listen to mundane words, meaninglessly flowing in and out of their consciousness, for they are caught in a daydream, or having **one** watch, listen, perceive, become?

It only takes one to become the magnificent God that they all are to be a Light to everyone else. Best you help one entity [rather] than trying to make an effect upon everyone: one by one, and only as an incidental part of your life. You understand?

*

I am not, entity, a ridiculous, cloistered, limited entity. I am a heretic, and I am pleased that I am, for I shan't guide anyone to religious following or prudent enslavement of beliefs, no matter who they are. That is not how you achieve this kingdom that I have spoken of.

To this hour, I have seen much and know much, entity, and have watched that which is termed this evolutionary process. And listen unto me when I tell you: 'Tis not discipline of any ritualistic act that brings God into one's being. And it is not the abstinence of life either. It is living life to the fullest measure and finding the Father in every bloom, in every feather, in every laughter, in every embrace. Then you are called happy. Remember that.

*

The peoples of this plane, you know, they lost priorities [as] to what life is. They got very confused into war, into religion, into governments, into creeds. And then to come back out of confusion, they found that the only way to truly live is to have relationships with as many people as they can, for that gave credence to their potency, it gave credence to their being, and it was the only thing that "gave a damn" about them according to their thinking. And in the course of that, they have become blind to the true beauty that really lies open-faced around them.

"Man, in his lust for himself, has denied himself life. To enjoy life is to have a lustful passion for everything: the wind, the night sky, the water—everything. Then Man can be greatly more appreciative in his diversification of himself, for then he does not have to have disheartening relationships in order to prove his state of being: he can observe it in life around him.

Enjoy this place. It is a grand place to visit, to come from, to belong to, to create upon, to express through, to find love upon. It is the emerald of this universe, and it has been a good mother."

Man, in his lust for himself, has denied himself life. To enjoy life is to have a lustful passion for everything: the wind, the night sky, the water—everything. Then Man can be greatly more appreciative in his diversification of himself, for then he does not have to have disheartening relationships in order to prove his state of being: he can observe it in life around him.

This is a very pleasurable plane to live upon. It is skillfully put together. It is artiscally majestic. It is wonderfully beautiful. It is the only plane of darkness and the only plane you do not hear music on; thus we have musicians who try to imitate what they once knew. This plane is vivid and robust and full of color. It is a delightful place to be a part of. When you find its beauty in even the small things, it enhances your appreciation of life. Then you do not have to find disappointment in your fellow men, because you [have] diversified yourself into the things that have learned to outlive them.

Enjoy this place. It is a grand place to visit, to come from, to belong to, to create upon, to express through, to find love upon. It is the emerald of this universe, and it has been a good mother.

*

Learning is a boring concept, entity; adventures are exciting. Who wants to learn, you know, to sit and to learn "learn?" What you need is to experience "experience." That is where the adventure lies.

*

Unlimited thought is not a hard thing to entertain; and, actually, you do not even know what you are going to entertain, for if you knew what unlimited thought was, you would already have it and be there and would not have to have all this fuss and the like.

Unlimitedness is an adventure--adventure. I have always taught my peoples, you, that in order for any one thing to be learned to its greatest peak of value [so] that wisdom can be ascertained, that what is being taught should be put into a splendid adventure. Lessons are very boring, monotonous, mundane, and no one wants them. And if God is nothing but a series of lessons, I'd rather you be what you are and forget about the business of being God.

Adventures unfold into Life. And the adventures of what you have learned here will take you far from this place into many households, into other arms, into greater intelligence, to the highest peak of the world, indeed into the lowest valley, for in teaching in an adventurous way, the entity expands his consciousness because [learning] is a natural function, because he is jolly happy with what he is doing. Happiness **promotes** unlimited thinking.

For all that are gathered here, adventures are planned, eloquently, wonderfully, as doors opening to the lot of you, that you may entertain God I AM, indeed Unlimited Self, the love of the spectacular entity; [and that you] come to appreciate these words—not only to say them, but to understand them. And for what purpose? [For] you to rise above your ignorance; to rise above that which can sequester you into dominion and take away from you your Unlimited Kingdom and thrust you back into that which is termed the slings and arrows of outrageous war. Adventure is a wonderful way to know who God be and [who] you be and to evolve [you] beyond the structures of death and disease and all that is associated with this.

Unto all that are here, I send you on your adventures, happily. And along your way, you shall be that which is termed the soothsayers that will pass your bit of wisdom by that which pass in your fields and in your adventures—and they shan't ever forget you! And living your light in grace and in easements allows you to realize, without pain, the virtue of your immaculate selves.

Adventures? Hmmm. They are jolly wonderful.

*

The world is a very beauteous place. Everyone thinks that this place is called "hell." Know what a "hell" is? It is an open grave, a shallow, open grave to where an entity would be put because he could not afford the drachmas or the rubies to be entombed. And because it was an open grave, the hyenas and wild dogs took their feed upon the embodiment. But that's all it ever meant, until a later translation.

There is no such place as hell; there never was and there shan't ever be. It was a dreadful thing to create to intimate, by fear, and coerce the masses into a controllable organization. God the Father is much too loving of your being and **is** all matter—every little grain in the sea, every little butterfly in spring, every vast star in the heavens. He is everything, and for Him to have had such a place would have been like a cancer in His body, and it would have eaten Him up.

There isn't [such a place as "hell"]. And there is no devil—Lucifer [as] he is termed. The entity was called Lucifer, but was far from the entity you learned him to be. There is only God, and for this place to be called a "hellish place" is most unfair, because it is the emerald of your universe.

The world is not in the marketplace, my beloved brothren. It teems there with life, but the greater life is to be found outside of the marketplace on top of a snowy mountain, indeed, where the wind is crisp and cold and clean, or at the base of a magnificent tree, or looking into a brook and putting your feet into it and being one with the fishes. There is so much more to this your plane of those who want to ascend it. You have not lived it and you have not investigated it. You have only been in the oppressive democracy of your cities.

This is the emerald of the universe. Go to all of these places. Be a part of them. Put down that which is termed your silks and jewels, and take your shoes off. Be cluttered with unfashionable simpleness and go and experience God and this your heaven that you have created. It is worth living for. It is worth being here for. I beseech you to do this, for you shan't have lived until you have lived in these places and been a part of their ongoing, forever consciousness.

I am called Ramtha the Enlightened One by my peoples; and so I have kept that name even unto this hour. An Enlightened One? I was a solitary entity that sat on a plateau while everyone else did all of the things that they do in their days, and through this alienation of myself in a wilderness, I found the Unknown God.

You have not lived until you have become solitary in such a wilderness and at peace with the midnight sky and a moon that waxes and wanes until the brilliance of dawn. And in all the dreams and the knowledge that comes to you, behold, you too will become the Enlightened One, for priorities change there. The wildness of the consciousness of [the] wilderness accepts you, beloved brothren--it accepts you. It expects you to be timeless like it is; and in such circumstance, can you grow boldly to become this God and to become steadfast in all the days of your life that are to come. I desire for you to do this.

The Unknown God is silence, great silence, and yet it will speak to you if you allow it to do so. Reach out and be a part of this continent. It is magnificent, so magnificent. And then one day, you'll be a little more like me, brothren even. So be it.

*

CHAPTER TWENTY-TWO

SEE THE SELF YOU LOVE IN OTHERS

"When you learn to see all of your brothren and attune to them as you attune to the wind or the sun who are unfailing, then you learn about you. These, your brothren, are great teachers and great refiners in the substance that is you. When you learn to see them in that view, master, it is easy to love them as you love you. It is a robust feeling of exalted compassion."

"Everyone that comes into our lives adds to the virtue, the clarity, the dignity, the expanse of our perception of ourselves. Every entity is purposeful, intentional, and is a blessing, for they help to round, to define, to glorify our own human existence. Without them, we could [not] understand that which we be, for they play an important part in our being to help us understand ourselves."

SEE THE SELF YOU LOVE IN OTHERS

Relationships can be as varied as people are varied, and they can be as adventurous and clever and exciting as people are in the secretness of their beings. Surprising, enchanting, alluring, wonderful--all relationships have this essence: an encounter with sublimeness, if but for one brief moment. And each time we encounter that briefness, it tenders a need, a satisfaction, a gratification, a part of our being now realized that we did not know was touchable before.

Each encounter puts us in touch with ourselves. And for that purpose, even if it for a moment, it is wonderful!

*

Relationships, indeed they are wonderful! To love another entity, to be a part of another entity's world and nature is Life, for the Father is in each and every face that you see, wherever you go. And each and every face has its own world, its own uniqueness, its own joys, its own sorrows, its own indecisiveness and its own conquering. Thus, relationships permit us to learn within the world of another and to add to our being by the spectacular being [that they are].

There are never bad relationships; all are good, for [always we] prosper by entering ourselves in another's reasoning, another's understanding. Love them all in freedom. Be careful not to lose yourself in their thinking. Always maintain your own worth and your own value and your own standard of goodness. But enjoy. The Father is in all of them. That is partaking of Life, the greatest gift there is.

*

A good way to love other entities is to look at the entity as if you are looking into a mirror and that entity you see is you. You will find it easier to smile at them, to understand them when they do no reciprocate the smile. When they bash into you in a crowd, look at them and smile and love them, for they **are** you. All the "you's" that you see, in the situations and uniquenesses that they portray, will teach you, the looker, to better refine what you desire ultimately in you; they are the giver of that unadulterated truth.

If you see one who is a thief, look at him as you. The taking from another's possessions, is that you? What more than the taking of an object has the thief done? He has betrayed a trust

"You know, you never really love another entity. How can you, for you don't know what they are to love. What others love in others is what they see of themselves in the other person, for that gives a clearer identity of their own imagery. What we really love in others is ourselves."

and an honor; he has encroached himself on a kingdom that he was not invited into. There is more to the thief than the act of thievery; there is the thought behind it. When you look at him, look at yourself, and what he is, become better in you.

When you look at the old woman who keeps looking at you because you are so lovely and it has been a long time since she felt as you look, look upon her and see you, and remember that once you were as she is. Think about her and her thought processes as she is peering at you, blatantly. See her as you and love her as you for admiring you so openly.

When you learn to see all of your brothren and attune to them as you attune to the wind or the sun who are unfailing, then you learn about you. These, your brothren, are great teachers and great refiners in the substance that is you. When you learn to see them in that view, master, it is easy to love them as you love you. It is a robust feeling of exalted compassion.

Lovers Are The Mirrors Of Our Own Identity

Those who have called romance and love "mistakes" or their "undoing" should learn not to see them that way. They should see it as adding to their understanding of people, adding to their understanding of, if nothing else, their own vulnerability, their own ineptness, and their own greatness.

*

[Your relationship] will last for quite a good deal if you allow it to by allowing the other entity to be who they are. After all, that is why you love them, for in them, you see who you are. If you try to change them, you will distort the image of what you are seeing within yourself and you will lose sight of Self seen in the other.

You know, you never really love another entity. How can you, for you don't know what they are to love. What others love in others is what they see of themselves in the other person, for that gives a clearer identity of their own imagery. And when the entity starts doing things alien and foreign and unfamiliar, then the image is lost; thus the love begins to be lost. What we really love in others is ourselves.

The search for ourselves seen in another human being--that intimacy and that depth is far greater than experience has ever been known. The embrace, the copulation, the sharing--all of that is, in actuality, Self. Allowing the other entity to be who

"How can you love another entity when you don't know what they think? If what they think, entity, is understood by what you think, then you have that which is called a relationship. But none here knows the Soul of another; they only know what they see of themself in the other.

Loving another individual, entity, is loving the reflections of Self. That is a wondrous treasure, for love in its interlude with one another helps explore that which is termed the vastness of each of ourselves. That is why it is such a rare and wonderful treasure and should always be held onto."

they are is the greatest treasure and gift that you can give in a relationship.

The truest marriage is of the Soul: that is Infinite Self shared by Infinite Self that time or measure or death or life or no things can take away. Achieving that is when Self is achieved.

*

No one here truly loves anyone else, if you wish to understand the science of it. For what they are loving in the other individual is the reflections of their own Self's identity. How can you love another entity when you don't know what they think? If what they think, entity, is understood by what you think, then you have that which is called a relationship. But none here knows the Soul of another; they only know what they see of themself **in** the other.

Loving another individual, entity, is loving the reflections of Self. That is a wondrous treasure, for love in its interlude with one another helps explore that which is termed the vastness of each of ourselves. That is why it is such a rare and wonderful treasure and should always be held onto.

[Many], master, have not had the opportunity, as it were, to open [their] beautiful eyes to see who [they] are in another [for] fear of seeing what [they] dislike in another because it is what is in [themselves].

*

You cannot love another entity. You do not love **other** entities; you love what you **see** in other entities that represent Self. To take and love another entity without any identity, you do not do that! You must have a **reason** to feel, and the reason that you feel is that Self identifies in another its own Self. **That** is what you love!

Once you have learned what it is to love yourself completely and to honor and to hold yourself above all other things, entity, then you will know what it is to love another entity, sincerely.

Love, it is the most prostituted word upon your plane. It is used to do more damage, all willing of course, than any other ideal. And ideal is the greatest destroyer; it destroys even greater than war does.

*

When marriage is the soul of an existence, one never marries another; he marries himself. You do not love another; you love only those aspects of Self seen in the other, for that is the only

"You and another make up one God that was in the Beginnings of all Beginnings, that your collective Self, expressive Self, represented one Infinite Entity that was grand enough to split itself to become two, that he may multiply the earth."

way we can identify them. And when embracing another, you are embracing that which is termed the truth of your own being. Thus, marriage of the Soul is marriage of Self. The love of another is the love of Self, for what we love of another is the virtues that we possess within our own inner beings.

*

Lovers help [each other] to understand themselves and prepare better for what is termed a " Soul lover." A Soul lover, there is only one. One. And that entity is the direct resemblance of Self but in an opposite gender. And that is often a very long journey to find such an entity. But those who desire it and are sincere upon the encounter of Self and loving Self and [who] look for the return of Self do find it.

When I speak of "lovers," I am speaking of a God who is in need of another God who is in need of that God, that the two exchange and learn of love and compassion and tenderness and what it is to have another tremble within their arms with anticipation and hope and all trust.

Love is mocked on this plane, as much as copulation is. But to be a lover and to respect and to feel and to tenderly hold another human being that is a God is an art that everyone here needs to learn. And when they have learned that, then they have touched on the premise of themselves. Then they are ready for that which is permanent and deep and everlasting.

Soul Mates: The God, So Defined As Two, Now Come One Again

You are the half of another entity. Together, the entity and you represent a Godhood of sublime power. Everyone has a Soul mate and they have only one. Everyone is searching for them, everyone, until they find that which gratifies their being; then they never look again. That is why women ponder men: for themselves. That is why men ponder women: for themselves. And without that draw to one another, copulation would never have occurred and the species would never have been, and God would still be the wind and the creation that blows through the hollows of flowers and tree roots, and storms that bay at the horizon, without one man to ever observe Its magnificent beauty.

Women, be glad you are woman, and men, be glad you are man, for you have added to the depth of emotion and love of one another and have provided for others to see this magic kingdom you have created.

*

You are a part of another collective energy. You are expressing in what is called the "negative" or the "positive" gender: the positive gender be Man; the negative gender be Woman. That is how the forces of the body electrum are made up. When you split that which is, you lower it, and the lowering of that which is into electrums will always be opposite.

You and another make up one God that was in the Beginnings of all Beginnings, that your collective Self, expressive Self, represented one Infinite Entity that was grand enough to split itself to become two, that he may multiply the earth.

Self is driven to find itself. A part of loving Self is the desirous completion of Self. Entities that have relationships upon relations, there is no thing wrong with that; they are merely looking for someone that reflects what they are unitedly.

When the two come together, they become a Great God. They are no longer "positive" or "negative"; they are One; they are what is called the "Is-factor." They are all-powerful; they have all-joy. The world not only marvels, but becomes notoriously jealous and envious of them, for they draw great splendor and attention around them.

A Soul mate does not only exalt one but drives one to near madness also, for in order to achieve true love, one goes through the loss of one's Self into the arms of another or the hands of another or the control of another into great jealousies, envy, hatred, despise, hurt: all factors they experience. But it is really a humbling process that is occurring, and the humbling is removing all of the insecurities that each have clothed so tightly around them for survival [to allow] the Pure Essence to emerge.

You will go through this with your mate, as she will go through that with you. You [will] tremble for you [will] not know what to do with what you feel. You will feel so great and yet so very small and helpless and insignificant. Love will do all of these things to you. It is not simply rapture; it is sorrow, it is hurt, it is the doing away with all of the negative forces which pull at you greatly. But then one day, mastery after mastery, and the two stay together, light is achieved. Then, the workings of both together in harmonious form create the powerful union, [and] they are never separated again.

When such [a relationship] is realized, it answers all of the reasons why of the failing of relationships, the disappointments in love or marriages or whatever, thinking it to be the "real thing." Relationship upon relationship, [entities feel] there must be something better, there must be something more. But no one has ever described to them why they feel that way. Well, this is why.

The moment that [the existence of a Soul mate] is felt and understood, the Spirit begins to magnify itself to draw to it itself. Your [Soul mate] could be an entity on another plane, and it will be drawn here to be born, even at this time, to meet you in your life. Or [it] could be in another place, and all of a sudden, the "doors" would open to allow the entity the opportunity, upon one wondrous working of strategy, to meet in a most unexpected place. You choose when, and so does your mate; that is not for me to see. But I will tell you: [when] it is known [to exist], so it becomes quickly.

*

Everyone wishes to have their Soul mate, but not everyone is prepared for their Soul mate, for their Soul mate is the identum that they are. For you to be [prepared], be everything that you are desiring to have in another: be loving of yourself, respecting of yourself, and, by all means, never be enslaved by time--be patient with yourself. And be kind to others no matter what their attitude toward you is. And when that becomes harmonious within your divine structure, when you completely love Self, that is when the Soul mate appears.

Your Soul mate comes when you least expect it to come, when you are the busiest loving yourself, and it does not matter if no one loves you, [for] it does not change how you feel; that is the moment of birth!

Your Soul mate will come when you love yourself and are complete within yourself: that is what draws them together. And simply knowing that there is such a creature also draws the entity to you: [you] only have to [your] capacity to receive and understand; complete knowingness has everything. Those who do not know about Soul mates rarely, if ever, meet them. Those who know, draw them to themselves for they are no longer ignorant.

*

All that find [their Soul mate] become accelerated entities into their Mastership, into their Goodness, into their Joy, and the remembrances of who they are come unhidden upon them. For when they come together, there is no thing beyond their reach; there is no thing that can hurt their joy, their peace, their beauty, for they are the God, so defined as two, now come One again.

*

"Who be friend? All be. Comradeship is that what we are, we are to all peoples, all Gods. And in finding ourself, truly we do not find it with the closest intimates of our being, but in all beings.

When we look and we love and we perceive and we justify our beauty by seeing it in others, friendship, wonderful friendship indeed, is achieved."

Though one [soul mate] can advance more rapidly than the other, they always try to be simultaneously "in time" with one another because they know, infinitely within their being, that they are the Perfect Coming Together.

Who Be Friend? All Be Friend!

Now, let us speak in regard to that which is termed Friendship. It needs, indeed, a learning upon.

In all beginnings, in all purposeful understandings, when Soul mates were splitting themselves from Gods who were anxious for the experience of life, also in groups of Gods were there gatherings, many gatherings. And all that were in the groups [creating the] evolvements of that which is termed plantum, that which is termed animal source, mineral source, aqueous source, cellular source and the like, all had a common bond unto one another, for they were experiencing commonly the sameness unto one another. Thus, their experience brought them close to a sharing point, a common interest, as it were. And when the common interest was seen, each added their own ideas unto that which is termed the object of their creation and perfected [it] little by little.

Comradeship amongst the Gods goes back to the beginnings of the breath of life. Friendship, indeed, is a prized and noble thing. It is as close [as] anyone can get [to another], save unto that which is called the deep and wondrous intimacy that mates share unto their beings. Friends, indeed, imitate [that] sharing, but not on that which is called a physical level or that which is termed a "life-love" level. They share on a comradeship level: they are truthful, they are steadfast, they edify each other and are hopeful unto one another. Friendship indeed is a wondrous thing to have. It means a trusting knowingness in one another.

Man, in his understanding and consciousness, though in all of his history being an enslaver, a warrior, a competitor and a wretched thing in some light, he also is a lonesome thing in all lights. Man, who hath none to glorify him, who hath none to heighten his beauty or deepen his respect or put him into laughter, he vollifies himself and becomes inward of himself; and not inward to the point that he finds himself, but, often, [to where] he begins to destroy himself, wishing to become to whatever will let him become unto; [and] that, more often is the cause of him not knowing who he is. That **is** of Man.

[In friendship], one will have the strength the other has lacking, and the one that has a lacking will have a strength the other has [a] lacking in. They more often have [the] same feeling and same beings and same understanding as the other. When there is two instead of one, the two find strength in one another.

Friends glorify and never abuse. They love, indeed, and never misuse. They are indeed the trusted source of all growth. Gods unto Gods, in friendship, begin to find the beauty in all Gods by seeing [it] first within [each other] and then in others. And friends, masters, will be the first to be the recipient of this wondrous understanding, this wondrous being, that you have now begun to be!

But then you take it a bit further. Who else is a friend? Have you ever asked a stranger to be your friend unto you? If you sit complacently and listen to him, his heart will soften, and a new glint will be born in his cloudy eye, and his raspy voice will become clear, and he will become hopeful that he hath found a newness that adds, perhaps, to the lacking that he has. And then the adventure begins.

Who be friend? All be. Comradeship is that what we are, we are to **all** peoples, all Gods. And in finding ourself, truly we do not find it with the closest intimates of our being, but in all beings. When we look and we love and we perceive and we justify our beauty by seeing it in others, friendship, wonderful friendship indeed, is achieved. If one dishonors even a stranger, he has dishonored the trust, the coveted beauty of what is called "shared expression" through friends. Even one!

[In friendship], one learns to covet and to cherish the beauty that others have within, that tranquility and peace is allowed when they are together. If he abuses this, indeed he has abused it within his own Soul, within his own being, within his own purposeful understanding. Nay, you should never do that.

Friends are, in essence, loved of our being and are the being of our being which we are seeing and being gratified in. A friend, a good one, if truly love be there, will stand for you in the midst of fire, will stand for you, indeed, in the midst of a great gale, will stand with you indeed when a whole nation turns their sabres upon you. A friend, entity, will love you for all and what you be, **regardless** of how you are expressing. That, entity, is the deepest friend you could possibly find, and there are few in this audience who know even one!

Now, if you do not have **one**, then perhaps you should look at you and how you express. [Of] the things you be wanting in a friend, do you, indeed, project, do you, indeed, live within your own uttermost parts of your being? If you are expecting one to stand with you in fire, yet you yourself will not stand by them, why think you to expect it of them and not of you?

Friends that are around you will only be as good as you, entity, realize that they are unto your own being! If they have "failed" you, [it is] not **they** [who] have failed you, [but] **you** who have failed you, for who is the receivership of "failure?" [It] is only you, not them! And only you, in the uttermost parts of your being, know what failure is; thus you have contemplated it, thus you have become it, and thus you have betrayed yourself!

To have a rally point of love around you does not mean that you need to succor every moment of your life and to care for the friend to make sure they are there! But being earnest in your own being and respecting in others what you respect within you will always have a point of reference with always a multudious of friends. Thus, any moment that your hour comes that strength is needed, the strength that you have put forth, indeed, and seen in **them** will be born innately of them, and they, entity, will rally with you in your moments. It is a truth!

Man on this plane, he is a child of his society; he is a child of fashion; he is a child of illusion! He is, in all regards, a fatalist to the overall consciousness. If one God feels that he is a failure and sees himself inept, the consciousness will feel the ineptness. Thus, when it comes time to turn to them, they will feel so inept, entity, that they will never fulfill. That is a truth!

To think properly, to think justly, to think purposefully, to think beauteous of one's being and to love one's being above all things, and to be honorable and trustworthy and just and good and beauteous unto you permits you to see that in others who may not have ever seen it in them[selves]. And once you see it in them, it is **born** of them, and they will never forget it!

And behold, an unlimited reality of esteemed emotion is born forth, and the emotion goes forth to perfect, to rally, to serve, to glorify them who hath never known it. And thus all the virtues of [you], the giver of virtues, are now being realized in the receivership of the receiver. Thus, that which is with you, entity, begins to realize all that you are. And behold, beauty and honor, indeed love, indeed the preciousness of esteemed being is realized in them, and it will be returned unto you in steadfastness. And they, indeed, will find it overwhelming and engulfing within their own beings, that when they look at yet others around them, all that they can see within **them** is what they are themselves. Thus, it goes on and on and on!

The importance [in] understanding this is seeing what you be. Do not, indeed, judge yourself harshly, but refine yourself. Do not become the victim, as it is so termed, of harsh judgement of so-called "friends," for if they judge you in the barbaricness of their beings, they are indeed judging themselves! Let them be, and stand away from them. Love what you are and hold it in the highest, most purposeful regard, that who you be will someday be a light unto a receivership that **will** stand with you

"You know, there is no man, no friend, entity, that is so bad [that] he cannot be forgiven, for there is no consciousness so diverse that it cannot be made perfect, for the basis of it is good."

and will love you.

All are friends, all are Gods, for they are **all** our blessed and most esteemed beloved brothren and they add to the glory of life felt and understood.

Unto all that are here, you all rally toward some of your friends, and [from] some you have felt failure, and [from] some you have felt exaltedness, and from others treason! That is good. Now that you have experienced all of that, it is time to experience the greater virtue of what friendship is. And do not seek it in another. Be it first within you. Round it forth there.

You must understand that you are the ideal, the **purposeful** creator, and that all that you are, see, perceive, be, must first round itself within you and **then** become.

Many of you are weak. I understand weakness; but I also understand strength, and once strength is seen, there is no sense in being weak again. Strength carries you forth.

Of all that we succeed in all audiences to understand, be it in friend or be it in lover, be it in husbandman, wife, mothren, fathren, child, whatever it is, the purposeful understanding here will always be individualized **You** and making that point understood and realized in **you.** And each teaching that we bring forth in this audience, all here will experience the depths and the heights of it to find a common balance with it.

I do not teach for the sake of having you listen to my myriad words to be understood and misunderstood and [for you to] try to put [them] into use later. All that I say will affect all that are here. And you will learn, indeed, first and foremost and **always** of you! If but one was here and he listened and he became, he is enough to light your world for an eternity!

Listen and become. Stretch into unlimitedness; your body will take you there. Love what you are seeing there. Be changeful. Be ongoing. Be loving. The experience alone will rally you unto your being a greater gratification, and that can be seen as a greater gratification in those around you.

You know, there is no man, no friend, entity, that is so bad [that] he cannot be forgiven, for there is no consciousness so diverse that it cannot be made perfect, for the **basis** of it is good. Change, entity, in attitude is also change in others. Once we have perfected you into change, into not being fearful of change as some ninny, and put you forth, then the change will come about that there is no longer a fear to love others, for the love will steadfast itself within you and you will no longer **be** at the hands of insecurities, at the hands of a fearful existence! And that we will do this day.

"I am a servant unto you, my dearest, most splendid brotherhood, and I cherish you all. I have not chosen to cherish you; do not misunderstand me. I cherish you because you are me; because the closer we become unto ourselves, the closer we become unto one another and the closer do we become unto the secrets of who we be and what we be unto the mysterious force called "God."

You will understand this, to be sure, in your time, as time that you count on passes in its own inequities. You will understand, I assure you."

My friends, they are without number, for each particum of Light Source is beloved unto my being. And where you will judge and only let a few in, entity, I have let them **ALL** in, and the Allness, entity, has made me a **complete** ongoingness! **All** I love, entity. There is not one I do not! It matters not how they are feeling unto me, for I consider them The All, and it be wise unto **you** to follow such examples! Indeed? So be it.

We Be Unto One Another A Brotherhood: The Composite Of The Mind Of God

I am Ramtha The Enlightened One. Indeed. And who be I, as it were? I be that that loves God Almighty, that has [a] supreme alliance with Him that is all things, that is all truth, indeed that is all being, all presence, all knowledge, all understanding. Thus, I have aligned myself with that which is called the Splendor of Life, indeed the Creative Cause, indeed the Divine Principle.

And who be you that have gathered amongst yourselves unto this that we term "audience?" You be God, selectively chosen to become unique in beauty, indeed the divine power, the love that is called You in all your essence. You be unto you as unique and lovely as I am unto you.

And what gives unto us this kinmanship, this love, this understanding? It is recognizing [in] full truth and all knowingness that what I am in the fullness of my being, indeed of the understanding of my being, that you are also. This gives unto us a purpose in character, a uniqueness that is not separate but together. It is called "brothers."

Brotherhood is not singular, as man is defined singular against woman; but brotherthood is a uniting force that has gained itself into what is called a family mode or unit that is surrounded against and becomes one central figure that is called the Fatherhood, the Mother-Father Principle that be God Divine. We are subjects of His thoughts for we be the subjects of Him. Thus, [in] the beauty of our being do we share unto one another the same Fatherhood, the same purpose, the same cause. Thus, that which we be unto one another be brothren unto one another. You be, in all your splendor and purpose, my brothren who I love greatly.

You see, I cannot be God Divine, I cannot be professed to love that which is termed God, the Life Force, if I do not love myself. And, above all things, my greatest mastery was loving myself against the duality called a hateful and revengeful heart that I sought in the lifetime of my existence. But I became the master of my being by loving me. Thus, I can profess that I love the Force, the Cause, the Principle Understanding, and can love you because I love me. And because I love that which we are unto one another, that binds us in supreme beauty, in sublime peace and a foreverness and understanding as to what we mean unto one another, indeed do I love you.

You are God; that is the same God of my being, that your beauty is the same beauty of my being, that the life force of my being is of your being. Thus, if I am a servant unto the Power that emanates Life, that is the directive cause of Life, then I am a servant unto you, my dearest, most splendid brotherhood, and I cherish you all. I have not **chosen** to cherish you; do not misunderstand me. I cherish you because you are me; because the closer we become unto ourselves, the closer we become unto one another and the closer do we become unto the secrets of who we be and what we be unto the mysterious force called "God." You will understand this, to be sure, in your time, as time that you count on passes in its own inequities. You will understand, I assure you.

Thus, I serve ultimately the Life Force and none other things, for there is no other thing save the Life Force. It is an all-encompassing, all-wise intelligent purpose that is the Splendor of Life. Thus do I serve you, my beloved brothren.

CHAPTER TWENTY-THREE

JUDGE NO ONE LEST YOU JUDGE YOURSELF

> **"Entities judge other people because in judging they are also trying to identify themselves. That is where the real truth is and that is why it is very forgivable in the assets called God.**
>
> **When you are looking at everyone else and condemning them for whatever it is, what you are doing, in essence, is you are condemning those aspects of Self within you that you have readily identified [within them]. They have been merely the tool [for you] to notice it."**

"When you bring forth judgement upon another entity, you do not change their life. What you are doing is you are recognizing an altered form of creativity which will be your own.

You create every moment. Every moment you think, everything you do, is a creation which you are the recipient of! That is how it is. If you judge another entity, you are creating an altered state, you are victimizing yourself because you are creating what you are seeing in another for yourself.

When you know who you are and truly love who you are, you will see the folly of seeing anyone else [as] other than perfection."

JUDGE NO ONE LEST YOU JUDGE YOURSELF

Whatever you see, whatever you feel of other people, whatever you perceive in regards to them are the very things that are beginning their procession in your own life. Thus, if you love and abide in the beauty of another, you know that that love and beauty have found a truth and perhaps a more formidable reality in your own existence. Therefore, you can "identify" with the other individual.

But if you find them despicable and lacking in character and judge them harshly at whatever they do, then it is what they are doing that you have found yourself judging yourself for. It is a truth! It gives you a clearer view of who and what you are, naked into your Soul. It has you look at your reality closer.

And soon you find that you do not wish to be despicable or be despising or judge, and in place of those things, you find love and kindness and tenderness, the warmth of character and being that promotes a zest for life rather than somberness for life.

Then, as you begin to look at others, you will find that there are no longer despicable peoples around, that there is only beauty around and God expressing in whatever chosen fashion and being he so desires to express in. That is how we rectify ourselves.

There are many that have yet to learn this. It is a simple secret in identifying yourself and mastering yourself for greater hopes and purposes in being. The steadfastness will occur, master, when you continue to look earnestly [and] intentionally for the good.

*

When you bring forth judgement upon another entity, you do not change their life. What you are doing is you are recognizing an altered form of creativity which will be your own.

You create **every** moment. Every moment you think, everything you do, is a creation which **you** are the recipient of! That is how it is. If you judge another entity, you are creating an altered state, you are victimizing yourself, because you are creating what you are seeing in another for yourself. When you know who you are and truly love who you are, you will see the folly of seeing anyone else [as] other than perfection.

A bum in his bumdom, entity, he is a happy soul. Who is to say that he is not? If perhaps the clothing on his back or the millet in his cup is not what you would partake, who says that what he is expressing isn't the ideal expression? He is quite

"Everytime one judges, what they are doing, in reality, is judging themselves. And everything they put out, they are going to receive back tenfold; if they are a Christ, it is a hundredfold.

If you looked at things as an isness, you would not ever have to worry about judging. Those that are Gods, they simply are and know and be, and they know there is no thing worth their judgement, for if it was, it would mean they would have to be lowered in their own kingdom in the return of their words, and there is nothing worth that. Who wants to be altered once they become unlimited?"

happy in what he is or he wouldn't be it! And who says, entity, the Nubian is anything less than the white man? Who says they are less, that they are not God? They are, entity, the same as you are. And who says their truth is not heard by the Infinites? It is, the same as yours.

When you learn that they are that way because they **wanted** to be that way, and that for their experience they are doing that, and that the God-fire that is within them is the same within you, you will love them. The same with the yellow race, entity, and even the green race and all that there are. Who says they are not beautiful? And who is to say they are imperfect? No one is! They are all perfect.

When you infinitely love yourself and know you have become you for a perfect reason of expressing, experimenting, understanding, and when you love that which you are--all of You!--you will have the compassion to love everyone else. No, you do not need to go and take care of them and change them. Leave them alone: that is the greatest thing you can do! Love them and let them do whatever they wish to do. Then, master, you have become a great God, a great light unto the world!

Everyone here is doing **precisely** what they need to do, and there is not one of them that is "wrong," entity, for they are all going to live through it and they are all going to learn and they are going to be anew and better for it. It is **not** your place nor are you so great that you have set a precedence above the Father to judge what is good and bad. You are not that great, nor do you have the power to change it. The Father, that is the infiniteness of all sorts, hath judged **nothing**, entity; what gives you the right to say and weigh right and wrong? You don't!

Thus, whatever you create in your perception, it will never interfere or inflict upon another; it will inflict upon you! When you learn to love yourself as the infinite Source who can be all things, they you will love everything and all of it! Then, you will let it be and continue to radiate and create and become.

No one is worth judgement, entity. No color of skin, no action, no anything is worth having to put yourself through the creative part you have just judged as a reality! When you love this wonderful fire within you, you will never judge another thing.

*

Everytime one judges, what they are doing, in reality, is judging themselves. And everything they put out, they are going to receive back tenfold; if they are a Christ, it is a hundredfold.

It is difficult [not to judge], for the consciousness on this plane says, "How do you determine beauty? How do you determine right and wrong? By judging what is." [Since] you are a part of the consciousness, that is a difficulty, [but] that is a mastery.

If you look at things and see them for the truth that they are, the truth of the moment says, "This is how it is." If you look at a man who is expressing very poorly or is expressing very vilely or very negatively, do not note the negativity in him. If you do, it means it is noted within you, [for] you cannot see in another what you don't already possess. If you look and love them and let that love just be, regardless of who they are, then you will always be held blameless and you will always be pure in your being.

Always look at things and determine if they are worthy to be judged, [for] whatever you judge it [to be], you will become. So, is it worth the value or that which is termed the return receipt of your judgement?

If you looked at things as an isness, you would not ever have to worry about judging. Those that are Gods, they simply are and know and be, and they know there is no thing worth their judgement, for if it was, it would mean they would have to be lowered in their own kingdom in the return of their words, and there is nothing worth that. Who wants to be altered once they become unlimited?

*

Judgement is final. When you judge another, you are judging them finally, for you cannot see them [as being] any other way, and, unfortunately, all times after that, they will always be judged for that. Seeing a truth is seeing it **in the moment.** There is no wrong in seeing a truth in the person at that moment, but [only] at **that** moment. If the truth carries over way after the moment is finished, entity, then that is the judgement, for then you are saying this person is this way for the next day or so when they may not be!

When God looks at you, He looks at the totality of the being seen **now,** and the totality of the being seen now is **always perfect.** If one say, "I have done this and I have done that," the Father will look at them and He will say unto them how they can be better. But the Father does not look at them [in judgement]; only Man looks at them that way.

The greatest way that you can help others without passing judgement of them or being speculative about their truth is to live your life in such a manner that you are the reflection of hope to them, that perhaps they will see in you one thing that they are needing in themselves, without [your] saying they are this or they are that [but] simply letting them be. That is pure love, entity, [for] it hath no shades of judgement in it.

One wonderful thing about the Christ that is subtle: His light is your light, [and] your light draws only to you the likeness of your being. You do not have to utter a word or think a word against the will of an entity. If they stay with you, that is because their light has become like [yours], and in that, entity, all you can see is yourself. If it hasn't, they will soon fall away. Let the Christ of your being be a splendid example, entity, and just be.

Now, [what one] man believes and knows and what his intellect is, is going to be different from one sitting next to him. [But] they are both equal in [that] their understanding [is] unique to them, yet they are different [in that understanding]. One will say that he sees this one [way], yet the other will say that he does not see [that] at all; he sees it this way. Both are correct and true, entity. The thing people must realize about people is that however they view themselves is how they will be. However we view them, entity, is only the thing we can recognize in them that we are recognizing in ourself.

The greatest thing you can do is to love them and let them be and let them express, however. Love them for them, the God that they are, which is an isness. Simply sitting here, they are to be loved; they do not have to do anything to enhance their being. The fact that they [exist] is greater than anything they will ever do, entity, good or bad, negative or positive. Love them for being, for as long as the are, you will be.

What is good for the Father is good for the Son. What is good for the mass of the "Is," is good for the singular of the "Is," If Man will pattern his thinking after the Life Force and **be** as the Life Force, he will **become** the Life Force--and nothing less! So be it.

*

Life is perpetual; it will go on. And moment into moment into moment, as we live it wondrously, we have opportunities to make ourselves as happy one moment as we [do] in the moments to come. But however we fill that moment, master, is according to our will and our fulfillment and our good. And if in the moment, we are driven to slay an entity, and if that moment satisfied some ancient hunger within us, then in the next moment we will live in awesome fear that somehow that will come back to us. Thus, our moments to come are not secured, save we forgive ourself for the act.

Now, the slain will come back, again and again and again. Life is perpetual; it is continuous. It is the only thing that is perpetual, yet it is all things. If I abhor and bring judgement unto the slayer, I have brought it unto myself. The [slayer] has already made his own judgement. He will be at the hands of whatever attitude he has perceived during the act, and he, in all understandings, will have to balance that out; it must be balanced.

There are plenty of people that will go and be horrified and will judge and will curse. But I love the entity that has slain the other, for how can I not? Is he outside of the providence and the will and the wonderment of the I AM that I am? Is he outside of God?

When you see such things, they are fulfillments occurring. In our moments, we have the option to fulfill moments in a way that we feel driven to or we feel enlightened to. That is our choice. That is the only republic man has: the republic within himself, deep within himself. Your government will try to govern the mass according to democracy, laws, but they will never govern the will of man that works in the secret thoughts; only he does. And each time he lives in a moment, he balances the moment according to his being.

The [slayer] chose what to do. Now he must be responsible for the act in his moments that will occur and [will] repeat themselves in a balance that he must deal with. I do not abhor it. I have reasoned it, I have understood it; I am beyond it. If I abhor it and come back and be judgemental, entity, then I am no grander for it, I assure you, and my life will be affected by it, for the I AM which I am [will] have taken a part of it[self] and separated it from my being; then I am no longer whole. You see?

I say in this audience that there is no grander teacher than you are. There isn't! And ultimately, we are responsible for our life accords. Are we not the ones who in thought do one thing? Is it not the manifestation of that one thing that will teach our thoughts to be more refined?

You can take a man and put him in prison, into the smallest, darkest, filthiest pit there is, but you will never imprison his mind and his thinking. A man with the body stifled is still active in thought, and he, entity, through contemplative understanding, will teach himself and cure himself and reason with himself--and judge himself. That is why not even murder or hacking a man into several pieces ever destroys him; that only makes it worse for yet another day to come.

Life is ongoing. If it isn't, entity, then it is time that you count all your miseries and worries and start putting them together, because if it ends when you close your eyes, entity, then you have done a lot of missing in this life.

*

Is it a judgement, entity, to keep yourself from being within the throws of [an] enemy because you know he is going to do harm to you? If love of Self, entity, matters at all, then you will remove yourself from the harm and bless it and love it. If it lays siege to you, take up arms against it. I will tell you why: murder is not a sin. It [may be] an outrage to hear that, but it is not [a sin]. It would only be a sin if you destroyed permanently an existence, which can never be done, for if you could, then you are destroying a participle of God, and you cannot do that!

If you take up arms and you are the victor, you have not sinned, as it were, for there is no such thing as a sin. You have defended Self. The entity has been taken out of his body to where he can no longer do harm in a physical realm until he has had time to think about it; and when he is ready, he'll come back!

It is much better to "turn the other cheek," entity, than it is to go at war--unless it is evoked upon you. For if you do that, then you make them think, and time and experience will perhaps lessen the hate of your enemies, and [their] understanding in the way God works in His realm will allow the entity the experience to understand you a bit better. Then you have put off a catastrophe, as it were; a catastrophe not [in the sense] that you destroy anything, but [one of] a guilt within the Soul which is long mending.

To see the truth as it is, is one thing. To judge it as being evil, ugly or good or whatever, that is the judgement! You can say that a man is a killer because he **does** kill; he enjoys doing it. To say that he is "wrong" in doing it is the judgement. Understand that in an infinite understanding.

And do not judge that which is around you that would judge you for your beliefs. Love them and let them be. [Though] oftentimes they place that which you be and your beliefs in a very crucial and unloving position, that is also a great overcoming; but always remember Self amidst it.

What we are teaching here is not that anyone here after their life has a choice of going to a beastly place called hell or a heaven; we have talked of that already. That is not how it is. Everyone that perishes, even the most beastly of entities, as you would see it, will pass from this plane into the utopia called God; there is no other place but that.

What I am teaching you here is that you have options, and to be wise in the things you confront everyday in your experiences for this one reason: The emotion that weighs on the Soul determines your destiny, and if you do any one thing that wroughts guilt within your being, then the days that are

"Man is not evil in his Soul; he is divine in his Soul. And 'good' and 'evil,' the polarity, exists on this plane in those who believe it, for [as] they believe so their kingdom is.

If you choose to believe that, [then] that is your truth, and you are not wrong, at all. And if indeed it is yours, entity, it collectively belongs to you because it is formulated in your opinion. As long as you have that opinion, it will always be real. Always.

'Good' and 'evil' will always exist for you who believe it. That is how it is."

beauteous, that are God, that are unfolding every moment, will be dull, hurtful, and insecure to you because you have guilt upon your being. And that is not worth it, entity!

I am teaching you to have your life the most splendid of all lives and never [to] be condemning of Self, but to love Self every moment. Then, when you pass into the utopia, you can recognize it for the utopia it is rather than feeling guilty that you must come back here. You see? Either way, you are a part of God: that is inevitable. It is how you make life easier is where I am expert in teaching. So be it.

*

Opinion must have a foundation of experience; that is the only thing you can base an opinion on. The experience is lodged within the entity formulating the opinion.

Those who have lived upon this plane, for eons have been flung into that which is termed the horrors and terrors of "good" and "evil." They have lived violently, violently. So [the] experience and knowingness within their being has formulated "good" and "bad" according to experience.

Master, Man is not evil in his Soul; he is divine in his Soul. And "good" and "evil," the polarity, exists on this plane in those who **believe** it, for [as] they believe so their kingdom is. If you choose to believe that [man is evil], [then] that is your truth, and you are not wrong, at all. **Your** truth, master; not mine or anyone else's. Yours. And if indeed it is yours, entity, it collectively **belongs** to you because it is formulated in your opinion. As long as you have that opinion, it will always be real. Always.

How does one overcome that which is set opinion? The same way he got it in the first place. When you change your attitude [to see] that all that was was necessary for the evolvement of this refined, delicate creature, [and] that rather than [being] "evil," [you] obtained "purposeful knowingness," which is not evil (How can knowingness be evil? Knowledge is an enlightening thing), then all things [that] come forth, rather than [being] referred to in the memory as "evil," [they will be] referred to as an experience, a knowingness. And soon the Soul will begin to collect **knowledge** that is no longer based on judgement. Then you become, indeed, like that which is termed the angel who looks upon enlightenment as the dawning of tomorrow.

Unlimitedness must be formulated in the Soul experience by experience in order for the degree of judgement to be overcome in its totality. Then, when you have lived for a little eon here and thoughts are coming forth to you for reference by the divine Soul, all it can say [is], " 'Tis life, 'tis life, 'tis God." Then there is no judgement.

"Good" and "evil" will always exist for you who believe it. That is how it is.

*

The reason that you get "stuck" to [your point of view], as you have so wisely termed it, is that your point of view has proven itself to be a reality for you. Thus, you are coming from a basis of truth, a nucleus of truth. Your point of view has worked quite well and has shown itself to be a reality to you.

When you find yourself "stuck" to it and find those that you meet do not see your point of view and have their own point of view--which [has been] a workable truth to **them**--then what you do is [to] speculate beyond the bounds of your point of view; go into the "unreasonable reasoning," and when you do so, you [will] find a point of interest that will be most intriguing to you.

Contemplate it. Look at the possibilities that there is truth everywhere, for there **is**; that your point of view, entity, perhaps can be an answer to someone else who is "stuck"; and their point of view can be that very speculative cause which you have contemplated on beyond your bounds of "unreasonable reasoning."

Learn to be open, master. There is truth at all places, and all express according to their will. Contemplate their point of view. It does not mean that you must accept it as a truth for you in your kingdom, your truth; but contemplate it to see its workable concepts for those who believe in it as arduously as you believe in yours.

The way you do that, master, is do not have a point of view. Be, in a state of Isness, a state of Divine Being. When you are in a state of being, there be no premise of one singular truth for you, but you be the reviewer of all truth and thus do not have judgement to alter truth; [you] accept it and explore it and find if it be workable in your state of being.

When you are in a state of being, then you do not judge other people; you do not have the **only** truth and cannot see any further than your nose. In a state of being, you are aware of all truth. And in a state of being, when the barriers are broken down [of] one truth clashing with another, it is at that point that you learn to see people, men, woman, children--Gods sublime--for the beauty they are.

What is the most important thing in life? Not [others'] point of view, but their "beingness"; it is a direct reflection of yours. And in that, entity, joy, peace, happiness, knowingness, comes to you equally and evenly. Then you begin to be fulfilled, master, moment to moment. As long as there is a "point of view," as long as their be a "point of judgement," then your being is altered, [then] you will never have the completeness of life and what it offers--and that be a direct truth.

Be. Go beyond thinking, entity, into being. You will not become an unlimited entity as long as you have a "statute of limitation" of belief. You will only be at the hands of belief and not of life. So be it.

CHAPTER TWENTY-FOUR

LOVE IN FREEDOM TO LIVE IN FREEDOM

"The purest love, noblest love, mother-father love of all emotion and feeling is expressly given and earned through that which is termed freedom—when we can love one another freely and let them express their truth."

"Learn to love in freedom and respect all's truth and opinion as well as you desire them to respect your [truth] and [to] listen to you and [to] love you in freedom. When that is procured, the love will be longstanding; it will never be thrown away, it will never, indeed, be forgotten, for it will be divinely unique, its principle good and earnestly noble. No entity forgets nobility, and no entity forgets freedom."

ALLOW OTHERS THE FREEDOM TO EXPRESS THEIR UNIQUE TRUTH

Truth--well, that is an enigma, is it not, for who has got **the** truth? And, indeed, what is truth? Well, the truth is, everything is [truth]: there is no such thing as untruth.

You see, if Man were not here, the elements would have no reason to be elements, the sun would have no reason to be blatant upon this plane, the flowers would no longer bloom, because Man feeds life through his own poignant consciousness to give meaning to life.

Every entity in this dream is a manifesting God; they are divine and eminent. They have created, according to their own desires, ideals that perpetuate their own inner beauty, however that is. And everyone's opinion of things differs vastly, vastly, [for] they are gathering the sum total of that opinion based on the understanding [or] misunderstanding [that] they have in their Soul up to the point to where they have learned, through experience, to judge what things are.

There are entities in this audience that have been every conceivable manifestation of Man--in every form, in every circumstance, in every way. They, above all, possess perhaps the most unlimited graciousness, for they have compassion for all peoples because they have **been** all people.

According to each individual God's expresssion of life--not only in this one, but in all the multudious lives before this one--hath he gathered an opinion based on experience. And everyone here has learned [at] different intervals. They have gained differently, but, nonetheless, all have gained. That is a truth. So, one will believe in something or another, and another will argue it because his belief is different. And the two cannot comprehend one another because they have not **been** one another. You see?

So who is wrong? None. Everyone is right. To the lowest ebbs of limited thought, to the graciousness of unlimited flight, they are all truth. For a man to tell you a lie, he is not telling you a lie; he is telling you a truth. Because consciousness is ongoing, [it] can allow a new creation of what was truth a moment ago to be seen. You see?

The truth is: everyone is right and no one is wrong. What each one must discern is to learn to love the whole of everyone and know with infinite wisdom that their truth is as valid as yours, and love them for the saying of it. You see? Great Gods, great, immaculate, divine souls that do this are beloved by

"What greater happiness could you ask for anyone other than that they be content however they see happiness to be. Leave them alone. Love them. Let them have the opportunity to discern their own happiness. You simply enjoy your life and be: that is the greatest thing you can give them."

hosts, for they are the peacemakers, the Heralds of Peace--not because they have abstained from life and have an innocent view on it, but because they have been it and can embrace everyone because of it.

What I teach here is wondrous truth. There is no other place on your plane that this truth will ever be taught in this unlimited virtue and context, for who dare call God "lawless," for if He is that, then they have no control over Him. But my truth, entity, embraces everyone else's. Let that be the same for you also.

*

Everything is truth. Truth is only the perceived theory of the one speaking it and feeling it. To the one hearing it, that cannot feel it, it is always questionable.

Everything is truth, master. And for as many Gods that inhabit this plane of one of billions of understandings, everyone's truth will differ, for they have the right to create the truth differently.

Everyone is right. The thing that makes the difference, as it were, is allowing everyone else their truth, graciously, for that is called Love--loving another to allow them their truth **regardless** if it is your truth or not. Because they believe, assert or live in a certain manner different from you does not mean they are wrong. It is simply their truth.

Allow the whole world to believe however they wish to believe. It is their right to express it. Just be yourself.

*

What greater happiness could you ask for anyone other than that they be content however they see happiness to be. Leave them alone. Love them. Let them have the opportunity to discern their own happiness. You simply enjoy your life and be: that is the greatest thing you can give them.

*

You know entity, everything here is a dream. You are like in slumber here, a thick slumber. This is a dream, and in its unrealities, the one reality you know exists is that which perceives the unreality called Self.

Loving one's Self happens in a moment, first to establish that there **is** Self, that you really are. But the unfoldment of that, entity, will take many days in your time, for much will you have to see and learn from and be steadfast with. That will take a little while, but it will all be worth it. [And] once you have gained that which is termed love for yourself, a wondrous, wondrous miracle happens. Then you can love everyone else in freedom.

Everyone here, master, they all believe differently than you do. And who is right and who is wrong? There is nothing **but** truth! There is not an untruth or a lie: everything **is** fundamental Life, and every God here is right, everyone. Even if they are in disagreement with you, they are all right, including yourself. Thus, they are all expressing truth.

When you have reached a stage of loving that which is termed the sublime Self, master, and realize that you did everything you did for the glory of you and because you wanted to, and because it was necessary, and because you needed the wisdom from it; and you have forgiven Self for feeling guilty, indeed, for feeling fearful, hateful, despise of self; and learn that it was all intentional, purposeful good; then you can look at anyone and no matter what they say of you, [even] if they hate you, you can love them, for they are hating you in freedom [in] as much [as] they are loving you in freedom. You understand? This, entity, is how a Master is and how they become.

Once you do that, you will no longer live for anyone but yourself; you will live in spite of everyone. For when you become who you are, you become what is called a Living Light to the world--to the world. Then, entity, peace walks upon this plane in sublime stature; God is unfurled here [in] you. Then you will have the capacity to live in freedom, to contemplate the vastness, unlimitedness. [Then] genius is born, [a] creative principle arises, the poet is born, the scribe arises, the wise man is seen.

When you stop living for everyone else is when God immerses within [you], comes to the surface. That I will teach you to do. And it will take a little while, master, but it will all be worth it. And in the interim, when one becomes critical of you, smile upon their countenance and love them, sincerely, for they are expressing freedom, and that is what you yourself must have in order to understand Self. Indeed? So be it.

*

What will help you [to understand others] is try not understanding other people. Stop trying to! Love them and allow them to be and accept their truth. **Don't** understand them---**Love** them. 'Tis not for you to understand. 'Tis for you to understand yourself and be at peace with that principle.

Everyone upon this plane, they are doing everything **different** than what you are doing because they must, because they **want** to; that is the determining factor. To try to understand someone else you would have to be them, and you are not! You are yourself. What allows understanding is [relating as] God to God—that is called Love. That, entity, allows everyone to be however they wish **in** their understanding.

*

The purest love, noblest love, mother-father love of all emotion and feeling is expressly given and earned through that which is termed freedom—when we can love one another freely and let them express their truth.

What makes us love one another is the identity that each possesses uniquely. We do not wish to possess that, to change it, to make it our own. We wish to love them in the state that they are perfectly expressing.

Learn to love in freedom and respect all's truth and opinion as well as you desire them to respect your [truth] and [to] listen to you and [to] love you in freedom. When that is procured the love will be longstanding; it will never be thrown away, it will never, indeed, be forgotten, for it will be divinely unique, its principle good and earnestly noble. No entity forgets nobility, and no entity forgets freedom.

*

Everyone has their truth, and to what degrees or fashions that it is formulated is entirely upon the opinion of that which is expressing it, according to altered Ego. For you to go and to change the world or insist or feel badly because they feel [a particular] way makes you a tyrant and an enslaver, for you are taking away their freedom of expression, of truth.

Love them, master. Love them. No matter what they do to you, love them. But do not allow them to inhibit that which is termed your own growth, your own broadening perspective base, as it were. Continue to accumulate, continue to grow strong, continue to become. And the more you become, the greater the gentleness and the greater compassion [you will have] for the whole of humanity and their expression.

One day, entity, there would come one that would slay you of your life, and would you lift a hand? Nay, for if it is for the benefit of that entity to get rid of you, he will, and you will allow it, because in the infiniteness of your knowingness, your life will never be gotten rid of; you will always be. And that great, great humbleness is the sign of eminent holiness, that which is termed God.

God loves us **whatever** we do, and, in that fashion, you do it unto others the same. Allow them to feel whatever they feel. Do not take that away from them. Do you understand?

When your love becomes unlimited, it can love, indeed, a movement that moves entirely outside of the realm of your own dominion because you love it. For those of a limited perspective, that are riddled with guilt and betrayal, entity, you can do nothing to change that nor **should** you, for their concepts of your being are going to be however they **perceive** you. That is not important to you. What is important is that you are **allowing** them their opinion: that is called Love, master.

MARRY IN THE SOUL: ALLOW PASSION THE FREEDOM TO BE

Student: I would like to do something to make myself happy. I've had an unhappy marriage for a number of years.

Ramtha: I am aware, entity.

Student: And I would like to leave this marriage, and I need your help to know how to tell my husband and my children that I plan to leave it very soon.

Ramtha: It will not be so difficult if you stop and consider, entity, the reason you are doing it. The reason is self-happiness. You have lived long enough for that which is termed the images of other people. Now it is time to live for self.

I will tell you, master: The only way to ever speak is in complete love, but even. And to speak even, entity, is to earnestly express how you feel--but in compassion. If you love yourself, you will do this, straightaway. And if they wish to be hurt, it is because they want to be hurt; that is their choosing. Their expectancy to expect you to be a certain way all of your existence is quite enslaving when God, the Father, changes every moment.

The only thing that is forever is you. Think about why and do it. That is all.

Student: I would also like to remarry, and I wonder when the best time for this will be?

Ramtha: Why do you want to do that?

Student: I want to marry someone I love and someone who loves me and someone who will not make me feel that I am a servant, as I have felt for twenty-nine years.

Ramtha: You will do perhaps what I tell you to do and listen carefully? Do not marry them. You already are [in] that you desire it in your soul. Do not marry them. If you do, then you have placed a limitation upon already that which is pure and virtue. Go and live together and be happy. That is bliss, and the mere fact that you are doing it, [it] never gets tiring.

And who sanctifies the marriage of soul? Your government doesn't even know where it is located!

Student: Ramtha, I don't know if I can live with someone without marrying them.

Ramtha: Why, because a document says that you are?

Student: Probably so, but I don't know. I haven't come that far yet.

Ramtha: You need to! Master, what utterly can you commit in this your reality that you have not already committed in your thought? If you contemplate lying with your man in your fantasy--which you do--you have already done it. You wish to sanctify it and make it acceptable? It never will be.

You are not marrying for dignity. You are marrying for passion and love--which have nothing to do with papers! And to sanctify it in the name of God, in the name of God it already has been, for love, entity, is the answer to that. Yah.

You, tell me what your vows are for marriage. Speak them to me.

Student: "To love, honor and obey"--is that what you mean?

Ramtha: And that is the same thing that got you into trouble all of these years! You committed to it and so you have it.

The greatest marriage, master, the **greatest** marriage, is the marriage of Soul. The marriage of Soul commits **nothing,** except feelings. It doesn't vow to do anything; it simple is. That is the purest love there is, the purest desire, the purest passion. And when you love that way, master, you will find happiness with another entity.

Don't mar it. The sanctity of marriage is not acknowledged in heaven as a "must." What is acknowledged in heaven, entity--and heaven be all understandings--is emotion, and that is **already** created. And don't do it for the sake of the man to please him. Remember, you are trying to get out of doing that.

That is my answer. If you love yourself and wish this earnestly, you will not do it. You will go and be happy with the man to whom you love and you will find your bliss, wonderfully.

So be it . . . God will never judge you, you know.

Student: But everyone else would.

Ramtha: And who are they? Will they die for you? Ask one of them to die for you. If they will not die in your place and save you from dying, why should you care, entity, of what they think of your living?

Student: It's very thought-provoking.

Ramtha: It is, indeed, master. And if you take it to the limits of its unlimitedness, entity, you will see that the only thing that needs gratification here is you, and that no one else really cares. All they care about is themselves--and that is wonderful, for that is how they should be.

Student: Thank you.

Ramtha: And the next time someone is very hasty in their judgement of your actions, look at them and bless them from the Lord God of your Being to the Lord God of their Being and contemplate for a moment if this person that is making a mockery of your existence would kindly die for you. And if they [would] not, send them on their way.

Student: Thank you.

Ramtha: I will help you and I will show you what I am speaking of. So be it.

Hmh! Everyone thinks God is full of laws and regulations and all of that. He has not got the time--He is too busy enjoying what He is.

*

Master, I speak evenly unto you, and listen unto me. This love that you have is for you and the entity and no one else. And if that which is termed the family disapproves, give them the freedom to disapprove and do not rush to make excuses, as it were, or try to convince them otherwise. You have nothing to do for that; you are involved with that which is termed this beauteous entity and not her family.

If you will start living for you and your wondrous relationship together and let the world do whatever it chooses to do, you shall find happiness. However, if you are weak enough to let them interfere, entity, then perhaps you must reevaluate your worth and deserving to be loved by someone. You understand?

*

The travesty of that which is termed "marriage," if you will--and permit me to express this--is that entities get together in a sacrament, and they have great passions running through their being, and they cannot live without one another. And the "heat" is so strong that they plot and plan on how to get together--legally. It is a truth!

And so they get together, and the first thing they are doing, they are working so hard so they can pay for a great structure that they "must" have to impress all of their friends about their greatness. And they incur indebtedness so that they have the proper attire, the proper furnishings, and Persian rugs, and Alexandrian glass, and all of that. And then, of course, they have to entertain. And, in order to do that, they must keep the glass polished and the carpets cleaned and the walls immaculate. And so they get together to represent to the community a legalized passion which really doesn't exist!

"In my time, marriage was a commitment of the Spirit; it had nothing to do with papyrus and filing and all of that! That is boring, ridiculous and costly! Marriage is the Spirit. It is the union of love."

And before you know it, their burdens are becoming greater and greater, because they want to do more, and they are taken further and further apart. And soon entity, what occurs is that there will come along another entity who sees in either one of them what they once saw in [each other]. And soon, romance and hearts are floating to the sky, and passion is deep and thick, and gossip is being covered up, and love is examined—all over again. And pretty soon, it causes "the great heartache," and no one understands why it happened.

The reason it happens is that man and woman are here for love and the creativity of life they are enjoying. The reason there are sexes, the reason there is man and woman, is to copulate, to bring forth more life, and, in the process, enjoy what is before them that they have created. Unfortunately, they have done so much creating that they are forgetting about love and the reason they got together in the first place!

So another will come to take either one of your places eventually, because eventually you will look around and wonder what happened to your youth; you will wonder what happened to the feelings deep within you. And someone will come along and say, "Here they are!" And, alas, you'll be born free with another individual, but with all of the hurt and the sorrow that follows. Then you are weighted down with guilt. And so it goes, on and on and on.

You don't have a house **worth**, nor do you have papyrus-work **worth**, nor do you have siblings **worth** the separation of the union of passion and ecstasy and love that the two of you heartily possess. And it would do you well to take a look around you and ask yourself if it is worth it all, and start [giving] some of the things that are "responsibilities" to someone else who daily enjoys doing that sort of thing and get back into the arms of your lover and become a woman again and let him express through his loins how to be a man. Then you will have wonderful times together, and love will be born again, and your cheeks will glow, and you'll wonder why you ever forgot about it in the first place!

People get married here only to be separated--by "priorities." You have too many priorities and not enough of what brought you together in the first place. If you don't become a woman, someone else will. And if he doesn't become a man, someone else will. There are entities who still think of such things and find them deliciously delightful. That is how it is!

Go take a look at your wondrous structure. Your walls may gleam, and your glass may shine, and you rugs may be soft, but ah, alas, what is left of you at the end of the day when you only want to turn over and go to sleep? The house doesn't need to be spotless, nor does your business, nor your children, nor your entertaining, nor anything else!

"Now there is a bit of advice I wish to give you here. Don't go off with the inkling in your mind that you want to engage in this practice of marriage with contracts. Do not ever commit yourself to forever; that has not been established yet. Learn to love in freedom. Love for the sake of being together. That is all that is important."

Allow yourselves time together. Your siblings are going to grow up and leave anyway, you know that! You are not going to keep them forever, nor would you want to! They are only going to grow up to leave you. Then what have you left then? The memories? Or hoping they will come see you? Their life is their life, not yours! Get in touch with what matters; it will last you all this lifetime, that you'll never spend a lonely moment, or a forsaken moment, or an unhappy moment. Learn to be a woman and relish the moment that you are [in]. Relish it! The same with your husbandman. There be not anything that either one of you are doing that is worth the loss of what you have shared in your intimacy. You think of that!

In my time, marriage was a commitment of the Spirit; it had nothing to do with papyrus and filing and all of that! That is boring, ridiculous and costly! Marriage is the Spirit. It is the union of love.

*

Now there is a bit of advice I wish to give you here. Don't go off with the inkling in your mind that you want to engage in this practice of marriage with contracts. Do not ever commit yourself to forever; that has not been established yet.

Live in the moment and be happy in the moment and expect only the moment to fulfill you. If you live in the moment preparing for the future, you will have missed the moment entirely, as you will miss the future moments when they come. Learn to love in freedom. Love for the sake of being together. That is all that is important.

*

Marriage is created in the Soul. It is a thirst, a hunger. It is a desire, it is a need, it is a compassion, it is an "isness" felt for another entitiy that is relective upon Self. You never have to marry and never should marry for the eyes of society or for creed or family. Marry within the Soul that accepts, loves, and understands. Any marriage other than that will only make you unhappy and cause you worry.

*

If you slumber and live and love and labor and share with an entity, what is the difference in marriage and non-marriage in this given circumstance? What does marriage do? What does it sanction? You want to do everything that it says that you can and yet you are already doing them. Do you need an approval?

"If love is based upon how another receives it, love can never be. Love is not born in the heart of another, it is born in yours. Be happy that you love and that the capacity of that doth exist in your own kingdom and is fulfilled in your own kingdom."

Marriage is born in the Soul. That which loves one another and shares in the wholeness and the adventure of one another is already "married." That is a term meant for contractual agreements, and if broken, will sorely be punished. That is a limitation.

But marriage already exists. And what is the term of how long it exists? However long happiness is shared and the adventure is still wild and free and the fever runs hot into your veins and the moment is secured in a jubilant of joy with the embrace of both peoples. That is marriage—always. The Soul determines that—nothing else, master.

So what you are trying to decide to become, you already are in an understanding that is more unlimited and sweeter to the being. So, you don't have to make up your mind about anything. Simply allow and be. Being is the freedom to express: know that. Understand you?

*

Where lovers "fail" is that they expect that all the sensations of love to be felt not only in their own being but in whom they share their love with. They expect [the] other to reciprocate unto them the equal amounts in givingness that they have given. They expect their lover to be faithful and true, and to be earnest, and, above all, to love them above all.

That is an error, for if love is based upon how another receives it, love can never be. Love is not born in the heart of another, it is born in yours. Be happy that you love and that the capacity of that doth exist in your own kingdom and is fulfilled in your own kingdom.

*

You do not have to live with anyone nor should [you] live with anyone and share their life if it is not through good will and love, for all have their individual lives to live. You are not "wrong" or [have] erred in continuing a marriage that have lost the meaning long ago. [But] you are far better off and more agreeable to permit yourself the freedom to find life and to find its joys, master, that are always awaiting for you if you but look.

And to those personages that hold on to a forgotten past and are relentless in their pursuit to make some poor soul pay for his grievous acts, for them the future in not possible, for they cannot see the good or the joy in another's eyes, for they are bent on bringing forth war on that which has dismayed them. Woe unto them that do this thing, for happiness will never be theirs. That is a truth!

"Your children are your brothers, born through the vehicle of man and woman. You may call them 'children,' [but] in understanding, they are your brothers, and they are as old as you are. Thus, your siblings have lived right along with you since the Beginning of Knowingness, and have lived and created and formulated a virtual paradise in the created Self."

ALLOW CHILDREN TO BE THE UNIQUE GODS THEY ARE

It is the notion for some time that [children] are created from the genes of both parents. Only the body is! [Their] Spirit was created in one expansion when The Father contemplated Himself and created Light, a highest principle of bodily existence. All Spirits were created at the same moment--**all** at the same moment!

Your children are your **brothers,** born through the vehicle of man and woman. Through copulation, seed is formed, mass is formed, [which] allows the birthing of an entity that [their parents] had no part in creating, only God! You may call them "children," [but] in understanding, they are your brothers, and they are as old as you are. Thus, your siblings have lived right along with you since the Beginning of Knowingness, and have lived and created and formulated a virtual paradise in the created Self.

Every entity--and listen closely--every entity's fulfillment is whatever he has never done before in being a participant in life. The Soul that is within them **drives** them to fulfill that which is not fulfilled or experienced. Some entities will experience being kings and others [will] experience being servants. Some will be mariners and others will be farmers. Some will be smithies and others winers, candlemakers, broadcloth loomers, weavers, harlots, whoremongers, vile men, corrupt women.

Everything that has ever been created in consciousness **everyone,** entity, has experienced or will experience for the value that it is a "creative conscious level" that the Soul has no data upon.

Thus, the Soul drives the entity to experience in his life principles what he has never experienced before. And [this was] quite well and good until judgement was created that there were certain rights and wrongs. Life was never conceived to be right and wrong; it was conceived simply to be Life--[to be] experienced [as] part of creation.

Each time each Soul-entity-self experiences a consciousness of Man, the clearer is the wisdom he obtains from it [and] the less he becomes judgemental of Life and his beloved brothren.

Your children possess knowingness that could teach [their] family. They know of things that you have not experienced, for they have already done them. And what you are doing now, they [may be] bored with, for they have **already** done them! Boredom is a sign from the Soul that [something] has already been done, [that it] is learning nothing more.

"The grandest way to help [your children] is not to tell them what you want them to do, but allow them to do what they want to do. They will not abuse the right, nor will they abuse you or any of your family. They will be drawn to their own knowingness to complete what is in their Soul. If they do not, they will go mad and rebel against your house and everyone in it.

Allow them to be. The greatest and most intimate love is love given in freedom."

[may be] bored with, for they have **already** done them! Boredom is a sign from the Soul that [something] has already been done, [that it] is learning nothing more.

The grandest way to help [your children] is not to tell them what you want them to do, but allow them to do what they want to do. They will not abuse the right, nor will they abuse you or any of your family. They will be drawn to their own knowingness, indeed, to complete what is in their Soul. If they do not, they will go mad and rebel against your house and everyone in it. Allow them to be. The greatest and most intimate love is love given in freedom.

Man and woman do not create the Soul or Spirit [of a child]; they create the body. The Soul and Spirit is infinite Godhood, and it will do whatever it wants to do. In rearing children, most make an error in thinking everyone needs the same. They do not. Your schooling should be diversified enough that the siblings should choose what they want to learn. If they were allowed to do that, you would have more genius prevalent on this plane. And you would not have entities rebelling because they are treated as 'mass' rather than individuals, for everyone is.

Your children, no matter what they do in this life, they are doing it to obtain "noble virtue," not abstaining from life, but living life to its fullest measure that they may learn from life, that they may gain wisdom from it. And one day, when they are heavy in age, they will be grand teachers to many entities, for they will have found exalted freedom to love peoples, however they are.

Tell them that you love them, that you understand that their priorities in this life [may] really be much different than yours, but so is everyone's. Then the love of you to them will never change, regardless of what they do, for, after all, love is the most important of the whole relationship. Tell them that whatever you can do to help them, to lighten their worries, to befriend them, that you are there at all times. Let them come [to you] on their own free will--and they will! But in seeking [your] advice, they will teach you, and be grateful for that.

[Remember]: It is their life, not yours. You had the pleasure in creating them; it is now their pleasure in living it!

*

Children were my greatest teacher for they could express without shame, they could express lovingly. They had a wonderful imagination--that is really abundant memory--and they could go and play with little or nothing for days on end and be exhausted and fall into their little beds and sleep with slumber that was so translucent that I would watch them and wonder where their dreams were. They never worried all night like I

"Being a God does not mean you have to understand [another]. You are not [even] equipped to understand because you are not the other entity. But love is the grace that abides within the character of all of [us] that will allow the entity—regardless of understanding—the freedom to be."

did. And they were up bright and early, running around the whole place, eating everything there was to eat, and would not stay still, for off they were for another adventure. 'Twas a wonderful life!

Children, unfortunately, are taught out of their common sense. They are taught how to be restrictive, limited, and negative by "don'ts," "can'ts"; and [taught] hatred and bitterness [and to] be prejudiced. And they are raised in cloistered cities where there is earnestly very little compassion to be found, where molesting of little children are around every corner and lie in every shadow. And they are abused, murdered, raped, tortured, and tormented. And even the wellest families there are, with the greatest intents, still manage to deter the natural instincts of their children and cut off their invaluable source that allows them to be free and energetic.

The greatest school and the greatest happiness for children is a dell and a holler and a stream and great oak trees and animals and flowers and frogs and rods and birds and fish.

*

There once was an age for adolescence. In men, it went through their thiry-third year. That should be the same with woman: they should be children until their thirty-third year. Then, when they have secured a mate, they will have lived, enjoyed, gained wisdom, learned of evenness, compassion, humility, and who they are. Then their lives would be happy for a long, long time.

Try to be, earnestly, a child until you are thirty-three. You will not age one day if you do this.

*

Master, if you do not agree with your child's ideas, then that is **your** truth. Does that mean he must forfeit his to be in accord with you? Being a God does not mean you have to understand. You are not [even] equipped to understand because you are not the other entity. But love is the grace that abides within the character of all of [us] that will allow the entity--regardless of understanding--the freedom to be.

You only have to understand this: Your child and you are two different Gods, indeed; that you are [both] sovereigns, indeed; and that he has lived myriads of lives and experiences and adventures that do not run in the same course as yours have done; very few ever do. Thus, what you have accumulated in your Soul through emotion through all of your experience is going to vary in what he has accumulated in his, for what he has done, you would not think of doing, and yet what you are doing he has [already done].

"Everyone is different according to their experiences, but that does not make them any less or make them any less loved by that which perceives and looks upon them. You, master, must allow your child to have his [own] ideals, for how else is he going to learn from them except to experience them.

Love should not be warranted upon agreeing or disagreeing. It should be there in a steadfast manner regardless. To expect your child to be like you is a gross enslavement upon your part, and you are a tyrant."

Everyone is different according to their experiences, but that does not make them any less or make them any less loved by that which perceives and looks upon them. You, master, must allow your child to have his [own] ideals, for how else is he going to learn from them except to experience them. Love should not be warranted upon agreeing or disagreeing. It should be there in a steadfast manner regardless.

To expect your child to be like you is a gross enslavement upon your part, and you are a tyrant. [For] your [child] to expect you to believe as he does, he is also a tyrant. What you do, master, is to say unto him: "This that you have chosen to have as your ideals is foreign unto my being. And I love you greatly for you, for the individual character that you are. I may not understand all of your ideals and do not promise to even try, but will love you simply for you and desire for you that wherever your ideals take you, that you learn from them, that you gain from them. And I know and understand that the accumulation of all of these ideals will help form a greater character in your being." That is how a true parent and a true God, entity, loves its sibling and another God.

You do not love people "on terms." You do not love them because they will be this way or that way. You love them because of the way they are, because you love yourself for the way that you are. The Father is individualized character, and His own experience lives vividly within each entity; thus, each entity is sovereign and different and unique and equal to everyone else.

Love your sibling. Listen to his ideals and understand that he is driven to accomplish them; his Soul needs it. Do you know what causes determination in a entity? When the Soul, in **this** life experience, has an opportunity to experience something it has never experienced before, [the entity] will be "possessed" and driven to do it, for the Soul need the adventue to gain the pearl of wisdom from it so it never has to do it in future experiences. Your child **must** do it; that is a part of his being. If you keep him from doing it, you are inhibiting that part of his being, that instead of having the experience and adventure, [there] will be regretfulness and hatred, and he shall despise you for inhibiting that to occur.

Let him have his freedom. It is his life, not yours. In the same understanding, when your sibling is wishing you to be certain ways that you are not, speak to him evenly and tell him that you are only your own being, and that what you have learned, you have learned because you needed to and wanted to; [that] that which he is learning, perhaps you have already learned a long, long time ago, and that it is not needed any longer. As you love him for who he is, pray let him love you for how you are also. Do you understand?

In rearing siblings, it is most important to let them establish their own ideals. The entity that is the parent should be an ideal of what they are teaching the child to be rather than living a duality. Do not say unto your sibling to be one way when you are not that way yourself. It is the ideal that illuminates the light of understanding.

How you live, entity, influences your sibling, certainly, and helps to build their own basis, their own premise of ideals and character. But allow them to formulate their own. If you become stagnated and embroiled in the murk and the mire and limited into what you are doing, your siblings will grow away from you, for you have nothing to offer them. And yet, if you have many adventures and go into many things and are varied and multifaceted, your siblings will stay near you, entity, for they will be drawn and illuminated by the character that you are that helps them to learn. You see?

Raising them means living what you are and loving what you are enough that the light [of what] you are helps to illuminate the character of their [light]. Let them grow; you will be exceedingly glad you did. And that which shall bloom from the growth, entity, will love you forever for allowing them to do so.

Everyone wants to copulate and have babes, and they are all well and good as long as they are helpless and you can bounce them around and do whatever you wish to them. [But when] they become forthright, stubborn, unique and spoiled, then you woe the day you ever had such wonderful dreams. 'Tis a wondrous truth! Poor siblings, if they could have been kept babes, they would have never grown up!

[Raising children] is all a part of growing up yourself, of refining yourself and understanding [that] life is not the ominous thing that most would have it be. It is really rather sweet and very good for those who pursue it.

*

There are many parents who cling to their offspring fervently and hold them tightly unto their breast as if life were to snatch them away. But they have come [to this plane] not to be coddled, but to live, to experience life! I say unto you: Let them be. Do not say, "[I] know that they are going to be lost!" for they are never lost. When mothren and fathren indeed understand this, then it exudes a sweet freedom, not only upon the mothren and fathren, but upon the offspring also.

When they are free to be is the time that they gain their wisest judgements; indeed, they put forth an understanding of the moment and how it is lived. When they are free to express this and [are] not in shackles or chains, they can learn what is clever and not clever. And what are adventures? They are only learning more of life and how it is presented.

When you take a small steed and put him forth into a small place [with] a fence, [that] he hath no room to even turn around, he cannot love you or run for you or be the gallant entity that he is. It is only if you give him room to grow do the luster of his coat, indeed the fire in his eyes, indeed the sweetness of the sound of his hooves give unto you a contentment and total realization of what a steed, great as he is, **truly** is. When he is in a fence, he is only an object. When he is free to grow, his movement, his expression, is God Sublime; and of his beauty you will learn much.

Give them room to grow and you will find that they will return time and time again to your sweet freedom.

*

To help little ones, or those who be the fruit and seed of our being, to realize their purposeful good is not to create it for them. [To help] them evolve into what they know best for themselves is to become steadfast, unequivocably, in your love for them and love them in freedom. And do not maintain them to be this or to be that, but to be themselves. Once you start choosing for your children a path to follow to find themselves, they will never find themselves on what **you** think the path would be. They must find it only through the experience of their own life.

Love them openly, in freedom, and be steadfast with your love for them. And always listen to them, master, when e'er they wish to speak to you, for I will tell you this: They are the blood of your loins and you have provided their body for the greatness of their Spirit to become, and they will carry on your lineage into generations to come. For the sake of your future generations, as it were, make time to converse with them, to love them. There is nothing so important that should take you away from this your future element.

And be pleased with them. Master, there are plenty of peoples on this plane who delight in expressing and finding, indeed, the direful negative, or sorrow and despair in everyone. Find the good in your children. Never expand upon mistakes; expand upon the good that they are, and love them in freedom. There are many out there in the world of our brothers that will find faults. Do not be the one that will lead the charge.

*

Would you have your siblings change their life to be your ideal? Nay! Don't change yours to be theirs! If you do, master, they will never know you, and you will wonder why, alas, they are estranged from your countenance.

If you are you, completely, there is a profound respect that the innocence of siblings have, [even] young siblings, for they detect and understand: 'tis the Spirit of their being that knows this. Then you are loved and, far greater, you have been a profound teacher that will teach them not to live as the image tells them to do, but as the Master has allowed them to do.

When you allow, they shall grow and become purposeful, not sick, bent, tormented, and confused; they will simply be what they are. If you shall live this, then you will be as I am to that which you love, and they shall become even as you are becoming unto me.

*

Children do not come into your life, master, to be like you. They come in to fulfill their acts in their life according to what they have obtained in their life prior to you. You are merely the divine and sweet mother that have given unto them the perfect body to exude their brilliance and their beauty in. They do not inherit the characteristics in mind that the mothren or fathren has, as they are independent agents of one another.

When you have difference of opinions and different truths, it can best be lessened through the understanding that all are right and all have the prerogative to express truth and right—but only to the point, master, that it does not infringe on another's kingdom and their truth.

*

Parents, master, are under the assumption, through that which is termed ignorance, that they somehow own their children, that they are the ultimate creator, and that if the sibling does do not react how [the parents] think they should react, then, of course, their world is torn to shreds, as is were, and they cannot understand how they could have created something that does not co-exist with them happily.

I will tell you: Your sibling is a sovereign entity. The entity is not your sibling, but the greater relation is that which is termed your brothren in God. The entity has lived thousands of lives before it has come to you; thus it has had great experience in life. That is a truth.

So the entity, in its collective existence, has collected that which is termed attitudes through experience and gained the treasure of emotion and wisdom to have that which is termed a physiological make-up of being the entity that it is. Parents are only vehicles, entity; they are instruments; they are not the creator, nor do they choose who shall come forth through them. When [you] realize that this child is as old and ancient, if you will, as you are, [you] must realize that this is another God, a God with the things that it must do and fulfill within its Soul.

*

Know you that if a child possesses knowledge of life as it is understood by the parent, and that knowledge is given not as a condemnation but as a form of that which is called enlightenment and education, then whatever they advance themselves to do thereafter, they are doing it full well-knowing of that which is called the consequences of divine experience. If you tell them "No," then you are an enslaver. If you teach them and give them the option, then you are a God!

Parents never realize how wise parents were until they became one. Teach, and if you do not know the answer, ask for the answer; it will come forth in runners and all sorts of avenues of knowledge, and it will teach on your behalf.

*

Entities come as siblings through that which is termed parents as a vehicle to come through to express. [They] are drawn to one or the other parent because of an association or a familiarity in thought processess. Then there are those that are not drawn to either one of them; they are simply a means through which the entity can come through and have a life of expression.

Now, what do you do with an entity that comes in as a little baby and that is helpless, that cannot control its environment? I tell you, being born into matter is a very risky thing, and yet life is all worth it, anywhere you find it. You love the entity; you protect the entity. It only needs to be loved for itself and allowed to live because of what it is—a human being that is driven by a divine Spirit that has given it life.

*

Children are a wonderful blessing. They hold a little life within them that is accepting the world in an innocent vein again. And their truth is very much like God in His truth: they smile at everyone and have a trusting for everyone, and their curiosity of life in all of its splendor is quite glorious. Perhaps the only error, in that which is termed the foundations of humanity, is that everyone grew up.

*

If I sit in audience with you for less than what is termed your hour and teach you, it doesn't mean you have learned any less than what I would teach you all day or perhaps a decade; it does not mean you have learned any less. What is important is that you have been loved, you have accepted that which is termed a truth, you have been compassionate to Self here: that is all that is important. Do the same with your siblings.

If perhaps, by chance, the moments that are spent are very few and not as great as you would like them, make them the grandest there are. And the grandest way is loving them, listening to them--listening to them--for they have their truth. Do not be so arrogant in your own truth to not acknowledge that which is termed the little ones coming forth, for they can always teach you a thing or two. So listen to them and love them. And in those moments, those are the sweet moments that the sibling never forgets and only wants more of, but also gratifies both.

Master, you do not have to be a rich man to give your children everything. You only have to be rich in that which is termed compassion and understanding and love, and humble yourself enough to try to understand them. Then, perhaps, you are the greatest parent ever. Of course, in their eyes that will be the truth. And whose eye would you rather have it in?

*

Student: I have something I am very concerned about. Two of my daughters . . . well, they're like Cinderellas. They, they sleep . . . . I mean, they don't sleep literally, they sleep in their lives. It's like they don't live. One, whose name is Jane, she seemed like the Prince had come, and then he was killed in an avalanche two years ago, and she's gone back to seeking again. And it's like, she says, she doesn't feel that she will ever find anybody to love her and for her to love again. And she sleeps. And the other one, she lives in a kind of apathy. She goes to Wyoming. She stays with one of her sisters, and she loves the baby. And she has a lover, but the lover lives with his mother, and he's sick, and it comes to nothing after ten years. And, and . . . I grieve for them. And . . . I feel guilty.

Ramtha: Indeed. Entity, what be Cinderella?

Student: Cinderella was a girl. When she was born, the good fairies came and they gave her beauty and intelligence and a loving heart. But the bad fairy hadn't been asked, and she got mad--or the invitation came late. So when she got there, she was angry, and she said that when Cinderella reaches a certain age--I can't remember when it was--she will prick her finger with a needle, like in a spinning wheel, and she will fall asleep. And then everybody in the castle will fall asleep too. And then a young Prince comes, and there are big thorns grown up all around the castle, and he manages to get through. . . . Oh yes, and he kisses her, and she wakes up, and the whole castle wakes up too. And so I see two of my daughters as Cinderellas kinda, you know--they sleep!

Ramtha: But why worry you, when the Prince is still to come and kiss them to wake them up!

Student: But I am waiting for the Prince! I don't know. One is thirty-three and the other--I know, this is silly--and the other is thirty, and it's like, it's like their life, their life is passing them by.

Ramtha: Perhaps **your** life is passing **you** by because you are living it in your Cinderellas.

Student: Well, that's what I thought for a while, but in the last year, many things have happened to me that are, that are great--it's what I wanted to do when I was young. And so it's like my life is going on and they're just sleeping away.

Ramtha: But master, how long did you slumber until you were awakened?

Student: . . . Sixty years.

Ramtha: Then why think you, entity, to take this advantage away from them? You are an enslaver.

Student: But I don't want them to wait sixty years!

Ramtha: It is not **your** life to do that with; it is their own.

Student: I know.

Ramtha: You do **not** know that or you would allow them the freedom to express according to what makes them happiness.

Who is to say what the guise of happiness is? Illness is a happiness to some, sorrow a happiness to others, reclusiveness yet happiness to someone else—and slumber, sweet slumber, a happiness to yet others.

You are not your siblings, nor are they you! And what be that which is termed your life is not theirs. They are sovereigns. Though they are born of your womb, entity, 'tis a God that has [been] manifested of God, and God alone. And of their life, they have come not here to please you or to live for that which is termed your approval or disapproval, but for themselves.

Lady, what is your priority is never going to be everyone else's. And if it has taken you sixty years to come alive, how wonderful it is that you have come alive. How wonderful! And if [it is] only for a moment, the whole of lifetime is worth that.

Your Cinderellas are Cinderellas; let them be that. They are doing what makes them happy or they would not do it. Mankind is an entity that does what he **wants** to do, and everything he does, he does because he wants to do it, entity.

Student: But they don't seem happy.

Ramtha: Who are you to say that? Are you living in the state of that which is termed Omnipresent Happiness that you have a declarative eye to see within that which is termed the actions of others to determine that?

Student: Yes.

Ramtha: If you do, entity, then you have been blinded severely, for what is their happiness, they are gathering the experience of, and that is the joy of this life—the joy of it to do what they please with it. Happiness is the ability to exercise the option to do whatever you want to do, regardless of anyone else.

Student: Yes, I see that, and its not . . . I guess it's because when I see them, what I think is "unhappy," you know—they look sad, that maybe I don't want to feel that sadness, so I want them to look happy, or to be happy.

Ramtha: Lady, then you are taking away their right to experience even sadness. Everything here is done in this dream for the graduated understanding of the Spirit that is upon this dream. What you see as "unhappiness" could have been your fortune and lot in this life, and very well has been. But to them, they do not see that. They are yet to experience that. So unto their beings, they are well and good. You are the only one that thinks otherwise.

Allow them gracefully to come to their own understanding and their own wisdom, as you have, and cease this intervention on your part to enslave them into happiness. Allow them to find that for their own beings; that is what this life is for. And think you that this is the only life they are going to live? Nay, entity it is not! It hasn't been and never will be.

You, mind your own business and love you. And at sixty years, go and frolic and enjoy this place, and do all the things that bring that which is termed merriment and zest into your being, and love that which is termed your siblings and give them the freedom to express however they choose. In that, you will have found this life to be even sweeter than ever you thought it to be. That is what I say unto you.

Student: Will they find . . . I know this is my--

Ramtha: Will they find happiness according to your opinion?

Student: No, no. Will they find husbands!

Ramtha: When one goes **looking** in a marketplace for a husbandman, they also settle for a bargain . . . and the bargains, entity, very rarely hold. Don't ever **find** a husbandman. Allow them the grace, entity, that whatever they are will draw to them whatever they are. Then they shan't find bargains but indeed will have a life and an interlude that is supreme and will last them forever. Leave them alone and love them in good grace.

*

CHAPTER TWENTY-FIVE

SEE YOUR PERFECTION IN ALL LIFE:

ALLOW LIFE TO BE

"Each time that you let someone express how they want to express without condemning them for that, you deepen your love and compassion for yourself and your ability to have it for them. Each time, entity, that you can find beauty in what is obviously not beautiful, that deepens and strengthens the love of yourself and also gives them a recognizing point that they are beautiful. That is love being seen in a most profound manner."

"[All] things, of their own creation and natures, according to the life force that emanates within them, hath created a uniqueness, through perfect thought, that gives them the essence of sublime Life.

All things are good. All things are perfect in their natural, uninterrupted state. They are sinless, they are guiltless, they are guileless, they are wonderfully free. It is only attitudes that Gods of splendor attach to them that divide them from their perfect course, their destiny.

Purposeful good is intentional life, that when one seeks out the good in life, he is purposefully looking for it; he is purposefully fulfilling.

Purposeful good allows the freedom of life to become. When you intentionally let it become, then you are refraining from being the enslaver of the good, but letting the good be. And soon, in your sweet realizations, when looking for purposeful good in all acts, practices and purposes, behold, you will have ascertained that that is all you see. And where there is only purposeful good, there is Life."

FIND PURPOSEFUL GOOD IN ALL THINGS

I am Ramtha The Enlightened One. Indeed! And who be I that have come forth and issued upon this audience a most boistful [boisterous] voice of mystical intrique? I be that that be a servant unto God Almighty.

[God] be the Life Force, indeed. It be the heavens. Indeed, it be the earth. Indeed, it be the sphere. Indeed, it be all that is Life. In His beauty, in His mystery, in His awesomeness, He has been a singular God to many peoples. [But] The Father is all things. He is the Source. He is the Exhuberance of Life. He **is** Life. He is the consuming factor of all that is. [And] the power to be All That Is is worth, indeed, the humble notoriety that we pay in the most supremacy of our beings [by] being [a] servant unto [Him]. That I am.

I am Ramtha The Enlightened One. Enlightened? Indeed I am! For who be I hath taken that which is termed the Source, the Principle Cause, the wondrous, sublime Life that is all things, and hath become it in my own being, in my own essence, into all that I be: God maintained in the highest force of vibratory understanding, the highest learning of contemplative thought.

[In] being the greatest in the facility that I am, I have become Him in a concealed, multifaceted entity: Supreme Life. To become this, indeed, is to become a Christus in Man. It is when God is taken from the forgotten spheres of nowhere and [is] brought forth in the crowning glory of your own being and made a driving force that illuminates, as it were, gives forth the abiding point of life to all around you, to all things that **are** Him.

That part that is spectacular that I have consumed in my own being, it is called God Living As I AM. God Living As You Are is the arisen Christus in Man—Man no longer ignorant, Man no longer in a pitiful state of being that begins and ends in one brief breath of understanding. [Then] Man **is** the supremacy of the Father; He is the Christus of the Father; He is the Son, the Heirship, the Totality of the Father, all in one. Thus, unto the Christ, the Power that can be maintained, recognized and brought forth in every jubilant form in Mankind, I am a servant unto.

I am Ramtha The Enlightened One, servant unto you, my beloved brothren. And who be you? You be, indeed, all things that I be. You be, indeed, Gods rearing forth your tiny heads into seeing a more splendid life of arrayance, that you too can become a great and mighty tree. You, my most beloved brothren, indeed are God sublime in the basis of your life forms, in the Christ recognized in your understanding. And unto you do I pay homage equally.

I speak to you from the Lord God of my Being. The Lord God of my Being is the sublime totality of my being. It is an evenness, indeed, that is forever. What I speak unto you this day in your time is that which is called, as it were, a recognized point of seeing the value of all things. Let us take an understanding of how things truly be.

[All] things, of their own creation and natures, according to the life force that emanates within them, hath created a uniqueness, through perfect thought, that gives them the essence of sublime Life. All things are perfect in their states of being. They emanate a trueness of character of their created form. They emanate a sinless, guileless, guiltless presence to all who see them.

Animals, as they are so termed, precious and close to the hearts of Mankind and to God, they are indeed the creations of Gods. They are predator [and] they indeed are prey; yet they never have the feelings of guilt. They are guileless and they are sinless in filling the belly that aches for hunger. In their state of being, they are all perfect and hold life in the balance of living the moment. I will show you:

A great and beautiful stag looks upon his herd and he greatly approves of them. There be in his herd those who have lived long in their times, that the teeth of their jaws are fetid with rot, that they are old in their limbs and they are slow in their movements. The stag looks upon the old, the unhealthy of his beings and knows infinitely that they have met their day, but [that] they shall return again.

And lo, he looks, and what see he? He see a flash of a silken coat of a color that matches the grass which it slithers through. Quickly the stag has caught the eyes that are ever so cold, seething eyes, searching for that tragedy of infinite wisdom that it has its destiny to fulfill.

The stag calls to order that which he loves. All are [now] alert unto the lion that poses, crouched, with [its] shoulders high abreast its backbone, with the slickness of its forehead bulging, searching with its cold, listless eyes, searching for the doomed light, light that is sick, light that is old, [that] shall fill not only its belly but that of its young that it has wrought forth into this world [and] that cry for that which to replenish [their] sources with. [All] are alerted. And they move.

The lion, searching, finds the light he is searching for. And as he keeps the light of his eyes eagerly upon it, he begins to move closer to it, and closer to it. And behold, the aged light is alerted to that of his prowl and begins, indeed, its futile escape.

Within moments the great beast hath climbed upon the back, and with one single plunge of the fangs within the neck of the animal, it is lost, lost that the Spirit of its being has recalled its Soul and that pain and agony are no longer felt. It is finished.

You [may] look upon this and say, indeed, "Wretched are the lions! Wretched are the beasts of prey! Why cannot all things be grazers? Why cannot all things be at peace with one another?" For there is a balance in the intricacies of Life. None have created a "wrong" here. The lion, it is sinless and guiltless. And the animal that is lost, it is not sorrowful or despaired. The stag looks upon that which is gone and licks his sides; and [he] studies his herd and how one less will give room for one more to come, for the one that has left, its light will come again.

To look at this and to know that creations express perfectly according to their wills, according to their developed form, [is] to see the "purposeful good," as it is so termed, in all that is. One God [may] assert himself and say, "That is wrong! There is something wrong here. It is not quite right." And [he will] see the poor helpless animal and the futile being as it struggles not even a little underneath the weight of the lion. And yet another [God] will look and see that the herd will sustain and become more bountiful and will stay strong and will flourish. That is looking for the purposeful good in all things.

If things [are] left alone, **as they are,** they have committed no wrong. Yet man, in his most willful attitude of attitudes, can look upon any one thing and find fault, judgement, error, incompletion, imperfection, and all in all distaste in that which originally hath found perfect form.

To find the lawful good is to find the purposeful good that is there. Purposeful is **intentional.** Good, as it were, represents **life. Intentional life** in all things is purposeful good.

When you attune yourself, Oh wise masters that come a-calling on my audience for great "wisdom" that sometimes is applied, this I will tell you: To change the attitude from a "wrongful, negative" thinking to a "good" thinking, permits life; it permits life not only to abound itself within your **own** inner personal beings, but permits life in all other beings that express perfectly. [When you] look continuously [and] earnestly, to the height of your being, [for] purposeful good in your existence, soon you become personal, purposeful good; that there has become no room to find that which is called "negative responses" or "judgemental attitudes" or those things, indeed, that not be in accordance with a sinless, guiltless, perfect state of perfection.

How do you find purposeful good? When you begin to find [intentional life] in your actions, in your inner chambers, [do] you begin to hearken purposeful good in others and in all things. [Then], true to form shall all things become lighted in their perfection; shall no longer illness or crippling attitudes [of] a harsh, sterile eye [be] debasing of perfection but rather that

"Purposeful good is allowing life to be. When you look for purposeful good in your blessed brothren, you are allowing them to express beautifully, sweetly, and kindly. You are lifting from their beings a most foreboding life of judgemental attitudes and allowing them to grow into their purposeful good.

All things grow into life, and fight for life, and maintain life, and are never distraught with life—if left alone!"

purposeful good hath created an entity of most grand standards. [Then] all life around you [will] abound around you [such] that birds that make their nest so high into the great tree will make their nests lower in the great tree; that sweet creatures, however they be, will not scamper to avoid the purposeful good entity [you are] but will come and sit at your feet and be a part of your all-conclusive being, for you are a blessed light.

Purposeful good is **allowing life to be.** When you look for purposeful good in your blessed brothren who know not even these words, you are allowing them to express beautifully, sweetly, and kindly. You are lifting from their beings a most foreboding life of judgemental attitudes and allowing them to grow into their purposeful good. And I assure you that not allowing things to "become" is an error. All things, master, grow into life, and fight for life, and maintain life, and are never distraught with life **if left alone.**

Loving others for what they be and how they be is a good thing on your part. And a good thing on your part becomes a greater good thing. And behold, indeed, your words become magic. Your thoughts, they are the very winds themselves. Your tears, they are never wasted [but] are cherished and loved. You have **become** an honorable, valued, worthy, loved, good, lifeful entity. That is what a Master is; that is what you become. That is where infinite wisdom of the ages becomes the infinite wisdom of the "nows" and life, to you, master, begins to radiate hope.

You cannot draw to you what you already are not. Thus, if you have become purposeful good in your attitude, sight, thought, being, then you have drawn equal standard unto you of purposeful good, that what you have minted [meted] out in your kingdom has become that which you have become; that all, indeed, who surround you are of purposeful good also. Thus, there is joy therein. When you lose the ability to have negativity or forceful judgements--the enslaving parts of your being--when you lose that ability, you gain a higher one, and always it gets better and better.

There are many who can sustain their character in a three-dimensional understanding. There are many who can put, indeed, material forms before you. But I will put before you a spiritual character that is more personal, that is forever, that indeed draws a kingdom nigh unto itself into greater parts of realms, of heavens, of kingdoms--whatever you call it--that will last you forever. And when you walk with me, you will learn, [and] what was once barren shall bloom before our feet. And when you walk with me, indeed, you will walk in earnest, in honor, [in] value and worth and personal good.

This be I, indeed, your humble teacher, who be not a teacher that presents items, as they are seen, but forever character that

"Life of itself is a continuum of harmony and joy and ever-expanding beauty, becoming more and perfecting and crystalizing [itself], and it knows no end. There is a reasoning for life; there is harmony in life.

Look for the purposeful good in all things. When looked for, behold, it becomes abundantly clear to you, thus allowing you in your life to interchange with purposeful good."

will hold you in Eternity, for that is where we will always be. Gain from the days to come in your time and the good that you shall excel with in your beings and in your fantasies. I assure you, you will rejoice with an open and kindred heart. And that, unto me, my most beloved brothren hath made this journey well worth its time. So be it.

"To worship God is, simply, to worship You! To love God is, simply, to love You! To love Life is to love that which you be in the experience of what God is. And to love Life is never to condemn it, never to alter it, never to damn it, never to hate it or despise it, but [to] envelop it, as it were, totally in the essence of your being."

SEE PERFECTION IN ALL LIFE

I am Ramtha The Enlightened One, indeed, servant unto that which is termed the Force, the Principle Cause, the Mother-Father Principle, the Ongoingness; that which is termed, indeed, Thought; that which is termed, indeed, God Almighty.

What be He—what is called "God"—that is the Force, the Life Principle that be all-consuming, that be the basis of all things? How be He, indeed, existent when existence must be contemplated in measured form?

The word "God" simplifies, indeed, an ongoingness [that is] all-conclusive, all-enveloping Thought [and] is formed in the highest parts of "light understanding" which emit sound, or "vibratory understanding." The word resounds with that which is termed "light synthesis" that manifests into the highest vibratory field of sound. "God" be, indeed, the word to which all things, all universes, all spheres, all infinity, all thought, all moment, all smallness, all greatness, all largeness, **all** is, in sound.

Now, God be Life Essence. God be the Thought-Light essence that gives its form through what is called "God" in His ongoingness. Ongoingness permits, indeed, that Life be ever-moving, ever-evolving, ever-involving, ever becoming into that which is termed Being.

The Father has not, indeed, the smallness of contemplative thought to illuminate Himself as a superior over the Ideals [i.e., entities] which have formulated themselves from Him to experience Him in all that He is. All Ideals, all thought, all understanding, are given forth as an emission from the Source, that the Ideal, formed into matter (or that which is termed "illusionary essence") can experience the Father in His ongoingness. [For] how [does] an Ideal understand its basis of being until it has become, and in the becoming, understands what its origins are?

"God," the word, the sound, the vibratory feeling, cannot be spoken enough, for the "enoughness" will eliminate the essence, the experience or the Ideal into a nothingness. God, the Source, the Supreme Cause, the Element, knows not, in all the encompassing of Its being to eliminate Himself into that which is called limited thought which would alter His basis of being, for then that which is termed the Ideal will not have the opportunity to become the essence that is contemplated "God."

If this be unto you complex, I wish and desire it not to be. But to understand God (and the word) to whom I worship and love, to whom **all** are accountable unto, one must bring down the

"The God to whom I love, who be, indeed, the essence of my being, who be the ongoingness of my being, be one that in the totality of Its existence permits ALL to be—in spite of all that is—through Love."

measure of time, the measure of space, the measure of distance, and have it no more as an "illusion" unto the **simple** understanding of what God is.

God is the river in front of your nose. He is the nothingness which all seem to be illuminated by. He is the ongoingness, the steadfastness. The beauty of what He is, is Life.

To worship God is, simply, to worship You! To love God is, simply, to love You! To love Life is to love that which you be in the experience of what God is. And to love Life is never to condemn it, never to alter it, never to damn it, never to hate it or despise it, but [to] envelop it, as it were, **totally** in the essence of your being.

To simplify the Father that you may become the Father in the ultimateness of your being--[and] the "door" that keeps that progress assured--is to understand who you be. And, in all the complexities of your being, you are rather quite simple. The simplicity basis of Life that you are is a testament unto the goodness, the Isness, the permeance of what is called "God."

God of judgemental character, God of hatredness, God of bitterness, God of divided kingdoms, God of prophesied "doom and end," is not the God that is the simplicity of life. [That] is the God that has manifested his ideal from the Source, hath altered Life through hatred, despised Life through the despising of his neighbors, and given forth indeed that God sayeth that "all things will end," that God sayeth that "all things be done and said," the God sayeth "man is sinner," that God sayeth "none can be perfect." Only man says that! And man cannot say any one thing about God lest he have first **been** Him! Only Man can take the perfection of Thought and alter it into "altered God."

Thus, the God to whom I love, who be, indeed, the essence of my being, who be the ongoingness of my being, be one that in the totality of Its existence permits **All** to be--in spite of all that is--through Love.

Unto Him, God Almighty, Supreme Life, Ongoing Isness, Conclusiveness, am I, Ramtha The Enlightened One, a lover of, a doer of, an isness of. And [it is] through that isness, indeed, that understanding, [that] permits the God of my being, the Supremacy of my being, to love and to see and to recognize, **indeed,** the wonderful evolvement and wonderful spectacular display of God that each of you be.

How know I you? How understand I you? For I **know** what **I** am, and when I know what I am, indeed, I can understand what you be and see you in a continuum when you refuse to see yourself in even the spectacular moment.

Now, of all that God is, I am. And to teach you of all that you are, that must be your definite ideal, your course, your pursuant in life: to be the God I Am. The God I am is an

"Never settle for that which is termed an alteredness. Never allow yourself to be given alteredness. Never allow alteredness to be a state of being, for if you do so, then the alteredness will become a collective attitude, shall become, collectively, a life to which you are doomed to live [for] the alteredness has become a resolve, a truth into your life and the wonderfulness of an Unlimited Kingdom are far missed."

involver in life, for he involves himself in himself. He is pursuant on happiness and joy.

To learn who you are, to be who I be, is to know and to love you, for, simply, that is God, for, simply, you be God! And to live His life, the progressive state of a continuum now, is to love Life to the fullest measure and not to alter it in shades or shadows of evil or misconstrued understandings, in diplomacy or dogmatic understandings that limit the progression of Man's mind, but to love Life [for] how sweet it is.

Now, this does not mean that you be passive in all things. It means that you be declarative in all things--sublimely so! To declare that you be God in your being is to **know** that you be God in your being! And if [something] pleases not you, entity, then reverse the process or the "molecular understanding" of what it is and make it into a pleasing measure, for a God hath, indeed, the ability, through the **simpleness** of his being and the opportunity for what is called life, to do that!

Never settle for that which is termed an alteredness. Never allow yourself to be **given** alteredness. Never allow alteredness to be a state of being, for if you do so, then the alteredness will become a "collective attitude," shall become, collectively, a life to which you are doomed to live [for] the alteredness has become a resolve, a truth into your life and the wonderfulness of an Unlimited Kingdom are far missed.

Now, how [does] one change, **great God that you be,** an "alteredness" into that which is termed "perfectness," an isness? If what is called reason hath no altered view, the eye will see that which seemingly to others is altered, will refine and move it into perfection, and the perfection of the object will return to that which is called its normal course of action--will be accepted unto the Soul of your being and the Spirit of your being and the Ego of your being as "perfection." Thus, no longer is one living with alteredness. One has the ability, **through the power of his being**, to change and make it perfect, simply.

What be the heightened realization of all manifestation? It is Thought: it is the "spirit" of the manifestation. You do not change the manifestation in its **form** and try to **make** it perfect through the re-design of molecular structures; you change it here. And when it is changed here, in how it is **perceived** from a God, it will change there.

Thus, [a] God, living in the totality of his uniqueness, God-Man expressing that which is called the Christ of his being, hath, through **simply** understanding, the ability never to alter his ability but to think in the Isness and never has in his kingdom anything that be altered or lacking. And what have been a disturbance in his kingdom, all be he to do is to change the power of the disturbance and make it a sweetness--all through his thinking! You think this to be too simple? If you think this is

"When alteredness begins through acceptance, either dispense of it or re-acclaim its virtue. We, entity, are 're-acclaimed virtue.' All that are here are made perfect. All that are here are growing into that knowingness that their perfection hath been obtained once again, for [though] we thought it to be lost, it is through the virtuous action of living life that we gain the wisdom to understand what perfection is, and to understand what is meant by Joy, elation of being, completion of being, for all of you, blessed be your names, you are a glory unto this world."

too simple, you will never know God! That is how it is!

All who be here have accepted in their being less of what their being deserves. And how know they "lessness?" For they have **known** that it is lessness, and the knowingness hath created it so. To run about in this world through the murk and the mire of the marketplace securing all things and ornaments that will make us somehow more perfect or more beautiful for a very critical eye of altered states is a most foolish thing to do. And beyond that, it makes you the slave and never the king. A God accepts the beauty that he is and, through the mere acceptance and knowingness, becomes the greatest beauty of all—beyond, indeed, words, despicable as they are.

Knowing God through thought, through Life, is learning about You. You know, there are many who will try to live You for you, but they can never do that: they will never accomplish joy **for** you. Only you, splendid God, have the right, the **inherited** right, to be that on your own. And if you wish to wallow in that which is termed sadness and despair and unhappiness, fretfulness of the bodily action, and all things that make you gloom and doom, then so be it with you God, for you indeed are the ruler of your domain, and being the ruler of your domain, [you] hath found this acceptable for you; thus, we will let you be. But those who wish to take it to that which is termed the "ultimate," the ultimate of Isness, entities, is to be the simpleness of yourself, to understand and to love yourself, and to live this life fully, completely, and have no thing be in your existence that be less than perfect.

And how [are] you to know "perfect?" How [are] you to know and to recognize perfection? When you look upon any one thing, entity, and you find no fault therein and no fault is seen, you have seen perfection; no matter how vile it may be, you have seen perfection.

Accept no thing in your life that is less than perfection. If your neighbor finds it altered, and if you accept his opinion, then behold, your beautiful perfection hath altered and dimmed its beauty, and now no glows, no radiates, no becoming [is] satisfactory for that which is worthy of a king. And what do you then? When the alteredness of it begins through the acceptance, either dispense of it or re-acclaim its virtue. We, entity, are "re-acclaimed virtue." All that are here are made perfect. All that are here are growing into that **knowingness** that their perfection hath been obtained; [that] we have obtained virtue once again. For [though] we thought it to be lost, it is through the virtuous action of our being, through living life that we gain the wisdom to **understand** what perfection is and to **understand** what is meant by Joy, elation of being, completion of being, for all of you, blessed be your names, you are a glory unto this world.

"You do not heal the world by hating what the world does, for then you are a part of the wallow. You love it, and rise above it, and allow it to be as the Father has allowed it to be in your millenniums in time counting.

Ramtha loves God; indeed, Ramtha be God. Masters love God; indeed, Masters be God. What greater love can you give unto the Father, **greater** that you can give to Him, than to be Him? What greater recognition do we give to those that we love and cherish than to imitate them, for are they not worthy of our imitations? Indeed, for the essence and the beguiling mystery of their being hath promoted our life into such a flurry that the indentation of them upon us hath been a good one. To love God is to be Him.

To love the Christ is to love God. Christ is, indeed, the sweet blood, the sweet love, the sweet essence that ties you into the knowingness state that you are God. Christ is Man, the **one** perfect image and the **only** image that begat itself of the Thought, of the Source, and retained the perfect image of the Source in a unique, singular form.

You cannot love God without loving the Son. And who be the Son? He be you! But if you love not your neighbor, then you love not you and you love not the Son and you love not he Father: you see, you have altered the Father.

How take you on an **erroneous** "responsibility" of loving all the world in their despicable, wicked states? By loving their despicable, wicked states! When you love a despicable wickedness, behold, it no longer stinks, it no longer is vile, it is no longer ugly--it is beautiful. And once beauty is seen by that which is termed a great God into that which is called wickedness, behold, the wickedness (which only is a gross state of alteredness) becomes a light shining into an Ideal that is looking upon it, and [it] will grow into the Ideal as [surely as] the wind is a breath of good air.

You do not heal the world by **hating** what the world does, for then you are a part of the wallow. You love it, and rise above it, and allow it to be as the Father has allowed it to be in your millenniums in time counting. If you wish to **be** as Him, understand what He has **been** all of this time and allow all of these things to be, for life rejuvenates and will be again and again and again: that is the Covenant of Eternity that is given to all the Sons of the Great Father.

How do you love a wicked world? By loving what they are. The Loving Ideal gives them the light to change into perfection--**whatever** they term that to be! You see, you never help anyone by condemning them. Love them. Be unto them as a light. What they are will be a light unto you. And let them be in the freedom they wish to express. The world, beloved Gods, is going to be the explicit, greatest teacher unto them; not I, not you, not anyone else--not even the Father to which all of this is occurring in the moment! It is going to be themselves, for you know, it is in Man's nature to experience wickedness, to experience alteredness, to experience vileness. And when he has had his gut full, he will look for peace and happiness. Then he will have become a virtuous, wise man. Do you not know [that] that is where wisdom comes from? If you looked upon any pious, wise man and thought him [one] to behold, [know] he has done all of these things; that is why he is so wise; that is why you love him.

Now, in the eventuality, man will reach for his star, man will reach for his Ideal Light. And the Light can only be there if one other sees it for him, you know. He has no other way to identify it until he sees another possessing it, [for] it is **also** in Man's nature on this plane to possess what others possess. Man is a greedy lot, but he is going to learn through that greed to be a Sovereign, and **that** is a blessing!

Now, to perfect Godship and [to] do it through love, you, an understanding Father and, simply, Life--beautiful Life. You can break down Life into many scientific perplexities, and it will drive you mad! But look to it as a child looks upon life: through laughter and sweetness and always for yet another day, anxiously. [That] is how a God is in the innermost parts of his being.

To help you live this way, I be Ramtha, be God, speak to you as nothing other than God. And as long as you come unto me, and in your innermost thoughts, I will always recognize you as God, no matter how shameful you are yourself, and will love you in spite of yourself. And the great God I am, entities, will recognize **always** the great God that you be. And soon, the light and that understanding--and the word "God"--will seep through your understanding and will become you.

And one by one in this blessed audience, sweet morns, sweet evenings, one by one it will become a perfect alignment, a perfect understanding of pure thought. And one by one you will become God. And one by one you will leave my audience. And one by one you will live and placate yourself upon this life to be the Christus returned to the Hope of Men. And one by one you will affect them. And one by one they will become God.

And as this, indeed, is the hope that sitteth before you, is the hope that sitteth before me, do we [teach] this day in your time. And the enlightenment, through knowledge and then the doing of it, and accepting only perfection where perfection is known, and allowing growth to become where stagnation has been, and the exploration of life, is to help you understand better what it is. So be it.

Now, this learning is also a learning in the simplest form this mouth can work for those ears of yours to hear. You know, it has always been an amazement to me to watch scholars complicate a simplicity, for it elates their intellect into some form of ecstasy I have yet to see. Oh poor entity that is in the marketplace that be the simpleton that does not know foreign words and elaborated thoughts; only knows what life is. It is through the measure of keeping it simple, entity, that even the simple men will learn, for he too be God!

ACKNOWLEDGMENT

We sincerely appreciate the assistance of the following individuals in the preparation and publication of this book: Steven Bakker, Linda Barnes, Joanne and Carroll Cobbs, Richard Cohn, Carol and Wally Donaldson, Mark Goldman, Katherine Hogness, David Kerns, Judy Leadbetter, Bob and Eve Leander, Mary Lear, Sharon and Thomas Markham, Beverly McBride, Kellie McCurdy, Jerry McKinney, Karenina Muller, Patricia Muller, Mary Redhead, Sophia Sharpe, Bruce Sullivan, John Thompson, Alfred Weinberg, Miriam Weinberg, Myrl Weinberg, and Michaud Weinberg.

We especially would like to thank J. Z. Knight for her dedication in bringing us the wisdom and teachings of Ramtha and for her support of the publication of this volume.

SPECIAL ACKNOWLEDGEMENT

We would like to thank Douglas James Mahr for his comments, suggestions, and editorial assistance in the preparation of this manuscript.

REFERENCES

The material for this book was drawn from transcriptions of audiences conducted on the dates listed below. Several teachings were drawn from "The Portfolio," a publication of the Church I AM. The dates of these issues are also listed below.

Individuals wanting the specific reference for a particular teaching presented in this book may obtain it by writing to Sovereignty Publishing Company, P.O. Box 483, Eastsound, Washington, 98245.

November 9, 1979. Birmingham, Alabama
February 2, 1980. Birmingham, Alabama
February 3, 1980. Birmingham, Alabama
March 22, 1980. New York, New York
April 2, 1980. Wycoff, New Jersey
April 3, 1980. Wycoff, New Jersey
June 22, 1980 East Williston, New York
July 19, 1980. Mount Laurel, New Jersey
August 24, 1980. Mount Laurel, New Jersey
September 13, 1980. Wycoff, New Jersey
September 20, 1980. Birmingham, Alabama
September 21, 1980. Birmingham, Alabama
September 27, 1980. Chicago, Illinois
November 14, 1980. Mount Laurel, New Jersey
November 15, 1980. Mount Laurel New Jersey
December 7, 1980. New York, New York
December 13, 1980. Calabassas, California
January 10, 1981. New York, New York
January 12, 1981. New York, New York
February 15, 1981. Los Angeles, California
February 22, 1981. Patterson, New Jersey
February 24, 1981. Seattle, Washington
March 8, 1981. Boston, Massachusettes
March 22, 1981. Birmingham, Alabama
April 14, 1981. Seattle, Washington
April 21, 1981. Seattle, Washington
April 25, 1981. Los Angeles, California
April 26, 1981. Seattle, Washington
June 16, 1981. Seattle, Washington
July 15, 1981. Seattle Washington
July 21, 1981. Seattle, Washgington
July 26, 1981. New York, New York
August 22, 1981. Birmingham, Alabama
August 30, 1981. Seattle, Washington
September 21, 1981. Seattle, Washington

September 22, 1981. Seattle, Washington
October 19, 1981. New York, New York
October 11, 1981. New York, New York
November 1, 1981. Seattle, Washington
November 6, 1981. Birmingham, Alabamaa
November 22, 1981. Boston, Massachusettes
January 23, 1982. Denton, Texas
January 24, 19812. Denton, Texas
February 6, 1982. Calabassas, California
February 7, 12982. Calabassas, California
February 20, 1982 Birmingham, Alabamaa
February 21, 1982. Birmingham, Alabama
March 7, 1982. New York, New York
March 21, 1982. Seattle, Washington
April 9, 1982. Boston, Massachusettes
April 25, 1982. Denver, Colorado
April 18, 1982. Birmingham, Alabama
April 22, 1982. Denton, Texas
July 18, 1982. New York, New York
July 25, 1982. Calabassas, California
August 7, 1982. Seattle, Washington
August 8, 1982. Seattle, Washington
October 3, 1982. Boston, Massuchesettes
October 10, 1982. Calabassas, California
October 11, 1982. Calabassas, California
November 6, 1982. San Francisco, California
November 7, 1982. San Francisco, California
November 14, 1982. Aspen, Colorado
November 21, 1982. Birmingham, Alabama
December 5, 1982. New York, New York
December 11, 1982. Seattle, Washington
December 12, 1982. Seattle, Washington
January 8, 1983. Calabassas, California
January 9, 1983. Calabassas, California
February 13, 1983. Honolulu, Hawaii
March 13, 1983. New York, New York
March 19, 1983. Seattle, Washington
May 8, 1983. San Francisco, California
May 20, 1983. Seattle, Washington
July 16, 1983. Calabassas, California

Portfolio

December, 1979
January, 1981
February, 1981
March, 1981